D1422799

Britain's Railways 1948-1998

A Personal View of 50 Years of Change

Gavin Morrison

Ian Allan
PUBLISHING

Front cover top:
Garforth-allocated unrebuilt 'Patriot' No 45550 shuts off steam as it approaches Thwaites Junction for the stop at Keighley at the head of the Bradford Forster Square portion of the evening Morecambe residential service on 16 May 1962.

Front cover bottom:
Sporting the original InterCity 125 livery, an HST passes the south end of Doncaster on its way to King's Cross on 26 March 1986.

Back cover top:
Class 90 No 90002 was the first locomotive to be painted in the striking Virgin Trains livery. It is seen in the yard of RFS Doncaster before re-entering service on 6 March 1997. The locomotive has since been named *Mission Impossible*.

Back cover bottom:
On 30 July 1992, Construction-liveried Class 60 No 60095, which was then named *Crib Goch*, prepares to leave Swinden Quarry, on the old Grassington branch, with a Tilcon train bound for Hull.

Previous page:
The end of the 'Scarborough Spa Express' was a great blow to local enthusiasts in Yorkshire. The climb from Leeds up to Bramhope on the return journey was the highlight of the trip, and some remarkable performances were achieved with locomotives such as *City of Wells*, *Union of South Africa* and others. 'King Arthur' No 777 *Sir Lamiel* was not attempting any record breaking on 25 July 1995 as it crossed the River Aire on Kirkstall Viaduct at the start of the climb.

Below:
No 37428 in the special maroon livery for working the 'Royal Scotsman' leaves Muir of Ord past the golf course en route to Keith for an overnight stay on 22 May 1998

First published 1999

ISBN 0 7110 2629 7

All rights reserved. No part of this book may be reproduced or transmitted in any form or by any means, electronic or mechanical, including photocopying, recording or by any information storage and retrieval system, without permission from the Publisher in writing.

© Ian Allan Publishing Ltd 1999

Published by Ian Allan Publishing

an imprint of Ian Allan Publishing Ltd,
Terminal House, Station Approach,
Shepperton, Surrey TW17 8AS;
and printed by
Ian Allan Printing Ltd, Riverdene Business Park,
Molesey Road, Hersham, Surrey KT12 4RG.

Code: 9901/A2

All uncredited photographs were taken
by Gavin Morrison

GNER power car No 43114 heads the up 'Highland Chieftain' as it enters Carrbridge at 10.10 on Sunday 24 May 1998, power car No 43112 at the rear.

Visiting the East Lancs Railway No 5029 *Nunney Castle* in BR green arrives at Irwell Vale en route to Rawtenstall on 25 January 1998.

INTRODUCTION

*I*t came as a great surprise when Ian Allan approached me and asked if I would be interested in producing this book of 600 photographs covering the period from 1948 to the end of 1997.

I gave the proposal a considerable amount of thought, because I knew that I couldn't produce anything for the first few years, and in the early 1970s I had taken very little in this country. It was emphasised by the publishers that they wanted it to be a book which conveyed my experiences over the years as well as my own photographs. So I must make it clear from the outset that this is not a definitive work on the events which occurred year by year, but rather a story in pictures and words of what I did in this country in any one year. If you want a book to highlight the events of each year from 1942 to 1992, I strongly recommend *Ian Allan's 50 Years of Railways* written by my good friend Rex Kennedy, who willingly gave me permission to use his introduction for each year as a basis for my own.

Obviously having lived in Yorkshire for most of my life, there will be a tendency for the north to be better represented than the south, but I have managed to cover locations from Wick to Penzance and most areas in between. I know of other enthusiasts who have comprehensive collections of steam or diesel and electrics, but there are relatively few who have kept going with equal enthusiasm from the steam era to the present day.

My railway interest started in 1943, when my father bought an *Ian Allan 'abc'* to keep me occupied on a journey from Leeds City to Glasgow St Enoch; incidentally, this train was hauled by the first rebuilt 'Royal Scot', No 6103 *Royal Scots Fusilier*, which had just arrived at Leeds Holbeck. This inexpensive little book, which I still possess,

was to be the start of my lifelong interest in railways and eventually photography a few years later. I became hooked on train spotting and by 1959 there were only 12 locomotives on BR's books which I had not seen. Armed with a copy of *The British Locomotive Shed Directory*, priced 7s 6d, I travelled the length and breadth of the country. The book was written by Flt Lt Aiden L. F. Fuller ACA and it still has pride of place on my bookshelf. Even today I have the ability to visit a shed and remember nearly every locomotive present without writing anything down for days afterwards, but names of places and people, well that's an entirely different matter.

My first picture, which is illustrated below, was taken with the inevitable box Brownie, at Llandudno station. I was soon to learn that this camera was not suitable for anything moving and that you got better results if you didn't put a finger across the lens when taking a picture. I then graduated to an old Super Ikonta 2¼ x 3¼, which seemed to let more light in via the bellows that by the shutter. Fortunately, my father owned a Rolleiflex with a f3.5 Teisar lens. Unfortunately, he was reluctant to allow me to use it, with some good reason as I once left it on a train at St Blazey after falling asleep. A gentleman handed it to me out of the carriage window as the train departed as I walked down the platform.

I have always wanted to find an excuse to use the first picture that I ever took with my box Brownie. It shows rebuilt 'Patriot' No 45523 Bangor backing on to the Sundays Only 4.5pm Llandudno–Birmingham New Street service during the summer of 1949. The locomotive is in the lined black BR livery, with 'British Railways' on the tender. No 45523 was allocated to Crewe shed at that time.

During the late 1950s, Eric Treacy, whose Lime Street Cutting photographs I still consider as some of the finest action shots ever taken, was transferred (if that is the correct expression) to Halifax Parish Church. Luckily for me, my father and Canon Treacy (as he then was) became acquainted and so I began to attend Sunday evensong, for photographic guidance in the vestry rather than any spiritual matters. This did wonders for my processing techniques, although I do remember him saying to me once when I said I had tried a colour film: 'Leave it alone, it will never catch on for railway photography.'

After obtaining a motorbike, I travelled around the country getting to all the places where public transport was non-existent, but after losing control and landing in a gorse bush whilst trying to chase a train from Scout Green to Shap Summit, I decided that four wheels were safer than two and purchased a red Volkswagen Beetle. This became a familiar sight to railtour passengers as I followed the specials all over the country. More time devoted to ordinary railway traffic rather than specials would have produced a better balanced collection.

It was in the early 1960s, when I worked in Leeds, that I got to know the drivers and staff at Holbeck shed. In return for pictures, they would happily position locomotives for me, the crews laid on the 'clag' and I had an open invitation to travel on the footplate over the Settle & Carlisle to Carlisle and Glasgow. These were fantastic days and I am eternally grateful to all these railwaymen who gave me so much pleasure. I wish I had spent more time taking pictures of people at work in the sheds rather than just the locomotives, but it was just another opportunity I let pass; it wasn't until I visited places like India 20 years later that I managed to take these type of pictures.

As the 1960s headed relentlessly towards 11 August 1968, I, together with thousands of others, rushed around the country trying to record the last of classes and closing lines. I did this with a certain degree of success, but should have had the sense to record the early diesel classes as well. I well remember being at Shap one day and watching Nos 10000 and 10001 pass on the down 'Royal Scot' without even bothering to point the camera at them, but photographing the next dirty Class 5. I did get a little better at taking the modern traction in the late 1960s, but never made a trip purely to record diesels until well into the 1970s. I am sure there were many others who made the same mistake.

After steam finished in August 1968, I thought the world had come to an end, although I had, since 1966, started venturing abroad for steam and since then have continued to travel abroad, thus covering a good part of the world. I think that my collection can produce steam photographs from 31 different countries, but now that genuine steam has nearly vanished I have taken to visiting the USA for that country's impressive diesels.

The opening of the Keighley & Worth Valley softened the blow of the end of steam, but I now view this as a mixed blessing as I spent most weekends photographing on the line and thus producing a massive collection of pictures covering six miles of track which now seldom see the light of day. At the time I should have been recording the BR scene as well. It will be obvious from the photographs in the book, that I was not getting around very much at that time.

The revival of steam on the main line got me out and about the country again, covering huge distances for very little reward; however, in 1975 I started to take modern traction in quantity and, with the purchase of a 6x7 camera around that time, my activities returned to pre-1968 levels.

For the last 22 years I have been taking an average of about 1,200 black and white and 1,500 colour slides each year and so what you are seeing in this book is but a fraction of my efforts, a fact which made the selection very difficult.

My railway enthusiasm has been going on nonstop for 55 years and I have never given it up for a single day, much to my wife's dismay. She believes it is an incurable disease and she is probably right, as I don't think I could give it up even if I wanted to!

I am not interested in the technical aspects of photography; my object is to take photographs which please me. Having been a member of railway photography portfolios for over 30 years and more recently a local camera club, I have come to the conclusion that those who offer the most advice, are those who seldom produce the best results.

For the record, my black and white work has been on Pentax 6x7s since 1977, virtually all on TRIX film and developed in D76; before that it was mainly a variety of 21/4 square cameras. My colour slides have nearly all been taken on robust and simple Pentax K1000s or similar models, and mainly on Kodachrome 25 up to about five years ago when I moved over to Fuji Sensia film for a variety of reasons. I do have a couple of Minolta Dynax 7000 and 700SI, which I am using more frequently of late.

We are currently going through a very interesting period of railway development and I am making efforts to keep pace with the present and not spend too much time on the past. Had the publishers asked me to do this book in three years time, I could have hopefully covered all the 50 years myself, so my thanks are due to those who have helped me out with the first few years.

I come back to where I started by saying this is a personal account of the period. The pictures are just the visual part of the hobby; what really counts for me are the experiences, the places visited and the wonderful people all over the world that I have been privileged to meet through my hobby. I hope this book will revive happy memories for all its readers.

Gavin Morrison
Mirfield
March 1998

On 1 November 1997, 48 years and 35,000 negatives after the picture of the 'Patriot' at Llandudno, I took this extremely ordinary picture of Class 142 No 142068 leaving Widnes for Warrington on the former CLC main line. The young enthusiast on the platform was waiting for the arrival of a Class 56 on a Pathfinder special; it is a rare event for a locomotive-hauled passenger train to pass through Widnes these days.

1 9 4 8

This was one of the most important years in our railways' history as the 'Big Four' were nationalised on 1 January. The 19,414 route miles were split up into six regions — Eastern, London Midland, North Eastern, Scottish, Southern and Western — with the largest, in terms of route miles, being the London Midland followed by the Scottish. The legend 'British Railways' started to appear on the sides of locomotive tenders and on tank engines very quickly. The famous 'Locomotive Exchanges', which have been extensively documented elsewhere, commenced in April.

Diesel-electrics Nos 10000 and 10001 started trials early in the year, just as the last 'Princess Coronation' and the first 'A1' Pacifics were completed. The famous LNER Garrett left its home territory to work on the Lickey Incline.

New Pullman services were introduced; these were the 'Tees-Tyne Pullman' and the 'Thanet Belle' whilst the 'Queen of Scots' was reintroduced. The 'Royal Scot' name was reinstated on the 10am Euston-Glasgow service. The nonstop King's Cross-Edinburgh service also restarted on 31 May.

It was quite a year for reinvigorating the railways after the war, although there were a number of derailments caused by the poor condition of the track.

No 10000 in LMS livery heads the 4.45pm St Pancras-Manchester express on 29 March 1948 past Sheet Stores Junction.
J. C. Flemons

There were four Class A4 Pacifics fitted with double chimneys when new and these were generally considered superior performers to the rest of the class. It was not surprising that the Eastern Region selected them to represent the region in the 'Locomotive Exchanges'. No 60034 Lord Faringdon passes over the water troughs at Bushey at the head of the down 'Royal Scot' (10am ex-Euston) on 19 May 1948.
C. C. B. Herbert

1949

The British Railways Board announced the new livery scheme for locomotives: plain black for freight, lined black for mixed traffic, lined green for passenger locomotives and lined blue for express locomotives. Unfortunately, the blue livery was short-lived; I well remember the 'A4s', 'Kings', 'Merchant Navies' and 'Princess Coronations' in this livery and very smart they looked too.

Many new named trains were introduced and some familiar names from prewar days reappeared. On the Southern, O. V. S. Bulleid retired as CME, but not before his double-deck four-car EMUs appeared and trials began with his 'Leader' class steam locomotive.

All the locomotives converted to oil firing during the war had been returned to conventional coal operation by the middle of the year, the last so treated being 'West Country' No 34046 *Braunton*.

Whilst new locomotives continued to appear, some old classes disappeared — such as the ex-LNWR 'Prince of Wales', 'Precursor' and 'Claughton'. Other casualties included the last 'Aberdare' on the Western.

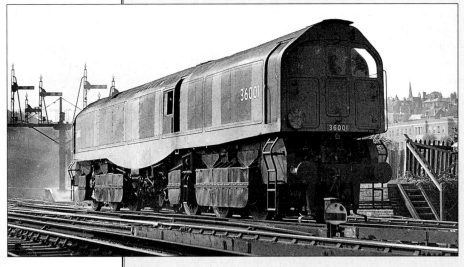

The first 'Leader', No 36001, commenced trials during the year. Built as an 0-6-6-0T, the firebox was situated in the centre of the locomotive, from where the fireman operated in very hot conditions. There was a driving cab at either end. The type never entered revenue-earning service and, in fact, Nos 36002 and 36003 were never completed. No 36001 is shown running bunker-first through Lewes on a trial run from Brighton to Crowborough on 31 August 1949.
C. C. B. Herbert

There are few details attached to this photograph other than the fact that it shows ex-London & South Western Class N15 'King Arthur' 4-6-0 No S453. The photograph must have been taken between February 1948 and March 1950, as the locomotive only carried the 'S' prefix between those dates. These prefixes — 'M', 'E' and 'S' were allocated — were applied by British Railways until it was decided to renumber the ex-LMS stock in the 4xxxx series, the ex-LNER stock in the 6xxxx series and the ex-SR stock in the 3xxxx range. The legend 'British Railways' was only applied for about two years before the 'Lion' emblem was introduced.
Ian Allan Library

1 9 5 0

The British Railways Board announced a massive locomotive building programme of Standard designs, plus a small number of inherited designs. In addition, a further 34,000 wagons and 2,400 coaches were to be constructed. Naturally this programme led to the withdrawal of some older designs. Two notable casualties were the last of the Highland 'Clan' class, No 54767 *Clan MacKinnon*, and the first of the GWR 'Castle' class, No 100 *A1 Lloyds*.

The first gas turbine locomotive, No 18000, arrived in the country from Switzerland having taken four years to complete. North British-built diesel-electric No 10800 also appeared on the scene; this locomotive was allocated to Willesden, but only lasted in service until August 1959. The first of the 'EM1' electrics for the Woodhead route, Nos E26001-3, were sent to Ilford for trials.

The 'Irish Mail' was involved in a bad accident at Penmaenmawr, when headed by rebuilt 'Royal Scot' No 46119 *Lancashire Fusilier*. The train hit 'Crab' 2-6-0 No 42885 resulting in a number of fatalities.

During the year, Crewe Works completed the building of its 7,000th locomotive. This was Ivatt 2-6-2T No 41272. To mark this fact a special plaque was attached to the locomotive; this plaque can be clearly seen in this photograph located beneath the BR crest.
Ian Allan Library

King's Cross-allocated 'A4' No 60003 Andrew K. McCosh *heads the down 'Capitals Limited' past the border sign at Lamberton Toll on 12 August 1950. The locomotive was running in the smart lined blue livery, which it kept for only 18 months before being repainted into BR Brunswick green. The train had been introduced the previous year. No 60003 was originally named* Osprey *but renamed in October 1942. The name* Osprey *was eventually to be carried by 'A1' No 60131. No 60003 was withdrawn from King's Cross in December 1962.*
E. R. Wethersett/Ian Allan Library

1951

This was the year that the first of the BR Standard locomotives appeared, commencing in January with Class 7MT No 70000 *Britannia* from Crewe. In May, Standard Class 5MT No 73000 emerged from Derby, with Standard Class 4MT No 75000 from Swindon during the same month. The first of the Standard Class 4MT tanks, No 80010, appeared from Brighton. Most of these new designs had a working life of only 10 to 15 years. A second gas turbine, No 18100, was built by Metro-Vickers; whilst two new 1Co-Co1 diesel-electrics, Nos 10201 and 10202, were constructed at Ashford Works.

This was the year of the 'Festival of Britain' and 'Britannia' No 70004 *William Shakespeare* was exhibited on the South Bank before being allocated to the Southern Region, where it became for many years a regular performer on the 'Golden Arrow'.

Two events were portents of developments over the rest of the century: 133 branch lines were identified for closure whilst, on a brighter note, the first preserved railway in Britain, the Talyllyn, reopened.

The first brand-new BR Standard Class 5MT No 73000 was photographed at Neasden on 25 April 1951 before entering service at Stratford. By November the locomotive had moved to the London Midland Region, where it spent most of its working life until withdrawn from Patricroft shed at Manchester in March 1968.
C. C. B. Herbert

The new 1,600hp 1Co-Co1 main line diesel No 10201, built at Ashford for work on the Southern Region, is shown leaving Derby at the head of the 12.5pm train to St Pancras during January 1951. It was initially allocated to Derby and finished its days at Willesden, going into store in January 1963 before being cut up five years later.
J. Lakin

An early picture of BR Standard Class 7MT No 70000 Britannia. It was allocated when new to the Eastern Region for express services between Liverpool Street and Norwich. It later moved to the Midland Division, finishing up at Newton Heath from where it was withdrawn in May 1966. Happily the locomotive is preserved and has been seen in use on the main line in the 1990s.
Ian Allan Library

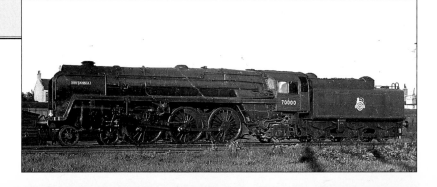

1 9 5 2

A glance through my notebook makes fascinating reading for the year. The ex-GNR Class N1s were still hard at work pounding the 1 in 50 gradients of West Riding, whilst on another line I knew well — that from Ashchurch to Malvern via Upton — services were still in the hands of the Midland 0-4-4Ts in BR lined black livery, Nos 58051 and 58071 being the regular performers. I also had my first trip on the Somerset & Dorset, with haulage provided by Class 5 No 45440 — a locomotive which had a long association with the line.

Apart from seeing the English Electric diesel No 10202 at Exeter, I don't think there was any sign of things to come, unless I saw No 10000 at Shap (which I never bothered to photograph). I note that I 'copped' 'Clan' No 72009 at Kingmoor in September; I suppose that it is just coincidence that as the new class was introduced so the last of 'Clan Goods', No 57954, was withdrawn.

The Fell diesel entered service during the year as did gas turbine No 18100. However, the year will always be remembered for the disastrous Harrow & Wealdstone accident, the details of which have been written about many times, but even with the passage of time the terrible statistics of 112 fatalities and 354 seriously injured are still frightening. The other major event was the funeral of King George VI on 15 February when, because the correct No 4082 *Windsor Castle* was in works at the time for overhaul, the locomotive exchanged identities with sister No 7013 *Bristol Castle*.

When I lived at Halifax, the local L&YR shed was Sowerby Bridge, which still had some Fowler '7F' 0-8-0s, L&YR 0-6-0s, 'WDs' and a few 2-4-2Ts at the time. Still with LMS lettering after four years of Nationalisation, No 50752 is pictured just outside the shed building.

I lived at a place called Ovenden, just outside Halifax, until 1961 and my local line was the ex-GNR/L&YR joint from Halifax to Holmfield, whence the GNR continued to Bradford and Keighley and the Halifax High Level branched off the Pellon. The regular motive power on passenger trains was the 'N1' class 0-6-2Ts, with help from 'N5s', 'C12s' and others over the years. The freight traffic was in the hands of 'J39' 0-6-0s, 'J50' 0-6-0Ts, 'B1' 4-6-0s and various others, including 'K2' 2-6-0 No 61723. The Halifax High Level line was worked by locomotives from Wakefield or Sowerby Bridge — Fowler 0-8-0s, L&YR 0-6-0s, two Stanier '8Fs' for a period and one regular Fowler 0-6-0. I spent many hours at Holmfield, where this picture was taken of Class N1 No 69443 leaving for Halifax. Occasionally, I was invited into the signalbox and also had footplate rides to Pellon and St Pauls. On one occasion I helped shunt with Fowler 0-8-0 No 49540 in the yard and, whilst on the same duty the following day, the driver collapsed at the station with a heart attack and died; an extremely sad event. I travelled on the last train over the route; this was hauled by Newton Heath Class 5 No 45339 on 29 June 1960.

There were 168 of these North British Class C 0-6-0s, which became classified J36 by the LNER. Built between 1888 and 1900, some members of the class put in between 66 and 75 years' service. Two of the class had cut down chimneys for working the Gartverrie Sidings and were allocated to Kipps shed. No 65287 is at the shed along with 'J83' No 68444 on 7 September 1952.

Five of the BR Class 5MTs, Nos 73005-9, went new to Perth shed in 1951. No 73005 is pictured passing St Rollox shed on a morning Glasgow Buchanan Street-Aberdeen service on the stiff climb, mainly at 1 in 79, to Robroyston. I spent many hours at this shed, as a cousin of my father was shedmaster here at the time, and he organised a shed permit for me for all the sheds in Scotland at any time. I later obtained a lineside pass for the region. I am still eternally grateful for the shed pass, as it seemed to gain me access to any shed in the country.

The prototype Fell diesel was only about two months old when I took this picture of it in Derby Works on 20 April 1952. The locomotive only had a six-year career, being used primarily on Midland main line passenger services. It was withdrawn in November 1958.

Undoubtedly the family holiday I spent at Exmouth in 1952 was one of the worst I ever spent with my parents. Watching from our hotel there appeared to be a nonstop procession of trains passing along the other side of the estuary on the GWR main line when all I could see at Exmouth were some ex-Southern Class M7 0-4-4Ts. This caused a considerable amount of friction. I wanted to spend all my time at Exeter, whilst my parents thought I should spend my time on the more traditional summer holiday activities. I did escape on more than one occasion and saw blue-liveried 'Kings' and unrebuilt 'Merchant Navies'. A memorable Saturday at Newton Abbot on 16 August 1952 produced 'King' No 6012 King Edward VI on the down 'Cornish Riviera', which paused on the through line to attach 'Castle' No 111 Viscount Churchill for the climb over the banks. The most notable locomotive seen was 'Saint' No 2920 Saint David which arrived on a down train; unfortunately, my photograph of this is not really suitable for publication.

Another escape from Exmouth one afternoon allowed me to take some pictures at Exeter St David's on 22 August 1952. This shows No 1011 County of Chester leaving on a Manchester-Plymouth express in lined black BR livery. To the left is 2-6-2T No 4532 and an unrebuilt 'West Country' or 'Battle of Britain' ready to leave for Central. I would give a lot to be able to point my 6x7 Pentax at a sight like this today. No 1011 did not receive its double chimney until November 1958 and was the last of the class to be withdrawn, in November 1964.

I am extremely surprised that I bothered to take a picture of English Electric 1Co-Co1 1,750bhp diesel No 10202. It was caught on 14 August 1952 about to leave Exeter Central for Waterloo. I am now glad that I did, as it is one of only two photographs I have of the early main line diesels.

1953

*M*y activities this year were almost entirely confined to excellent shed and works visits, which were organised by a local group, although my parents restricted these to school holidays; this had been typical of my railway activities for a number of years. I did manage to take a few pictures on these shed bashes, but the object in those days was to get round as soon as possible so that we could gain enough time to fit in an extra shed at the end of the day; not exactly conducive to good photography!

Fortunately, I still have detailed records of all my 'spotting' days right back as far as the summer of 1946 and they now make fascinating reading; one could easily see 1,000 locomotives in a day on certain visits, when Crewe, Derby, the Toton area and Colwick were visited. I note from my records that on 26 April, 980 locomotives were seen and I copped 308 in the day!

Serious flooding started the year in the south and East Anglia. The year saw the last ex-Highland locomotive, No 54388 *Ben Alder*, withdrawn, as well as the last ex-Caledonian 4-6-0 (No 54650 from Hamilton) and the last 'Saint' (No 2920 *Saint David* — a locomotive I knew very well from the time I was living in the Worcester area; I remember I thought it looked very smart in its lined black livery).

New named trains — such as the 'Pembroke Coast Express', the 'Elizabethan' (replacing the 'Capitals Limited'), the 'Manxman' and the 'Man of Kent' — were introduced. Also making their appearances were the 'Starlight Expresses' from London to Glasgow with their return fares of £3 10s.

Branch closures continued and there were some bad accidents, the worst being when 10 people were killed when a Manchester Victoria-Bacup train hit an electric unit causing the first coach to fall 90ft off the viaduct.

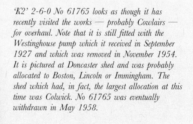

'K2' 2-6-0 No 61765 looks as though it has recently visited the works — probably Cowlairs — for overhaul. Note that it is still fitted with the Westinghouse pump which it received in September 1927 and which was removed in November 1954. It is pictured at Doncaster shed and was probably allocated to Boston, Lincoln or Immingham. The shed which had, in fact, the largest allocation at this time was Colwick. No 61765 was eventually withdrawn in May 1958.

Stratford-based Class L1 2-6-4T No 67726 is pictured on Doncaster shed, probably en route back to London after overhaul at Darlington Works. The class as a whole had a relatively short career, most members only achieving a working life of 12 or 13 years. The type was used primarily on suburban services out of Liverpool Street and Marylebone, with some also allocated to the northeast. After electrification of the Liverpool Street suburban services, the class was dispersed to a number of different sheds.

One of the large Class S1 0-8-4Ts, ex-Great Central to a design by Robinson and built in 1907 for shunting the massive coal yards at Wath-on-Dearne, is pictured at Mexborough shed. Wath-on-Dearne at one time served no less than 50 collieries. No 69901 was fitted with a booster, which had been removed in 1943. The first four members of the class were built by Beyer-Peacock in 1907 and 1908. A gap of 24 years then followed before Gorton Works produced two more; this pair was booster-fitted from new. The class was extremely successful, working around the clock except on Sundays. Two were eventually transferred to March to work Whitemoor Yard, but others were tried with little success elsewhere. Nos 69901 and 69905 were the last to be withdrawn, in 1957.

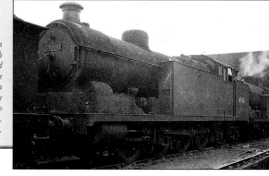

There were very few modifications undertaken to the famous Hughes 'Crabs', although five of the class were fitted with Lentz rotary cam gear until 1953, when they were modified with the Reidinger rotary valve gear. No 42818, which was one of the quintet involved, is pictured on 20 September 1953 outside the main erecting shop at Horwich Works. It is probable that during this works visit the Reidinger rotary valve was fitted. The shed plate 21A indicates that the locomotive was allocated to Saltley.

Little remains of the shed roof at Southport at this time — 20 September 1953. One of the 448 Aspinall-designed ex-L&YR Class F19s, No 52161, is at the shed in the company of local Class 5MT No 44989, Midland Compound No 41163 and an ex-L&YR saddle tank.

The London & North Western Classes G1 and G2 eventually totalled 301 locomotives; these were built between 1912 and 1922. They were simple, rugged locomotives and were the backbone of LNWR freight operations, some of them giving 50 years' service. Springs Branch shed, Wigan, where No 49352 is pictured on 20 September 1953, had a large allocation for many years.

There were seven of these ex-GCR Robinson-designed 0-6-0Ts, which became LNER Class J63. Six were built at Gorton in 1906 and the last, BR No 68210, did not emerge from the works until 1914. The class was primarily used at Immingham and surrounding sheds. Two were fitted with condensing equipment and used as station pilots at Liverpool Central, staying in that area until 1935. No 68208 was the first to be withdrawn, and is pictured in that condition at Gorton Works on 20 September 1953.

Photographs of the famous Gresley 'A4' No 60022 Mallard *seldom show it looking dirty and minus driving wheels. Obviously it had run hot on a main line duty and is caught here dumped at Doncaster shed awaiting attention.*

On 31 May 1953 'A3' Pacific No 60072 Sunstar *passes Pilmoor station at the head of a Bristol-Newcastle express. The locomotive was allocated to Heaton and Gateshead sheds for 34 years and was one of the members of the class to have a very brief spell, of nine months, at Holbeck for working over the Settle & Carlisle. After this it returned to Heaton and was withdrawn in October 1962. Pilmoor was the junction for the line to Boroughbridge and Harrogate; this closed in May 1958 when the East Coast main line had the additional up slow added.*

1 9 5 4

The BR Standard locomotive building programme continued in earnest, with examples of virtually all the types being constructed during the year; this, of course, included the now very famous No 71000 *Duke of Gloucester*. Whilst not exactly finding favour with the crews on the West Coast main line at the time, the locomotive has, of course, after modifications become one of the finest main line performers in preservation. To put matters into perspective, a total of 237 steam locomotives were built alongside 69 new diesels; also introduced were the 'EM2' (later Class 77) electrics for the Woodhead route.

Many locomotive classes, however, also became extinct. These included the last Cambrian-built engine, the last example from the Brecon & Merthyr and the last of the Cleobury Mortimer & Ditton Priors pannier tanks. Pacific No 46202 *Princess Anne* was also officially withdrawn after having been in store since the Harrow & Wealdstone disaster.

The 'Cornish Riviera Express' celebrated its 50th birthday, whilst the 'Bristolian' was reintroduced on its fast 1 ¾ hr schedule; this produced many performances of the train running in excess of 100mph. The most spectacular accident was when a little Class J88 0-6-0T ran away and plunged into the dock at Kirkcaldy; it was withdrawn after it had been recovered from its watery grave.

I continued to undertake extensive shed and works visits during the year, with trips over the country from Cornwall to Scotland. As the photographs will show, this resulted in little action photography. Mind you, my little Super Ikonta could not really cope with speeds in excess of 20mph anyway!

Hawksworth 'County' class 4-6-0 No 1012 County of Denbigh was originally allocated to Plymouth Laira when it entered service in February 1946. Initially the class was confined to Paddington-Penzance and Paddington-Wolverhampton services, but then eventually operated over virtually the whole ex-GWR network. In lined black livery and with a single chimney, No 1012 is leaving Plymouth on 19 August 1954 at the head of the down 'Cornish Riviera'. The ugly double chimney was fitted to No 1012 in September 1957 and the locomotive was withdrawn from Swindon shed in April 1964.

'Hall' No 6913 Levens Hall *of Plymouth Laira shed gets to grips with the 1 in 80 gradient out of Truro as it heads west on the 'Cornishman' on 19 August 1954. Built in February 1941, the locomotive is in BR lined black livery. It remained in service until June 1964.*

It must either have been a Saturday or school holidays judging by the number of schoolboys at the north end of York station on 10 April 1954 to observe one of the roller bearing-fitted Class A1s No 60156 Great Central *passing through the central road nonstop on the down 'Flying Scotsman'. The locomotive was built at Doncaster in October 1949 and was unnamed until July 1952. It emerged, when new, in the smart lined blue livery, which it retained only until July 1952 when it was painted into the lined green BR livery. It was allocated to King's Cross and Grantham until April 1959, before moving to Doncaster for five years; it was withdrawn from York shed in May 1965.*

Also on 10 April 1954, the up 'Flying Scotsman' was in the hands of Gateshead 'A1' No 60150 Willbrook. Built in June 1949, the locomotive had one month allocated to Heaton before being transferred to Gateshead, where it remained for over 11 years before ending its life at York shed in October 1964. It is pictured approaching York from the north round the sharp curve into the station.

One of the not very popular Thompson Class A2/2s, No 60505 Thane of Fife, pulls out of York station on 10 April 1954 at the head of the 8.35am Glasgow Queen Street-King's Cross service. This was the first of the class to be rebuilt from the 'P2' 2-8-2 in 1943. All of the class returned to their old stamping ground between Glasgow and Aberdeen on rebuilding, but were sent south in 1949 where they did a further decade of service based on York and New England sheds. No 60505 was withdrawn in November 1959.

There were few places where one could see 'Princess Coronations' and 'A4s' side by side; Carlisle and Aberdeen being possible locations if you were lucky. I was very lucky in August 1954 to have this photograph organised for me by the shedmaster at Eastfield, Mr Elliot, when No 46231 Duchess of Atholl made a rare visit to the shed to use the wheel drop. Haymarket 'A4' No 60027 Merlin was on shed so I had the 'Princess Coronation' pulled out of the shed for this line-up. Not the best of results from my very old Super Ikonta, but still an interesting picture.

The Brown-Boveri gas turbine No 18000 entered service in May 1950 and was based at Old Oak Common, where it is seen on 21 April 1954. It was withdrawn in December 1960 and sent to Austria. It was rescued for preservation in the UK and is now on display at the Crewe Heritage Centre.

Six of the BR Standard 2-6-2Ts, Nos 84010-15, were allocated to Low Moor, Bradford, when new in 1953 for local services. They only stayed for around a year to 18 months before moving on. Nos 84014 and 84015 are pictured ready to depart with local workings from the east end bay platforms at Huddersfield on 9 January 1954.

One of the seven highly regarded Class 47xx 2-8-0s No 4705, which I believe were originally intended for express freight workings but which proved capable on passenger duties, is shown at its home shed, Old Oak Common, on 21 April 1954. The locomotives are perhaps best remembered for their summer outings on extra trains from Paddington to Devon. No 4700 emerged from Swindon in May 1919, and all the class put in more than 40 years' service.

Compound No 40933 was built at Vulcan Foundry in June 1927 and remained in service until April 1958. Photographed at Willesden on 21 April 1954, the locomotive was attached to a high-sided tender during this period and allocated to Monument Lane shed in Birmingham. I believe it was used to pilot expresses from the area to Euston. Other members of the class, such as No 40936, also ran with this tender.

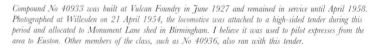

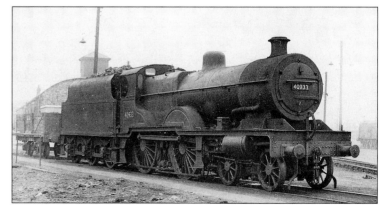

The famous ex-LNWR 'Cauliflower' class of 0-6-0s was built between 1880 and 1902, with 69 still in service at Nationalisation. In their later years the survivors were to be found on services around the Lake District. One of the last in service was No 58412, which is shown on 6 September 1954 in store at Carlisle Upperby shed.

One of the 10 Deeley dock tanks introduced in 1907, No 41529, is pictured on 25 April 1954 after attention at Derby, its home shed. The locomotive survived until 1965.

The Class 57xx 0-6-0PT and its derivatives eventually totalled no less than 863 locomotives, making it possibly the most successful 0-6-0T ever built in this country. The type was just as capable on passenger duties as it was on freight. Ten members of the class were fitted with condensing equipment for working over the London Transport Metropolitan/Central lines to Smithfield goods depot. They were normally to be seen on empty stock duties around Paddington; one of these 10, No 9702 (built at Swindon in 1933), is on shed shunting duty at Old Oak Common on 22 April 1954.

1955

At this time, my photography was somewhat limited; I see from my records that I only took about 150 photographs in the year and it was very much on a hit or miss basis. Most pictures were taken during shed visits, which, in spite of using public transport, covered a wide area from Scotland to London as well as East Anglia.

The BR Standard classes were still being built in quantity; the year's products included the batch of Franco-Crosti-boilered Class 9F 2-10-0s. This batch was allocated when new to Wellingborough.

The diesel era was just getting under way, with the Napier 'Deltic' prototype starting trials from its base at Speke Junction, Liverpool, and various new shunters also entered service. Lightweight DMUs started operation in the northeast on Middlesbrough-Newcastle workings. However, the Modernisation Plan foreshadowed radical changes to the BR fleet and the eventual elimination of steam.

Pullman services returned to the Western Region with the 'South Wales Pullman' from Swansea to Paddington. Also on the Western, comparative trials were conducted between 'Princess Coronation' No 46237 *City of Bristol* and 'Kings' on the main line.

In another hint of the future — this time preservation — the Ffestiniog Railway reopened on 23 July between Portmadoc and Boston Lodge, eight years after closure.

The 120 members of the Raven-designed 'Q6' class were, along with the 'J27' 0-6-0s, the backbone of freight operation in the northeast for some 50 years. On 18 September 1955 No 63391 is seen at the coaler at Blaydon shed, having recently returned from an overhaul at Darlington Works. Built in September 1918 at Darlington, No 63391 remained in service until April 1965.

A selection of headboards are seen hanging outside at Grantham shed on 9 August 1955.

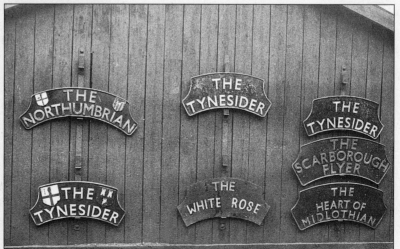

The Great Eastern Class S69 4-6-0s were built over a long period, from 1911 until 1928, and were classified B12 by the LNER in 1923. They were successful and handsome locomotives, both in their original and rebuilt form. No 61568 was built at Stratford in June 1920 and was rebuilt as a 'B12/3' in April 1941 and survived until August 1959. Pictured on 25 August 1955, it was at this time a Norwich engine and is seen alongside a 'J39' 0-6-0 at Cromer shed.

There were four of these little 0-4-4Ts built for the Highland Railway in 1905-6. They will always be associated with the Dornoch-The Mound branch, although they did work other lines as well. Only two survived through to Nationalisation; of these, No 55053 was fully lined out after its last overhaul at St Rollox in 1955, but had only two years' service after that date. Its partner, No 55051, was withdrawn in 1956. No 55053 is pictured, with myself on the footplate, on 4 July 1955, at Balornock shed, Glasgow (65B).

One of the once numerous Ramsbottom 'Special' 0-6-0STs built for the LNWR between 1870 and 1880, No 3323 is pictured at Crewe Works on 25 April 1955. A total of 258 of this type were constructed, of which 243 passed to the LMS in 1923; however, they were replaced thereafter by the Class 3F 0-6-0Ts (the 'Jinties') and only six survived to Nationalisation, all in the departmental fleet. Curiously No 3323 was renumbered 43323 in 1949 for a short period, but this duplicated another locomotive and it soon reverted to its original number. The last of the class were withdrawn in 1959.

Twelve of these Class J70 tram locomotives were built at Stratford between 1903 and 1921. They were mainly to be found at work at the docks at Yarmouth and Ipswich and on the Wisbech & Upwell line; they were displaced from the latter duty in 1952 by the arrival of Drewry diesel-mechanical 0-6-0s. No 68223, having been withdrawn in July 1955, is pictured on the scrap line at Stratford in September 1955.

The 'Y1' and 'Y3' classes of Sentinel locomotives did not appear until 1927. Most had relatively short careers of around 20 years, although some lasted longer in departmental service. No 68183 was one of these survivors and as late as 1955 received a major repair at Doncaster and was pictured there on 2 October 1955 awaiting its turn in the paint shop. This locomotive was to last until 1959, although two others of the type lasted until 1964.

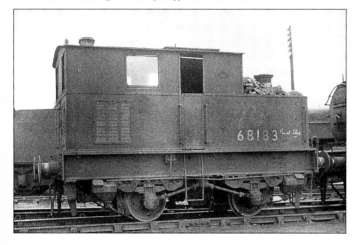

There were four members of the 'A2/1' class; two of the class started work in England before No 60507 Highland Chieftain headed across the border to join Nos 60509 and 60510. No 60508 Duke of Rothesay remained in England until withdrawal. No 60507 is pictured storming up Cowlairs Bank in April 1955 with a banker on the 4pm Glasgow Queen Street-Edinburgh service. No 60507 accumulated 786,505 miles in service before being withdrawn in December 1960.

Rebuilt 'Royal Scot' No 46105 Gordon Highlander *was a Polmadie locomotive for many years. It was on that shed's allocation list in 1933 and 1947 and was withdrawn from the shed in December 1962. In April 1955, looking in good external condition and with 'blood and custard' coaching stock, the locomotive makes a fine sight as it pulls out of Glasgow Central station with an afternoon working to Edinburgh.*

'Dukedog' class 4-4-0 No 9012 was rebuilt from the frames of 'Earl' class No 3405 in March 1937 and was allocated the name Earl of Eldon, *which it never carried as that name was applied to 'Castle' No 5055. The 'Dukedogs' were mainly employed on the ex-Cambrian lines and No 9012 is seen ready to depart from Oswestry on 15 July 1955 at the head of a local train to the west. The locomotive was withdrawn eventually in July 1957.*

The history of the Great Central 'ROD' class is complex as a result of all the rebuilding that took place. A total of 100 locomotives were purchased by the Great Western, 20 in 1919 and 80 in 1925; the class gave excellent service working alongside the GWR '28xx' class. No 3023 entered service on the GWR in August 1925 and survived until October 1955, two months after this photograph was taken on 9 August 1955.

All the 10 Franco-Crosti-boilered Standard 2-10-0s were originally allocated to Wellingborough shed. They were not as successful as hoped in terms of fuel economy and were returned to a conventional form between September 1959 and July 1962. As a result of the smaller boiler fitted, this batch was not as powerful as the remainder and were classified 8F rather than 9F. They never received smoke deflectors and nearly all of them lasted until 1967. No 92022 is seen on shed at Wellingborough in original condition on 5 August 1955.

1 9 5 6

It has been some time since I had a close look at my pictures taken before 1956 and I was surprised to find a few reasonable negatives. I was fortunate to be able to borrow a friend's Voightlander Bessa II, which had an excellent Skopar lens, but the front end had a bad habit of moving when using the fast shutter speeds. On other occasions I used an old Rolleiflex, which was not in very good condition.

During 1956 a large number of shed visits were made; this included a weekend trip when all the sheds in London were covered — this was quite an experience. I remember that Stratford (30A) had around 300 locomotives on shed on the Sunday and I am sure that, even then, I didn't manage to see them all.

There were some notable events during the year. On a sad note for enthusiasts, the famous Lickey banker, 0-10-0 *Big Bertha*, was withdrawn. The locomotive had managed to cover over 838,000 miles in its 37-year life, virtually all of it travelling up and down the incline. The Liverpool Overhead Railway closed; this was one of the first electric railways in Britain. BR Standard class locomotives were still being built in quantity and the first rebuilt 'Merchant Navy' emerged from Eastleigh Works.

As a result of the temporary withdrawal of the ex-GWR 'Kings', the ex-LMS 'Princess Coronation' and 'Princess Royal' Pacifics were to be seen on the South Devon banks at the head of the 'Cornish Riviera Express' and other workings.

The Welshpool & Llanfair Light Railway ran for the last time under BR ownership and another disappearance saw the abolition of Third Class tickets.

Looking back, it was quite a productive year; no thanks, however, to my extremely unreliable BSA 250cc motorcycle, which I had expected to perform like a much bigger machine and didn't.

Buxton was originally an LNWR shed, but always seemed to have a selection of ex-MR engines on its books. Coded 9D in the LMS reorganisation of 1935, Buxton still had this ex-MR 0-4-4T No 58083 (Midland Railway No 1420) which appeared, when recorded on 6 July 1956, to be in working order and was possibly used on trains between Buxton and Millers Dale. Originally, there were more than 200 of the class and the last was withdrawn in 1960.

The Class D49 'Hunts' and 'Shires' were seen in the Leeds area for many years. No 62774 The Staintondale is pictured on 7 August 1956 at the west end of Leeds City station, probably getting ready to work a train to Harrogate as it was allocated to Starbeck shed.

Ex-Great Western Mogul No 5381, of Wolverhampton Oxley shed, passes through the centre road at Beaconsfield on 13 August 1956 at the head of an up freight for London. Beaconsfield is on the former Great Western & Great Central Joint line from High Wycombe. Today, passenger trains over the route are operated by Chiltern Railways.

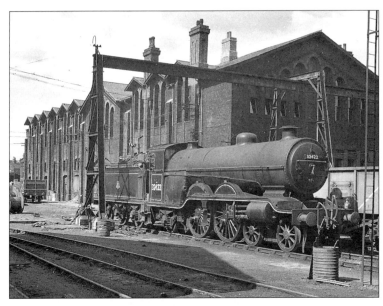

One of the handsome Marsh Atlantics, No 32422 North Foreland, is at Stewarts Lane shed awaiting possible repair on 12 August 1956. The locomotive had failed, with a broken left cylinder and, as it was withdrawn a month after this photograph, I doubt whether it ever received attention. It was built in July 1911 at Brighton and, like many others of the class, probably ran over a million miles during its 45-year life. It is a great pity that none of the class survives in preservation.

A fine selection of ex-GWR locomotives was lined up around the turntable inside Swindon shed on 2 September 1956. From left to right can be seen an unidentified 'Modified Hall', 'Castles' Nos 5000 Launceston Castle and 5009 Shrewsbury Castle, 'King' No 6023 King Edward II (still with a single chimney) and one of the fine 2-8-0s, No 3836. A sight to please any GWR enthusiast.

One of the best known and most interesting regular workings in my home area was the Heaton-Red Bank (Manchester) empty van train. This ran across the Pennines over the Calder Valley route and offered a great variety of motive power, either side of York or Leeds where locomotive changes took place over the years. The train could include up to 25 vans, which always resulted in double-heading. The service remained steam-hauled until July 1966, although there had been a mixture of steam and diesel working prior to that date. Even after it went over to diesel haulage a wide variety of classes was used. On 23 July 1956 Newton Heath locomotives, 'Crab' No 42701 and Class 5MT No 45284 head west over Luddendenfoot water troughs.

Another fine-looking 4-4-0, this time one of the famous ex-North British Class D30 'Scotts', No 62437 Adam Woodcock, is caught on 29 August 1956 working a freight out of Portobello at the north end of the Waverley route. This was not the type of work for which the class had been built between 1914 and 1920. The locomotive still had nearly two years to go before it was withdrawn, but I doubt that it did a great deal of work during that time.

One of the handsome ex-GCR Class D11/1s No 62664 Princess Mary finds itself in unusual surroundings at Manchester Exchange on 4 May 1956. As can be seen, the locomotive is in excellent condition as it had been prepared specially to work an Ian Allan 'Pennine Pullman' railtour over the Calder Valley route at the weekend. Together with No 62662 Prince of Wales, No 62664 had been loaned to Newton Heath shed for a short period and when recorded here No 62664 was being used on a local train; this was possibly to check that all was well and to familiarise the crew with the locomotive.

1957

*T*his was the first year that I started taking colour slides. Not many were taken and many were discarded. With a film speed of 8ASA and a Voightlander Vito B camera, with a maximum aperture of f3.5, it was very difficult to record anything moving.

The main activity during the year was still represented by shed and works visits. As illustrated, the main trip was to Scotland, when I managed to persuade my father to lend me his Hillman Minx. He was very protective about his cars and didn't think that 'shed bashing' was a good use for them. I don't think that I made it plain at the time that I intended to visit Wick and Thurso and, as a result, I had a great deal of explaining later about the 1,900 miles added to the clock in four days. It was a very memorable trip with good weather and, apart from returning still wanting to see ex-CR tank No 55126 (which was out at Kyle of Lochalsh), I had seen all the steam locomotives allocated to Scotland. I was using the 35mm camera for black and white work, which was much more successful than the colour results.

On BR it was a bad year for safety, with a number of major accidents. The worst of t hese was at Lewisham, when 90 people lost heir lives.

As normal there were 'firsts' and 'lasts'. The last steam locomotive to be built at Doncaster, Standard Class 4MT No 76114, emerged on 16 October, whilst the first maroon 'Princess Coronation', No 46245 *City of London*, appeared as did the first rebuilt 'West Country', No 34005 *Barnstaple*.

New diesel-electrics to appear for the first time included the Type 2s later designated as Class 20 and the Class 31/0s. The former were initially allocated to Devon's Road whilst the latter were split between Ipswich and Stratford. In Scotland, cross-country DMUs built at Swindon were introduced on Edinburgh-Glasgow services, whilst on the Southern Region, the Hampshire DEMUs, which have given such excellent service, also made their first appearance.

No 62387 was one of the last six of the famous Worsdell 'R' class 4-4-0s in traffic. It was made available for the Railway Correspondence & Travel Society 'Yorkshire Coast' railtour on 23 June 1957. It was specially cleaned up for the occasion and is pictured waiting for the stock to arrive at the east end of Leeds City station. It hauled the train as far as York, where 'D49/1' No 62731 Selkirkshire took over. The 'R' class was designated Class D20 by the LNER and the last were withdrawn from Alnmouth shed in September 1957.

The 'Yorkshire Coast' railtour was the first of many on which I travelled. It was organised by the West Riding branch of the RCTS. Part of the tour was along the Easingwold branch in open wagons. The branch locomotive at this time was 'J71' 0-6-0T No 68246, which had been built in 1889. The passengers are seen here climbing aboard ready to depart from Alne, having just seen 'A4' No 60028 Walter K. Whigham *pass by at speed on an up express.*

A busy scene at the north end of Stirling station is recorded on 8 June 1957. BR Standard Caprotti No 73146 has just arrived on a Glasgow Buchanan Street-Dundee service, whilst Kingmoor Class 5 No 45334 waits on the carriages that will form an evening local service. To the right a locally-based Standard tank, No 80125, carries out some shunting.

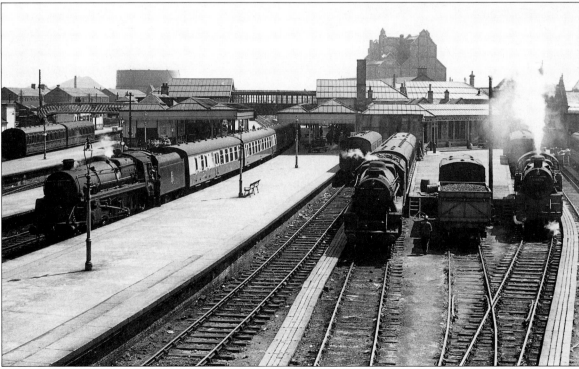

Rebuilt 'Royal Scot' No 46100 Royal Scot is nearly complete after overhaul on 16 June 1957 as it waits for its tender to be attached outside the erecting shop at Crewe Works.

Midland '2P' 4-4-0 No 40541, of Bournville shed, stands alongside Midland Compound, No 41199 (which was allocated to Sheffield Millhouses), around the open turntable at Derby shed (17A) on 24 March 1957.

The pictures on these pages were taken on a mammoth shed 'bash', when, in four days, I visited with three friends every shed, including sub-sheds, in Scotland north of Motherwell, except for Kyle of Lochalsh, Fort William and Mallaig. I managed to 'cop' my last Class 5, No 45477, and as a result of the trip the only locomotive allocated to Scottish Region which I had not seen was Caledonian 0-4-4T No 55126, which was the Kyle of Lochalsh pilot. I never, in fact, saw the locomotive. This picture, taken on 9 June 1957, shows the famous water tower at Inverness shed, with Perth-based Class 5 No 44924 present.

Caledonian 4-4-0 No 54491 stands outside the shed at Wick on 10 June 1957, with Inverness Class 5 No 45319 in the background. I remember that the evening before I had been taking hand-held pictures on the shed at 10.30pm.

A very quick visit to the Aberfeldy branch on our way home on 10 June 1957 found ex-Caledonian Class 439 No 55209 working the service. The locomotive is pictured at Ballinluig Junction running round its coach.

Three more pictures from the Scottish shed 'bash'. A busy scene at the coaling plant at Kipps shed on 8 June 1957 shows Holmes-designed ex-North British Class J36 No 65225 having its tender filled, with the last of the Gresley 'N2/3s' No 69596 awaiting attention. At the end of the 1920s, there were 44 of the 'N2' class allocated to Scotland.

The Class Y9 0-4-0STs were introduced by Drummond, although normally are credited to Holmes. These little North British tanks were built between 1882 and 1899 and most put in more than 60 years of service. The majority were allocated to St Margaret's shed in Edinburgh and could usually be found working in Leith docks. On 8 June 1957 No 68101 was at Dunfermline; it remained in service until October 1962.

Only two of these fine-looking Class V4s were built, in 1941. Records suggest that wherever they were used, the pair appeared to be liked by the crews and performed well. They were tested in East Anglia, the West Riding of Yorkshire and on most of the LNER lines in Scotland. By this date, 9 June 1957, No 61700 Bantam Cock and No 61701, generally known as Bantam Hen, had little work at Ferryhill, where I persuaded the shed foreman to pull the latter out of the shed for photographs. It was withdrawn four months later.

1958

Looking back 40 years to 1958, it would appear that this was the year that diesel traction really became a major force in this country, although electric power had been around, particularly on the Southern Region, for many years. In hindsight, it does seem very odd that we rushed headlong into diesel traction, rather than phasing out steam more gradually and expanding the electric route network, which would have benefited the railways more in the long term.

Main line diesels to appear for the first time included various Type 2s (the Classes 26 and 27), the English Electric Type 4s (the Class 40s) and the Metro-Vick Co-Bos (the Class 28s). On the Southern, the 2,500hp No E5000 was also introduced; and the first of the future Class 73s. On the London Midland Region, the first 25kV ac trains operated between Wilmslow and Mauldeth Road. Lightweight railbuses started operation and the experimental battery-powered multiple-unit was introduced on the Ballater service in Scotland.

As this was happening, Crewe Works turned out its last new steam locomotive — Class 9F 2-10-0 No 92250; this was the 7,331st locomotive built at Crewe.

This year was, as far as I was concerned, probably the last one that I devoted to a lot of shed visits around the country, choosing to concentrate more on the lineside photography. However, I still enjoy the occasional depot visit. As the selection of photographs show, there was reasonable coverage of the country from London to Fort William, largely due to the trusty Triumph 21 motorcycle.

Unrebuilt 'Merchant Navy' No 35019 French Line CGT waits at the ash pits of its home shed, Nine Elms, for servicing on 13 September 1958. The locomotive was built in June 1945 and originally numbered 21C19. It was rebuilt in May 1959, running for six years in its rebuilt guise.

A general view of the ash pits at Nine Elms on a Saturday afternoon — 13 September 1958 — sees 'Merchant Navy' No 35026 Lamport & Holt Line, 'Lord Nelson' No 30861 Lord Anson and unrebuilt 'Merchant Navy' No 35024 East Asiatic Company awaiting servicing.

No 30909 St Pauls was one of the
Maunsell Class V 'Schools' fitted with a
multiple-jet blastpipe and large-diameter
chimney. It is shown on 13 September 1958
coming off the turntable at Stewarts Lane shed,
where it was allocated at this time. Built in
July 1930, it survived until February 1962.

An almost new DMU (later Class 104) arrived
at Hawes on 6 September 1958 with a special
organised by the Yorkshire Publicity Association.
The station, is still in existence as a tourist centre.
Opened on 1 October 1878 it lost its passenger
services on 16 March 1959. I believe that this
was the only occasion that a DMU visited this
section of the Garsdale-Northallerton line.

Before entering service, the first North British Bo-Bo No D8400 (later Class 16) is pictured outside Doncaster Works on 17 August 1958 alongside BRCW Type 2 (later Class 26) No D5300. The North British locomotive was allocated to Stratford shed during its brief career of 10 years. Fortunately, No D5300 (later No 26001) has survived into preservation after 35 years of service on the main line.

The ex-North London Railway shed Devon's Road, coded 1D, was the first all-diesel depot in the country and the British Thomson-Houston Type 1s (later Class 15s) were amongst the first locomotives to be allocated to it. No D8200 was nearly one year old when I photographed it on shed on 13 September 1958.

The mill chimneys of Sowerby Bridge stand out clearly on the skyline on 10 August 1958 as the crew prepare for what was likely to be a fairly rough ride on 'WD' 2-8-0 No 90650 if they were to keep time as far as Wakefield. The train had arrived from Lancashire and was split here, the first portion heading to Bradford Exchange and this section going to Wakefield.

In 1958, the ex-LNWR Class G2 0-8-0s were seen along the North Wales Coast main line regularly, No 49416 is arriving at Llandudno Junction with an empty ballast train on 8 April 1958. The train was probably heading for Penmaenmawr. Note how clear the embankment is on the right; today, in comparison, it would not be so easy to stand at this location.

A familiar sight at Tebay shed for many years were the Fowler 2-6-4Ts that were used as bankers on Shap. Nos 42396 and 42404, which performed these duties for many years, stand outside the shed on 11 August 1958 awaiting their next call of duty.

The down 'Waverley' approaches Crossflatts, just north of Bingley, on 8 November 1958 headed by an unidentified Stanier Class 5. Rather surprisingly, the nine-coach train is having the assistance of Holbeck-allocated '2P' 4-4-0 No 40491. The fifth vehicle is a 12-wheeled dining car.

This is one of my favourite 'Princess Coronation' photographs and shows green-liveried No 46241 City of Edinburgh making a steady ascent of Shap past the little signalbox at Scout Green on 26 May 1958. The locomotive spent the majority of its time allocated to Camden shed, which is probably the reason why it averaged 72,202 miles per annum during its life, this being the third highest for the class. It was withdrawn in September 1964.

No 46256 Sir William Stanier was the last Pacific to enter service under the LMS; the last of the class, No 46257 City of Salford, entered traffic after Nationalisation. The two were regarded as improved members of the class, although it appears that their performance was much the same as for the rest of the type. No 46256 became the last of the class to be withdrawn after working a special from Crewe to Carlisle and return on 29 September 1964. It is seen in its red livery hauling the up 'Royal Scot' near Preston Brook on 4 August 1958 when allocated to Camden shed.

On 19 June 1958, what appear to be new brakevans are shown at the rear of an up freight as it passes south past York shed.

I don't know why I happened to have a piece of chalk in my pocket on 17 August 1958, but it came in useful to highlight the M&GN lettering on the tablet-catcher which was fitted to the tender of Ivatt Class 4MT No 43069 when I saw it at Goole shed.

An interesting sight in the yard at York shed on 14 June 1958. I don't know if they were loading or unloading, but one girder is on the wagon and the second is on the ground.

At this time the 'Coronation' observation car used to be attached to the rear of the 10.15 Glasgow Queen Street-Fort William service during the summer months. This would have given a splendid view of the banking engine up Cowlairs Bank. The coach was turned on the turntable at Fort William shed ready for the return working at 4.20pm. Local Class J36 No 65300 is ready to return the coach to the station on 1 September 1958, whilst 'K2' No 61788 Loch Rannoch is dead on the shed. Ben Nevis can be seen in the background.

March shed, coded 31B, was primarily for freight and served the large marshalling yard at Whitemoor, where trains were assembled and despatched all over the Eastern Region. The shed also had a few passenger duties and back in 1958 it had an allocation of Class B17 'Sandringhams'. During a visit on a Sunday evening, 4 May 1958, Class B17/4 Doncaster Rovers is dead, whilst No 61633 Kimbolton Castle, which was a 'B17/6', is being steamed along with 'K1' No 62020. The photograph gives some idea of the variety of classes to be seen at this shed in 1958.

In good external condition on 21 September 1958, No 61653 Huddersfield Town, which was a Class B17/6, leaves March with a local train heading for Ely.

Spalding was a sub-shed to New England and a variety of dead locomotives were to be seen on a visit early on a Sunday morning, 4 May 1958. From left to right are Ivatt Class 4MT No 43062, 'K2' No 61750, '4MT' No 43083 and 'J6' No 64191. There were a further five Class J6s and five more Ivatt '4MTs', plus a 'J69/1' 0-6-0T and a diesel shunter No 11160, on the shed as well.

1 9 5 9

This was a year of considerable development on the railways, albeit in small isolated patches. For example, electric traction commenced between Victoria and Newhaven (using Class 71 locomotives) and the first 25kV locomotive for the West Coast scheme was handed over to BR. Colchester-Clacton went over to 25kV and the Bury-Manchester services received new units (the future Class 504s). Many new diesels appeared, such as the first 'Peak' No D1, but at the same time some of the early diesels, such as the 800hp diesel-electric No 10800 and the SR diesel-mechanical shunter No 11001, were being withdrawn.

Several steam classes became extinct. The most significant, as far as I was concerned, was the demise of the ex-GNR Class N1, since these had operated the local services in the West Riding for many years. Another notable casualty was the unique ex-LNER Class W1 4-6-4 No 60700.

I appear to have had an active year, the most significant trip being to the ex-Great North of Scotland lines to the north of Aberdeen. As usual, I had left it far too late as most of the traffic was now dominated by the BR Standard Class 4MT tanks, but I did manage to get some pictures in spite of the

bad weather. It was a memorable trip as we camped out, getting fairly wet, and was completed using a brand new Ford Popular. This had a three-speed gearbox and did not like going above 55mph. I remember my friend's father complaining that the new family car had got 900 miles on the clock after a week!

For myself, most trips were by motorbike, a Triumph 21 Twin which managed a maximum speed of about 80mph and a fuel consumption of 80mpg. With petrol at about six shillings a gallon, I could have a good trip to Scotland for under £2; but that was half my weekly wage.

Little had changed on the local scene, but I made frequent trips to Shap where I took innumerable photographs. The future, in the form of the Type 4s on the Standedge route and the East Coast main line, was rapidly approaching. Looking back, I suppose that 1959 represented the lull before the storm, but unfortunately I did not approach photography in a logical fashion, spending far too much time around Shap where steam was to last for another seven years, rather than concentrating on the Great Western and Great Eastern areas where steam's disappearance was imminent.

This is one of the two ex-Great North of Scotland Class Z4 0-4-2Ts, No 68191, which spent virtually all its career shunting in Aberdeen docks, averaging about 10,000 miles each year of its 44-year life. There were also two Class Z5s, which were similar. Both classes were built by Manning Wardle & Co in 1915. All four locomotives were allocated to Kittybrewster shed. The date is 11 June 1959.

The BR Standard Class 4 2-6-4Ts, together with a few Standard Class 4MT 2-6-0s, virtually took over the workings of the ex-GNSR lines before the diesels arrived around 1960. No 80028 was working a freight to Fraserburgh on 12 June 1959 and is seen heading norh past Auchnagatt, situated between Ellon and Maud Junction. Sadly, today, virtually nothing remains of the ex-GNSR network, save for the line from Aberdeen to Keith.

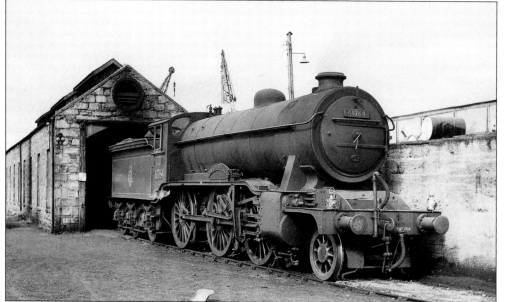

I was delighted to find Class K2 2-6-0 No 61764 Loch Arkaig inside the shed at Mallaig in light steam when I arrived on 22 July 1959. I managed to persuade the person in charge to move it out for a photograph and then asked if it could be substituted for the booked 'K1' back to Fort William for the evening train. This was also promised but did not materialise; he probably thought the best way of getting rid of me was to say 'Yes' and it worked. As a result, I never had a trip behind a 'K2' on the West Highland line.

Ribblehead Viaduct, without scaffolding, pictured on 16 May 1959. A clean Carlisle Kingmoor Class 5 No 44795, which meant that it was recently ex works, heads a northbound freight towards Blea Moor. The viaduct was built between 1870 and 1875; it has 24 spans in its 440yd length and a maximum height of 100ft.

I was extremely surprised when 'Princess Royal' No 46212 Duchess of Kent appeared at the head of the down 'Royal Scot' on 14 June 1959 as it rushed through Tebay station. The train was virtually monopolised by the 'Princess Coronations', although I did see it running with two 'Jubilees' over Shap one Saturday around this time. The Birmingham-Glasgow service, which was often hauled by a 'Princess Royal', passed a few minutes later behind 'Princess Coronation' No 46248 City of Leeds.

Red-liveried 'Princess Coronation' No 46243 City of Leicester makes steady progress with the up 'Royal Scot' past Harrison's Sidings, just north of Shap station, on 29 August 1959. Judging by the amount of coal on the tender, I would assume the locomotive had taken over the train at Carlisle. This locomotive was the last of the class to lose its streamlining, in 1949. It was eventually withdrawn on 12 September 1964.

In the days before the Worth Valley line became famous, Ivatt '2MT' No 41325 is pictured on 15 August 1959 arriving at Oxenhope station with the push-pull train from Keighley. The line originally opened on 13 April 1867 and lasted until December 1961. The story of the next 7½ years of negotiation and hard work by members of the preservation society has been told many times and, today, after 30 years of operation by the society, the line has become one of the finest preserved branches in the country.

One of the three ex-Great Central Class C14 4-4-2Ts transferred to Barnsley in 1957 for working the Doncaster-Penistone services was No 67445. As it turned out, this was the last of the class to survive, being withdrawn in December 1959. It is seen, on 9 May 1959, at Dodworth on a Saturday afternoon service. My belated thanks are due to the very friendly crew who waited for me to get off at every station to get a photograph.

A large number of the ex-LNWR 0-8-0s, plus ex-LT&SR 4-4-2Ts and 0-6-2Ts, were dumped awaiting scrapping on the Winsford branch in Cheshire when I recorded the scene on 27 September 1959. They were presumably despatched to Crewe Works for disposal.

Springwood Junction was situated between the tunnels about one mile to the west of Huddersfield station. It must have been a dirty and depressing signalbox to work, as at times it seemed to be covered continuously by smoke. On a fine summer's day, 22 May 1959, the signalman observes the passage of a Hull-Liverpool express from his open window. The train was headed by Farnley Junction Class 5 No 45204 and Patricroft 'Jubilee' No 45563 Australia; this was a regular combination for these trains.

Rebuilt 'Patriot' No 45531 Sir
Frederick Harrison *was a regular
performer on the Leeds-Newcastle
expresses through Huddersfield in the
1950s. It spent 13 years allocated
to Edge Hill shed in Liverpool,
having been rebuilt in 1947. It is
pictured emerging from the gloom of
the tunnel into the sunshine at
Huddersfield station on
27 September 1959 at the head of
the 9am departure from Liverpool
Lime Street. The locomotive would
return from Leeds back to Liverpool
at around 1pm. The services went
over to diesel traction in early 1961.*

*A well turned out Great Western
Class 45xx 2-6-2T No 5541, in
green livery, heads the up
'Cambrian Coast Express' — note
headboard — along the banks of
the Dovey estuary, between
Aberdovey and Dovey Junction,
with the Pwllheli portion of the
train on 28 March 1959. It
will be combined with the
Aberystwyth portion to be hauled
towards Shrewsbury by a 'Manor'
class 4-6-0. Aberystwyth and
Machynlleth sheds kept
locomotives well cleaned for this
train at that time.*

A busy scene at Bala on 29 March 1959. Class 74xx 0-6-0PT No 7428, still with GWR lettering after 11 years of British Railways, comes off the single-coach train which has just arrived from Blaenau Ffestiniog (Central) over the very scenic route, whilst No 8727 waits to attach itself to the train to take it forward to Bala Junction to connect with a Ruabon-Barmouth service. Passenger services ceased here in January 1965.

Once a daily sight at Swindon, ex works locomotives were run in on local duties before returning to their home sheds. On 7 June 1959 No 6811 Cranbourne Grange, still with a small tender, stands out amongst the other dirty locomotives before returning to its home shed of Bristol St Phillip's Marsh (82B).

1 9 6 0

The selection of pictures for this year shows that the majority of my photographic activity was in my home area plus frequent trips to Scotland. The big event locally was the allocation of Gresley 'A3s' for working the expresses over the Settle & Carlisle line to Glasgow; I had got used to the rebuilt 'Scots' ever since the first, No 6103 *Royal Scots Fusilier*, arrived at Holbeck back in 1943.

There were plenty of developments on British Railways. These included the introduction of the 'Blue Pullman' services on the Midland main line, the introduction and withdrawal of the electric Blue trains in Glasgow and the virtual elimination of steam on passenger workings in East Anglia.

The building of steam locomotives finally came to an end with the emergence of No 92220 *Evening Star* from Swindon Works. Another tradition came to an end when the last slip coach was dropped at Bicester on 9 September. Several well-known steam sheds — including Bristol Bath Road — lost their steam allocation, but sheds designed to handle the new diesel traction — such as Leeds Neville Hill on 17 June — opened.

Many steam classes became extinct. These included the Class B17 'Sandringhams' and the ex-North British Class D30 'Scots', the latter with their wonderful Scottish names such as *Wandering Willie* and *Jingling Geordie*. It is hard to believe but it is now 38 years since the electric operation of the West Coast services between Crewe and Liverpool or Manchester commenced; no wonder most of the line today requires modernisation.

On the diesel locomotive front, the first of the BRCW Type 3s (later Class 33s) appeared; at the time of writing, in early 1998, the last few of the type are still in service. Also the first English Electric Type 3s (later Class 37s) were introduced; many consider these to be the finest diesel locomotives built in this country and many remain in service today.

Modernisation of the railways was well and truly underway. However, it depended on where you lived as to how noticeable these changes were; fortunately, in the West Riding, steam still reigned supreme except for some DMUs, but it wasn't to stay that way for long.

Edge Hill (8A) rebuilt 'Royal Scot' No 46124 London Scottish *is ready to leave Leeds City on the 10.10am Newcastle-Liverpool service on 28 February 1960. The train had arrived from the north behind Neville Hill 'A3' No 60086* Gainsborough. *During the week, this train was often double-headed from Leeds for its journey over the Pennines, very often with a locomotive which was recently ex works from Crewe. In spite of the ample power, these trans-Pennine trains seldom seemed to produce any sparkling performances and often ran late. The good performances were to come in the dying years of steam, when on summer Saturdays local 'Jubilees' and Class 5s produced some very lively journeys.*

On the previous day, 27 February 1960, rebuilt 'Royal Scot' No 46124 London Scottish was also at the head of the 10.10am service, but was on this occasion being piloted by rebuilt 'Jubilee' No 45736 Phoenix, which was allocated to Crewe North shed at the time. This powerful combination is seen passing Farnley Junction shed on the climb out of Leeds to the summit in Morley Tunnel.

The first of the Southern Railway dc electric locomotives appeared in 1941 as No CC1. It was followed by No CC2 in 1945, but it was not until after Nationalisation that No 20003 arrived. There were differences in design and technical specification between the trio and, in my opinion, it would have been difficult to design a more unattractive locomotive. Nevertheless they gave good service, initially on freight and later on the Victoria-Newhaven boat trains, for which they will always be remembered. The last, No 20001, was withdrawn in January 1969. During their careers, the locomotives carried several liveries and No 20003 is seen in BR green during a visit to Eastleigh Works on 11 September 1960.

There are usually more passengers than this on the Keighley and Worth Valley line at Ingrow station today. Ingrow is a suburb of Keighley which once possessed two stations, this and Ingrow East on the ex-GNR line to Queensbury. Ivatt 2-6-2T No 41326 was a regular locomotive on the line in the branch's last years and was fitted with push-pull equipment. In preservation the station has been rebuilt and the yard relaid with old-fashioned 'setts', which makes it very attractive. At the bottom of the yard are the sheds which house the collection of the Vintage Carriages Trust. The date is 3 June 1960.

I couldn't believe my eyes when Gresley 'A3' No 60092 Fairway appeared at the head of the up 'Thames-Clyde' express at Gretna Green on 4 June 1960 and was even more amazed to see a 55A — Holbeck — shedplate attached. I had no idea that the rebuilt 'Royal Scots' and the 'Britannias' were being supplemented by the ex-North Eastern Region-allocated 'A3s'. However, they only had a very short spell, about 15 months, working the Scottish expresses over the Settle & Carlisle and ex-Glasgow & South Western main line to Glasgow; there was one exception, No 60038 Firdaussi, which survived longer and which was usually diagrammed for the 10.35am Leeds-Glasgow St Enoch service.

An unusual view taken from the footplate of Ivatt 2-6-0 No 46456, on an RCTS special along the old Cockermouth, Keswick & Penrith Railway at Penruddock on 4 September 1960, as one of the very early Derby lightweight DMUs passes. The special was double-headed by Nos 46442 and 46456, which had taken over the special at Workington and hauled it through to Penrith. The pair put up a remarkable performance, regaining more than 20min on this section after time had been lost with an unrebuilt 'Patriot' around the coast. Both locomotives were in immaculate condition, a tribute to the staff at Workington shed.

On a Sunday afternoon — 14 August 1960 — the down 'Royal Scot' with 17 coaches had been stopped alongside Carlisle Kingmoor shed before crossing over for wrong line working. No 46232 Duchess of Montrose, one of the non-streamlined members of the class, spent virtually all its days allocated to Polmadie (66A) shed. Along with other Polmadie 'Princess Coronations', its average annual mileage was around 10,000 miles less than the regular Camden and Crewe North locomotives. Perth-allocated Class 5 No 45473 waits in the loop to head north.

Two of my favourite LNER classes appear on this page, although sadly I don't have many pictures of them, particularly of the 'K2s'. The Scottish-based 'K2s' had a special appeal, possibly because most of them were named after Scottish lochs and because I vividly remember seeing two members of the class in apple green livery storming up the bank from Glenfinnan Viaduct to the station whilst I was being forced to watch some Highland Games at the head of Loch Shiel on a Saturday afternoon in August 1948. No 61788 Loch Rannoch is on the ash pits at Eastfield (65A) shed, Glasgow, on 12 August 1960, about 10 months prior to its withdrawal.

I got to know the Gresley 'V1' and 'V3' 2-6-2Ts well when I lived at Jordanhill, in Glasgow, during the late 1950s. I could hear their distinctive exhaust from my home as they passed on their way to Queen Street or Helensburgh. I used to travel each day into Glasgow behind one of the class, although occasionally a Class N2 or Ivatt Class 4MT 2-6-0 might appear. In those days most were kept in immaculate condition, in spite of spending so much time in the tunnels under Glasgow. By 1960 the condition of the locomotives had deteriorated, as the electric Blue trains were about to enter service (for the first time). On 11 August 1960 No 67605 is ready to leave Hyndland station for Airdrie.

The ex-North British Class C15 4-4-2Ts, which had worked the Arrochar-Craigendoran push-pull service on the West Highland line, were replaced by railbuses in September 1958. One of the railbuses, No 79971, a Park Royal unit built in July 1958, was working the service on 11 August. It is pictured approaching Craigendoran Upper station. The railbus lasted until February 1968 allocated to Eastfield; it was cut up in July 1984 at Mount Vernon, having been used as a staff mess room at Craigentinny since withdrawal.

The 'White Cockade' railtour ran on 18 June 1960 and was the last time, prior to preservation, that a Class K4 worked over the West Highland line. The locomotive involved was No 61995 Cameron of Locheil, which by this time was allocated to Thornton (62A) shed. The tour started from Glasgow Queen Street and headed to Fort William; photographic stops were made at virtually every station north of Crianlarich. On the return journey the train reversed at Crianlarich on to the Callander & Oban line for the return to Glasgow; this was possibly the only time that a member of this class ever worked over this route. The locomotive is shown taking water at Crianlarich Upper prior to reversing to the Low level. The trip was memorable for the fact that at Carlisle on my return home the terrible truth dawned on me as I wound my 35mm camera — on which I had been taking colour — on to frame 40 that the film had not been taken up on the spool for the whole trip; thank heavens for black and white.

A weekend trip on the motorcycle from Yorkshire to Fort William found me passing Ballachulish on 13 August 1960, where ex-Caledonian 0-4-4T No 55224 was on shed between duties on the branch to Connel Ferry. These locomotives were replaced by an Ivatt 2-6-0 shortly afterwards; which I believe was transferred from Colchester to Oban — quite a move. Passenger services over the branch ceased on 28 March 1966.

On a dismal summer's day — 18 June 1960 — the 3.15pm Fort William-Mallaig train passes the shed at Fort William at the start of its journey. Local 'K1' No 62052 was piloting, rather surprisingly, Eastfield allocated 'B1' No 61243 Sir Harold Mitchell; the normal motive power for the Mallaig line was usually 'K1s' or 'K2s'. A consist of one van and four coaches hardly warranted such power; possibly one of the locomotives was going to sort out a failure.

I don't know if it is generally realised that BR Standard Class 4MTs, and No 76001 in particular, used to be transferred in the summer months at this time from Motherwell to Fort William. I was fortunate to have a footplate ride on it — 13 August 1960 — and the performance of the locomotive was quite superb. It comprised of two vans and five coaches and we gained eight minutes on the schedule in spite of having to wait for me to take photographs at most of the stations; we also, incidentally, killed two sheep along the bank of Loch Eilt in the process. The train is shown here ready to leave Lochailort station. The return journey was made on 'K1' No 62011, which was in appalling condition, I have never had such a rough ride aboard a locomotive except in Turkey and India. I remember the Mallaig driver telling me that, after 22 years of service based at Mallaig, he had never been south of Spean Bridge in his life.

During the summer months the 10.15am Glasgow Queen Street to Fort William used to carry an observation car from the old 'Coronation' express at the rear. It was turned on the turntable at Fort William prior to the return journey. Standard Class 5MT No 73077, which is piloting 'B1' No 61396, went new with No 73078 to Eastfield shed in May 1955 and spent most of its life working the West Highland line before being transferred to Corkerhill in January 1963. The shed also received Nos 73105-9 new, but these locomotives always seemed to work Glasgow-Edinburgh expresses. On a stormy 13 August 1960, the train is shown approaching Tyndrum Upper. There are now so many fir trees at this location that I can't find the exact position where I took this picture.

1 9 6 1

For steam enthusiasts, 1961 must surely have been the year of the 'lull before the storm'. Most of the main line steam classes were still performing main line work, but large numbers of new diesels and electrics were beginning to appear. The year was to see the first of the following types: 'Deltics', BRCW Type 3s, 'Westerns', 'Hymeks', Type 2s for Scotland, 'AM5' electrics and trans-Pennine DMUs, as well as gas-turbine No GT3 and No D0280 *Falcon*. A formidable variety of power, which after driver training and sorting out really made their presence felt in the following year.

Electric services started on the London, Tilbury & Southend line and trans-Pennine DMU sets commenced operation between Hull and Liverpool. On the other hand, the last steam-hauled 'Golden Arrow' ran on 11 June and before the year was out Camden shed, the home of the Stanier Pacifics,

had closed; another casualty was Kittybrewster shed at Aberdeen.

My own activities were largely around my home area, but I still had my Triumph 21 motorcycle, so trips to Scotland and to Shap were also achieved. Many of the photographs that I took between 1958 and 1961 were as the result of travels on this bike — extremely economical and quite fast. It used to average 80mpg travelling at 75mph, but it came to a premature end as a result of an argument with a laundry van.

Outside the UK, I was also fortunate enough to travel on the footplate of a Nohab diesel on the Bergen-Oslo line during the Norwegian winter; this was an experience as one emerged from tunnels to hit snowdrifts that temporarily completely covered the front of the locomotive — definitely an experience never to be forgotten.

The driver on unrebuilt 'Patriot' No 45513 looks ahead as he gets the locomotive into its stride out of Leeds on the 1.54pm service to Carnforth on 7 June 1961. The picture was taken from the now long-demolished Wortley Junction signalbox, where I used to spend most of my lunch breaks when I worked in Leeds. This particular 'Patriot' recorded the highest mileage — 1,462,043 miles — for an unrebuilt member of the class, this figure being only 45,000 less than the lowest for a rebuilt locomotive.

This was how Neville Hill shed in Leeds turned out one of its Class A3s for my footplate ride on the 'North Briton' to Newcastle on 25 March 1961. No 60086 Gainsborough *had been allocated to the shed for many years and spent most of its time between the two cities on the 'Queen of Scots', the 'North Briton' and Liverpool-Newcastle expresses, via either Harrogate or York. The locomotive rode superbly at around 80mph north of York, which was in sharp contrast to some of the rather rough riding I had experienced on some of the Holbeck-allocated rebuilt 'Scots' at this time. I am eternally grateful to the officers of the Public Relations Department at York, who willingly organised such trips for me just because I supplied them with a few photographs; I don't think they ever appreciated what a great favour they were doing for me, in providing me with experiences that I still remember in every detail to this day. To think that I got a specially prepared locomotive, an inspector, lunch in the BR canteen at Newcastle, a return trip via Harrogate and Wetherby on an English Electric Type 4, all for nothing; how times have changed.*

After being rebuilt in December 1943, 'Royal Scot' No 46117 Welsh Guardsman *spent nearly 20 years allocated to Holbeck shed, working mainly over the Settle & Carlisle line on the Scottish expresses. Looking well cleaned on 15 February 1961 as it leaves Leeds City on the down 'Waverley', the locomotive would work to Carlisle and then return on the overnight Edinburgh-St Pancras service. No 46117 had been to Crewe for its last major overhaul one year earlier and so was probably still in good condition. However, I had a ride on it from Carlisle to Leeds one evening in 1962 and it was by then extremely rough, and rolling alarmingly in places.*

With the 'Deltics' and English Electric Type 4s working some East Coast main line duties, sheds like Doncaster (36A) found themselves with a surplus of Pacifics. This is the reason for Thompson 'A2/3' No 60520 Owen Tudor working the three-coach 2.5pm Leeds Central-Doncaster local on 21 June 1961. The train is seen approaching Holbeck High Level station, which had closed on 7 July 1958. The start of the spur to the lower level is on the extreme left of the picture.

There was still plenty of work for the Fairburn 2-6-4Ts at Beattock in 1961, although Caledonian 0-4-4T No 55234 saw little work, except possibly the occasional trip to Moffat. On 20 May 1961 Nos 42192 and 42205 appear to be ready for their next 20-mile round trip to the summit and back.

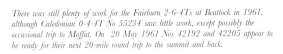

I have always liked this photograph of Carlisle Upperby shed, which was taken on a Sunday evening (22 May 1961), and shows all the Stanier Class 5s facing south ready to do battle with Shap on the following day. In the foreground, Newton Heath 'Jubilee' No 45700 Amethyst and 'Princess Coronation' No 46248 City of Leeds, a Crewe North engine at this time, are awaiting servicing.

The North Eastern Region painted two 'J72' 0-6-0Ts into this light green North Eastern/British Railways livery. On 20 August 1961 No 68723 was the station pilot at Newcastle Central. No 68736 carried out similar duties at York. As the photograph shows, they were kept in immaculate condition and made a very colourful sight as they pottered around the stations.

The three preserved Scottish locomotives were very active around this time, although North British No 256 Glen Douglas *probably saw the most use. The West Riding branch of the RCTS organised a trip from Leeds to the border country on 9 July 1961; the trip included a run along the truncated line from Ravenswood Junction on the Waverley route through towards the East Coast main line. The train travelled as far as Greenlaw and returned over Leaderfoot Viaduct (seen here), which must be one of the most elegant in the country. The train was hauled from Leeds to Carlisle by No 46247* City of Liverpool, *Carlisle-Hawick by double-headed 'B1s' and, around the border country, by 'J37' No 64624* Glen Douglas. *The return from Berwick to Newcastle was behind 'A1' No 60143* Sir Walter Scott *and a 'V2' from Newcastle to Leeds. The cost of the day — a princely £2 10s. If that was not enough, the 'Princess Coronation' covered the 17.25 miles from Hellifield to Blea Moor in 18min 38sec, passing the signalbox at 56mph with a load of 365 tons. Not a bad day out.*

Looking extremely clean for a Carlisle Kingmoor Class 5, No 44790 approaches Dent station on 13 May 1961 with the 3.40pm local from Bradford Forster Square to Carlisle. A feature of this train were the vans which were always attached to it, either at the front or rear. In the loop, blowing off, is 'WD' 2-8-0 No 90685 of Newton Heath, at the head of a Long Meg train.

There was still plenty of steam around the West Riding of Yorkshire, but the main services had by this date, 3 May 1961, had mainly gone over to diesel operation. One of the handsome — although I didn't think so at the time — trans-Pennine Swindon-built DMUs (later Class 124) passes Copley Hill No 3 signalbox as it heads west on a Hull-Liverpool express. This was not the usual route out of Leeds, which was over the viaduct above Holbeck shed, but the train had been diverted due to engineering work.

The Scottish expresses north from Leeds went over to 'Peak' (Class 45) operation as from the summer timetable in 1961. No D15 (later No 45018), which was based at Holbeck for several years, is at the head of the down 'Thames-Clyde Express' on 29 June 1961 near Otterburn. The locomotives appeared to perform well, although the train heating boilers gave some trouble, resulting in fairly frequent steam substitutions.

The Class 4F 0-6-0s had been passing through Chinley North Junction for decades, although by 1961 the more usual motive power for freights over Peak Forest tended to be Stanier '8Fs'. Trafford Park-allocated No 44250 crosses over from the Sheffield to the Peak Forest line with a rake of empty wagons on 4 March 1961.

There were still a few Midland '2P' 4-4-0s allocated to Stranraer and Dumfries sheds for working the 'Port Road' through Castle Douglas. No 40623, a Stranraer (68C) locomotive, is pictured ready to leave Castle Douglas on 1 July 1961. In the background is the branch train to Kirkcudbright, which was being handled by Stanier 2-6-2T No 40150. Services over the 'Port Road' ceased on 14 June 1965 with the Stranraer trains diverted via Ayr.

Hellifield shed still had this Midland '3F' 0-6-0 in 1961, although its activities were confined to shunting the yards. It is pictured at the shed on 29 June 1961. Other Midland types at Hellifield included several '4Fs' and probably '2P' No 40685, which used to pilot expresses over the Settle & Carlisle line.

In 1961 the ex-Midland '2Ps' were still busy piloting the expresses over the Mendips on the Somerset & Dorset. No 40700, which had been allocated to the line for most of its life, is seen on 12 August 1961 piloting Bath Green Park Standard Class 5MT No 73052 through Masbury station at the head of a summer Saturday express from Birmingham to Bournemouth. No 73052 was allocated to Bath Green Park from new and stayed there until withdrawal in December 1964; the same applied to sister locomotive No 73051. Note the tablet catcher on the 4-4-0.

This was the classic Somerset & Dorset combination — a 4-4-0 '2P' piloting an S&D 2-8-0 on 12 August 1961 — at Masbury summit. As can be seen, both locomotives are in terrible external condition, although during the summer months there was little time for locomotive cleaning on the line. No 40564 had been based on the line since before World War 2 and, of course, the 2-8-0 No 53810 never worked anywhere else. The train is the 11.12am Bournemouth West-Sheffield service. The '2P' would have been attached at Evercreech Junction. The '2Ps' lasted on these duties until 1962, but were often stored during the winter months.

1962

This was a significant year as far as locomotives were concerned. The last of many famous classes were withdrawn, including the Great Western 'Kings', the LMS 'Princess Royals', the Beattie well tanks, *Duke of Gloucester*, the unique rebuilt 'Royal Scot' No 46170 *British Legion* and the SR 'Schools', the finest 4-4-0s in the country. Other casualties included the 'WD' 2-10-0s, Fowler and Stanier designs of 2-6-2T and numerous others. On the plus side, although I didn't see it that way at the time, the first of the Brush Type 4s (later Class 47) entered traffic at Finsbury Park, the 'Westerns' started their short careers, as did the 'Claytons'; also appearing for the first time were the Class 73s on the Southern and the Class 07 shunters.

I find it very difficult to believe that it is now 36 years since *Princess Royal* was withdrawn, with a

similar time span for the 'Kings', but I suppose it is because we have been so fortunate to see these fine locomotives running in preservation for longer than their original careers.

During the year, the quartet of Scottish preserved locomotives was well used; the work included a final steam trip to the far north with the 'Jones Goods'. This was something that I missed and which I have regretted ever since. Elsewhere, all steam operation finished in East Anglia and was virtually eliminated from King's Cross.

Branch lines continued to close as did more important lines, such as that across Stainmore illustrated later. The 'Pines Express' was routed away from the Somerset & Dorset.

The year was a bad one for enthusiasts of branch line operation and steam locomotives.

The year got off to an interesting start in Mirfield, where I have now lived for 28 years although in 1962 I was resident in Halifax. Apparently, on 7 January 1962, the driver of Class V2 No 60954 thought he was on the main line; he was, however, on the down loop. By the time he realised his mistake, it was too late as the locomotive ploughed through the buffer stops and down the embankment. Fortunately, there were no injuries and the locomotive was repaired. It provided a good Sunday's entertainment for myself and others watching the rerailing process.

1 9 6 2

The last day of use for the famous Stainmore line, including Belah Viaduct, was 20 January 1962. The Railway Correspondence & Travel Society organised a special from Darlington to Tebay and return. BR Standard Class 3MT No 77003 piloted Class 4MT No 76049 on the train and the pair are pictured leaving Kirkby Stephen on the last westbound working. This ended 100 years of train services over the route.

Belah Viaduct was one of the most impressive viaducts in the country. Built in 1859 to the design of Thomas Bouch, the viaduct was 1,040ft long and 196ft high. It cost £31,630 to build. The last westbound train — the 'Stainmore Limited' — is pictured crossing the viaduct in weak winter sunshine on 20 January 1962. In spite of protests, the viaduct was dismantled in 1963.

It was unusual to see a Polmadie rebuilt 'Royal Scot' at Holbeck shed, but No 46105 Gordon Highlander must have been a last minute substitution on one of the previous night's sleepers and, on 6 June 1962, was now ready to leave the shed on the return diagram, which was the 10.35am from Leeds City to Glasgow St Enoch. The locomotive was withdrawn in December, having spent at least 15 years at Polmadie.

Unrebuilt 'Patriot' No 45543 Home Guard finished its working days on the Leeds-Lancaster trains, as did several other members of the class. Its time on these trains was short, lasting only about eight months until it was withdrawn in November 1962. On 6 June 1962 it was working the 1.54pm from Leeds to Carnforth and is pictured negotiating the sharp curve round the triangle at Whitehall Junction, Leeds. For me, the rebuilt 'Patriots' were amongst the most handsome locomotives I ever saw in this country.

'Deltic' No D9020 Nimbus, *the last of class to be named after racehorses was delivered new to Finsbury Park, and was only four months old when I took this picture of it heading the 5.29pm Leeds-King's Cross express past Beeston Junction, Leeds, on 7 June 1962. In the early years, No D9020 always seemed to be the Deltic at Finsbury Park to be kept in immaculate condition, but sadly it was the first of the class to be withdrawn, along with No D9001 (No 55001) St Paddy, in January 1980.*

In the very early days of the BRCW Type 3s (later Class 33), the class used to be diagrammed to work away from the Southern Region; at least this was the case on this cement working. Nos D6563 and D6579, both less than a year old, pass York on their way back to more familiar surroundings on 16 June 1962. The locomotives became Nos 33045 and 33063 respectively.

The Class 27s are today always associated with Scotland and, I believe, are known as a result as 'MacRats' in some circles. In fact, it was only the first 22 of the type that were initially allocated to Scotland, the others being despatched to Thornaby and Cricklewood when new. As a result, they were frequently seen on the East Coast main line north of York, and on 16 June 1962 Nos D5377 and D5374 (later Nos 27030 and 27045) were photographed passing Benningborough on a northbound freight. At the time the locomotives were only four months old and were based at Thornaby.

Being only two months old, Type 4 (later Class 40) No D386 is looking very clean as it approaches the outskirts of Keighley, past the bridge to the golf course, on a motley selection of non-corridor stock on 4 June 1962. This stock was used for a daily trip from Neville Hill to Appleby for crew training on diesel traction. The train became a familiar sight in the area and I believe that it ran for more than a year.

'Peak' No D67 was only a few days old when I captured this picture on 10 May 1962 of it leaving Bingley on an afternoon Morecambe-Leeds train. This was the last of the type to enter service and was named The Royal Artilleryman *in September 1965, becoming No 45118 under the TOPS code. It was withdrawn in May 1987 and passed into preservation.*

The 'White Rose' from King's Cross to Leeds and return ran for a few weeks in April with this rather startling headboard, advertising the woollen industry of the West Riding. 'Top Shed' allocated 'A3' No 60107 Royal Lancer to the train during the promotion and gave it the shed's beauty treatment. The train is pictured leaving Leeds Central on 9 April 1962 on the up working. Further coaches would be added at Wakefield Westgate from Bradford, which was being run, again with a headboard, behind very clean 'B1' No 61024 Addax.

The Leeds–King's Cross duties were generally shared at this time between Copley Hill 'A1s' and 'Top Shed' Pacifics. The 10am departure from Leeds was generally a King's Cross locomotive and on sunny mornings I used to manage to slip out of the office for half an hour to photograph it and the 10.10am 'stopper'; the latter very often had an ex-works locomotive off Doncaster. On 5 June 1962 No 60033 Seagull, which spent all its life at 'Top Shed' except for a four-year spell in the mid-1940s, is pictured passing Beeston Junction. The locomotive was withdrawn at the end of the year.

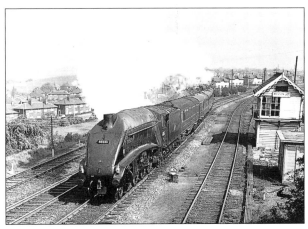

For no logical reason, No 60017 Flying Fox was always one of my favourite 'A4s'. It was one of the trio allocated by 'Top Shed' to the 'Silver Jubilee' and, according to records, worked the train 409 times out of the 1,952 occasions when the train ran in the four years prior to World War 2. After this period, it remained at King's Cross, except for the last four months before withdrawal in October 1963. The silver fox is clearly visible on the side; the locomotive always carried this embellishment. It is pictured on 29 April 1962 at the south end of Doncaster shed prior to working an up express to King's Cross.

I must have followed, or chased as some people prefer to describe it, hundreds of specials over the years, but this tour from Glasgow to Oban and back, on a perfect day and with little or no traffic on the road, must be counted as the best. The locomotives, in particular the Caledonian single No 123 in blue, looked superb. It is true that North British 'D34' No 256 Glen Douglas did much of the work, as West Highland territory was not exactly ideal for the single. The train stopped frequently and, as a matter of interest, I calculated how many photographs I took of it — a grand total of 51 slides and 34 black and white at 34 different locations and every picture in the sun! It makes today's trips seem rather hard work when usually one gets about four pictures and 300 miles on the clock of the car. The train returned via the old Callander & Oban line from Crianlarich and is pictured, on 12 May 1962, passing Glenogle in the lovely evening sun. Note the thistles engraved beneath the buffers of No 123; this had been done by one of the shed staff at Dawsholm. It may come as a surprise that, on this occasion, there were only two cars following the train, my own trusty and much abused Volkswagen Beetle, and a little green A35 van. Those were the days; I'm sure I'll never see their like again.

I have only travelled over the Central Wales line once and that was 2 June 1962 on the 10.25am from Swansea Victoria to Shrewsbury. A very clean green Standard Class 5MT No 73036, allocated to Shrewsbury is pictured at Swansea, and whilst I enjoyed the journey I remember wondering if we would ever get to Craven Arms; the journey seemed to take an awfully long time and nobody seemed to be in much of a hurry at the stations. I travelled from Shrewsbury to Welshpool on the down 'Cambrian Coast Express', then took the Mid-Wales line to Brecon, thence over the tops via Torpantau and down to Cardiff before returning to Swansea over the main line to collect my car. Not a bad day out.

I always regarded the Stanier Class 5s as fine looking locomotives, but I reckon this is about the worst angle one could take for any member of the class. Double chimney and Caprotti-fitted No 44756 is caught on the ash pit at Holbeck, its home shed, on 12 April 1962.

At Sowerby Bridge shed, ex-L&YR 0-6-0 No 52413 (with extended smokebox) had come to the end of its long working career by 8 April 1962. Other members of the class were also stored here, along with the shed's allocation of three Fairburn 2-6-4Ts, which had been made redundant by the recently introduced DMUs on the Calder Valley line. The shed's main function was to serve the Mytholmroyd marshalling yard and local services. The yard opened in 1919, but closed along with the shed in January 1964.

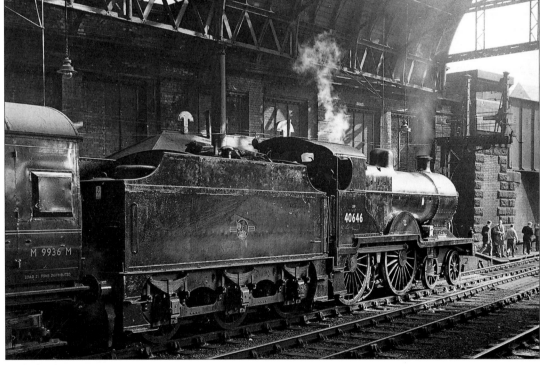

By 1962, there were only a few active Midland Class 2P 4-4-0s still in service. The Stephenson Locomotive Society in Birmingham had No 40646 well turned out for a special on 14 April 1962. The special ran via many cross-country routes, eventually getting as far as Hatfield on the East Coast main line. It returned once again cross-country, arriving almost on time having been, at one stage in its trip, more than an hour late. I feel that the atmosphere of Birmingham New Street prior to its rebuilding is well captured in this view; it is a source of regret that I only took relatively few photographs here or at that equally atmospheric station, Snow Hill.

A familiar sight for more than three decades was a Midland Class 4F 0-6-0 on a transfer freight or coal train pottering across Leeds from Stourton to Kirkstall power station or further up the Aire Valley. Stourton-based No 44044 passes the signal gantries between Holbeck Low Level station and Wortley Junction signalbox on 14 March 1962. In the background can be seen the girder bridge carrying the ex-Great Northern main line towards Leeds Central.

1963

This was the year that Dr Beeching presented his proposals for the reshaping of the BR network. It sent shock waves through enthusiasts and railwaymen as both groups realised the implications of the plans. The closure of lines accelerated, which resulted in the withdrawal of many classes of locomotive. Notable locomotives which passed into preservation included *Flying Scotsman*, *Mallard* and the prototype 'Deltic'. *Flying Scotsman* was, however, only out of traffic for a matter of three months before it ran its first special, on behalf of the Ffestiniog Railway Society, in apple green livery.

A piece of good news was the reopening of the Welshpool & Llanfair Light Railway on 6 April; otherwise the year was dominated by closures and the last of classes being withdrawn. It was also the year of the Great Train Robbery at Sears Crossing, when £2.5 million in total went missing. Class 40 No D326 was the locomotive involved.

As far as I was concerned, there was plenty of activity. The 'Jacobite' tour from Glasgow to Mallaig, the last with steam, was extremely enjoyable for all the wrong reasons, but my footplate trip on 'A4' Pacific No 60023 *Golden Eagle* over the Settle &

Carlisle, when hauling the 'Three Summits' tour, must have been the highlight of the year as we averaged 78.4mph from passing Mallerstang signalbox to Cumwhinton (40.9 miles) with a maximum of 95.4mph — the fastest I have ever travelled on the footplate of a steam locomotive. It is one of my regrets that I have never managed to travel at 100mph behind steam.

There was an interruption to railway activities in July, when I got married, but I did manage to persuade Eric Treacy to conduct the ceremony, as he had been a friend of the family for many years.

There were some interesting workings in my local area when Class A1 No 60114 *W. P. Allen* worked a special, which finished up at Blackpool, along the Calder Valley line. The most memorable sight, again for the wrong reasons, was 'Princess Coronation' No 46251 *City of Nottingham* storming over Beattock Summit in perfect sunshine at the head of an RCTS special; unfortunately, I did not wind on the black and white camera and so I only have a slide of the event. This is something that still upsets me 30 years on, but I have done the same thing many times since.

This was the sad sight which greeted me on 3 February 1963 on a visit to Doncaster Works. No 60014 Silver Link *had been withdrawn the previous month and was available, I believe, for sale at a little over £3,000, but nothing happened. Think how much the nameplate alone would be worth today! It was a pity that No 60014 did not survive rather than some of the rather less famous members of the class, but it was in the first batch to be withdrawn.*

Whilst No 60014 was at Doncaster awaiting scrapping, the most famous 'A4' of them all, No 60022 Mallard, was working an LCGB special from Waterloo to Exeter and return via the GWR main line on 24 February 1963. A stop was made at Tiverton Junction while the passengers had a very cold trip along the Hemyock branch in brake vans. The locomotive gave an excellent performance between Salisbury and Exeter, when we exceeded 90mph on four occasions, but as one Southern enthusiast pointed out, our time was still over a minute slower than that booked for a 'Merchant Navy' on the 'Atlantic Coast Express'. My last sighting of No 60022 in steam before withdrawal was the following week at Doncaster shed. The next time I saw it, the locomotive was in Doncaster Works receiving attention before passing into preservation and display at the Clapham Museum.

This year was the swansong of the 'A4s' in England. Those that were in a fit condition were transferred to Scotland to work the Aberdeen-Glasgow expresses, some going into store and being later reinstated as others were withdrawn. This was a sad occasion at Leeds Central when the up 'White Rose' on 15 June 1963 became the last steam-hauled train from the station to King's Cross. The condition of the locomotive was not what one had come to expect from 'Top Shed' over the years, but its closure was imminent. No 60025 Falcon made a dismal sight as it left the station and, for that matter, 'Deltic' No D9004 on the down 'Queen of Scots' was hardly any cleaner. No 60025 did not get transferred to Scotland, but to New England for a few months, where I suspect it did very little work.

Apart from the LNER Pacifics on the Glasgow-Aberdeen services, there was very little main line steam left north of Glasgow. This was one of the very rare occasions when I actually managed to get a picture of the North British Class 21s working; on 11 May 1963 Nos D6122 and D6108 are seen approaching Gleneagles on a Dundee-Glasgow Buchanan Street service. No D6108 was later converted into a Class 29, but No D6122 was withdrawn in December 1967 after just 12 years of service, and no doubt much of that time was spent out of service.

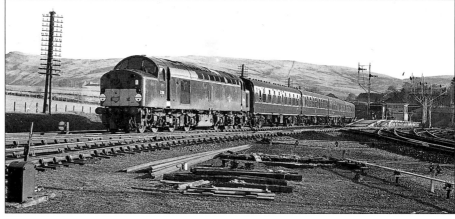

Class 40 No D296 catches the evening light on 11 May 1963 as it departs from Gleneagles on the last leg of its journey from Euston to Perth. The class was the regular motive power for these trains, having replaced the 'Princess Coronations' during 1962. The branch to Crieff, which lasted until 1964, is visible on the right of the picture. On this occasion, the branch service was being provided by a Standard Class 5MT No 73007 with a single coach.

The last steam special over the West Highland line from Glasgow to Fort William and Mallaig was the 'Jacobite', which ran on 1 June 1963. It was an operating disaster, with three of the four locomotives failing. The journey to Fort William was behind the preserved 'Glen' No 256 Glen Douglas and 'J37' No 64632, both of which failed with the latter being dumped at Rannoch and the former being rescued by North British No D6137. I suppose it was a change for the diesel to rescue anything. On the Mallaig section, a second 'J37' ran hot and whilst not being fit to return did at least reach its destination. The train returned behind Class 27 No D5351 (later No 27005), arriving back in Glasgow in the early hours of Sunday morning. The train is shown descending Glenfinnan. No doubt the Scottish Region authorities hoped that they would never run steam over the line again, but that is another story. As a matter of interest, there were only two cars following the train all day, myself and the late Bill Anderson, and even my car failed at Tyndrum Upper! Fortunately, it was repaired by the local signalman after I had pointed out that the engine in a VW Beetle was at the rear.

Following on from the comments in the previous caption regarding the 'Jacobite' tour, I got this picture of the two 'J37s', Nos 64592 and 64636, passing Corpach on 1 June 1963 when both locomotives were running well. The location was chosen to show Ben Nevis in the background, but the 'clag' ended that bright idea.

A rather unusual double-header on 28 September 1963 was a 20-coach empty stock working climbing the bank from Huddersfield to Marsden headed by Farnley Junction 'WD' No 90588 and Stanier '8F' No 48225. The fireman of the 'WD' seems to be having a look to see that all is well on the '8F' as the train passed Golcar in fine style.

After 1.5 million miles, No 46201 Princess Elizabeth *was withdrawn in October 1962. Eight months later the locomotive was still at Carlisle Kingmoor waiting to be hauled over the Settle & Carlisle to Ashchurch and preservation. It is one of my favourite preserved locomotives, possibly because I was very lucky to become the owner of one of the Hornby Gauge O models of the locomotive at the end of the war; fortunately, the model is still in the family. The 'Princess Coronation' behind is No 46247* City of Liverpool, *one of the class which was painted in red livery; it was placed in store in June 1963 and sent to Crewe for scrapping.*

Now in preservation, 'Jubilee' No 45596 Bahamas *with double chimney presented this rather unusual sight at Farnley Junction shed, Leeds, on 5 September 1963. Apparently, it had been in a minor collision with a Class 08 shunter and seems to have lost. The impact caused the tender body to become partly detached from its frames. There was, reportedly, no damage to the diesel. The ensemble was ready to be towed away to Crewe Works.*

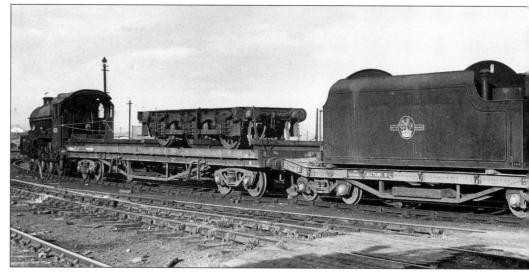

The North Wales Coast main line in the early 1960s used to see anything ex-LMS from a 'Princess Coronation' downwards to Stanier 2-6-2Ts, plus most of the Standard types. Class B1 4-6-0s also appeared and on 22 June 1963 No 61153 of Canklow had worked a special from Sheffield and was awaiting servicing on Llandudno Junction shed, along with Class 5 No 45271 and long-time resident of the shed '4F' 0-6-0 No 44389. Just out of the picture to the right was 'Crab' No 42700 of Bury, which is today being restored at Barrow Hill engine shed on behalf of the National Railway Museum.

The exhaust from Class 40
No D291 still hangs in the cutting
at Shap Summit on 24 August
1963 as the locomotive and train
pass at little more than 30mph on
a down Euston-Carlisle express.

By 1963 there were sufficient 'Peaks' to work some of
the Leeds-Morecambe services. On 23 May 1963 the up
afternoon train rounds the sharp curve at Shipley headed
by No D127 (later No 45072). The picture was taken
from the signalbox at Bingley Junction and the cars in
the background have since become 'classics'.

There was severe weather on the Settle & Carlisle in January and the line was blocked in Dent Cutting for several days, marooning, I believe, a 'Peak'. The line reopened on 26 January and by some miracle I managed to drive my car to Dent station and photograph the procession of trains. I was on my way back to the station after giving up any hope of getting to Rise Hill Tunnel, when the up 'Waverley' unexpectedly turned up with Gateshead 'A3' No 60073 St Gatien, and I found myself in the wrong position. This was definitely a missed opportunity, but I was only expecting a 'Peak'.

The Caprotti-fitted Class 5s were not very handsome and, on 4 June 1963, No 44751 was in terrible external condition as it passed Holbeck shed on the 11.15am service from Leeds City to Sheffield. Three of the Caprotti-fitted locomotives with double chimneys were allocated new to Holbeck — Nos 44755-57 — and the trio remained for many years. They operated over the Settle & Carlisle for a while, but were generally employed on services south of Leeds.

Great Western 'King' No 6018 King Henry VI *was specially reinstated to traffic in order to work a Stephenson Locomotive Society special from Birmingham Snow Hill to Swindon via Southall on 28 April 1963. The locomotive put up a superb performance, reaching 90mph during the day and must have made one of the most vigorous climbs of Hatton Bank from a standing start at Leamington for any member of the class. Looking at the locomotive at Swindon shed surrounded by 'Hymeks', it is hard to believe that it only had another 100 miles of service to run. Note the number on the buffer beam and the 'TYS' code, both of which had been added at Tyseley shed where the locomotive had been prepared. For GWR enthusiasts it was a sad occasion.*

The 77xxx series of BR Standards was probably the one class that never made its presence felt, partly because there were only 20 built. The type does not seem to have been photographed a great deal and were allocated to many different sheds with the result that the crews never really became very familiar with them. A few finished up at Stourton shed, Leeds, to replace the Midland '4F' 0-6-0s and were generally employed on local freights, never seeming to venture very far. On 17 September 1963 No 77001 is pictured arriving at Wortley Junction with some coal for the local gasworks, before heading further along the line towards Shipley.

Some works pictures are not always quite what they seem. Class A1 No 60117 Bois Roussel was visiting Doncaster Works for the last time and was parked up near the paint shop on 19 May 1963 attached to a Class A3 tender, which appears to be full of coal. No 60117 did not enter service with this tender but with a standard 'A1' type. The locomotive lasted until June 1965, but I suspect that it did little work after this repair. Mallard can be seen in the background.

The BR Standard Class 6MT 'Clans' may not have been the best performers of the Standard types, but for me they were the most handsome. No 72009 Clan Stewart was the last to be built, in March 1952, and it spent its entire career allocated to Carlisle Kingmoor until withdrawal in August 1965, except for a short period on loan to Stratford shed on the Eastern (which does not seem to have been a success). Pictured alongside on 6 April 1963 is 'Princess Coronation' No 46226 Duchess of Norfolk, which worked out its last days at Carlisle Kingmoor, mainly on the Perth trains. The two make a fine study under the coaling stage at Kingmoor and, in their green and red liveries, also made a nice slide. Kingmoor was one of my favourite sheds and I named my first house after it; this did not meet with my wife's approval. On the other hand, when she discovered that I wanted to name my second daughter after a South African Class 23, she put her foot down and I had to give in.

1 9 6 4

It was as long ago as 1964 that BR introduced the corporate 'rail blue' livery. Class 47 No D1733 and eight coaches were the first to be painted and the complete train set went into service on the 'Talisman' in June. Little did one realise at the time that, with very few exceptions, this would remain the corporate image for over 20 years. Now it is only seen in preservation. Other important introductions in the year were the Merry-go-round coal train and the 'Cartic' trains for the Ford Motor Co.

The diesel fleet remained fairly stable, although the short-lived Class 14 diesel-hydraulics appeared; most of these had a very short working life on BR although many were sold into industry or overseas and a large number are now preserved.

It was, however, a year when the last of many fine classes of steam locomotive became extinct on BR; the casualties included the ex-GWR Class 47xx 2-8-0s, the Hawksworth 'Counties', the LNER Class B16 4-6-0s, the Somerset & Dorset 2-8-0s and the LMS 'Princess Coronations'. Many of those withdrawn were in good condition. Even the 'Atlantic Coast Express' ran for the last time with steam haulage; other than on the London & South Western, main line steam duties were beginning to decline considerably.

As far as I was concerned, there was more than enough to keep me busy and, as you will see from the selection of photographs, some very unusual workings took place. The arrival of 'Grange' No 6858 *Woolston Grange* on a service train at Huddersfield must rank as the most unusual working I have ever seen in West Yorkshire. Over the years I did manage to photograph an LMS 'Princess Coronation' in Leeds, a 'Merchant Navy' and of course Gresley 'A4s', but these involved specials; unfortunately, I never saw the Great Western 'King' in Leeds during the 1948 Locomotive Exchanges as I was at school in North Wales.

My most memorable experience in the year was undoubtedly my footplate trip on 'Merchant Navy' No 35012 *United States Line* from Carlisle to Hellifield; the performance of the crew and locomotive was a privilege to witness, although the riding of the locomotive seemed very harsh compared to a Gresley 'A3' or 'A4'.

Class A4 No 60010 Dominion of Canada *spent its entire life at King's Cross until the shed closed in 1963, except for a very short spell at Grantham. It then enjoyed a final fling on the Glasgow-Aberdeen services, based at Ferryhill. It is pictured being serviced at Glasgow St Rollox (65B) shed on 31 March 1964; the shed was also known as Balornock. The locomotive had worked an up morning train from Aberdeen. Following withdrawal, No 60010 was preserved in Canada and is on display at a museum in Montreal.*

Passenger journeys on the scenic Barmouth Junction-Ruabon line were due to finish in January 1965, so on a frosty morning — 19 December 1964 — I went to photograph the remaining services on the line in the Bala area. Ivatt 2-6-0 No 46446 appeared on the morning service from Barmouth heading for Llangollen, having just shut off steam ready to call at Drws-y-Nant. The other services on the day were operated by Ivatt 2-6-2Ts.

My interest in football in the 1960s centred around which clubs were doing well in the Cup and what was the likelihood of 'footex' specials being run. Carlisle United usually did well in the early rounds and were well supported; this meant that specials were virtually guaranteed over Shap or the Settle & Carlisle. The local sheds, Kingmoor and Upperby, always cleaned the locomotives for the occasion and so, on 25 January 1964, when United were drawn against Bedford in an away match, 'Jubilee' No 45736 Phoenix and rebuilt 'Patriot' No 45527 Southport were to be found at Holbeck shed waiting for the return workings. Locomotives had been exchanged at Leeds Engine Shed Junction, with this pair being replaced by two rather dirty 'Jubilees' for the trip southwards. Being January, the photographic opportunities were limited.

A general view taken inside Holbeck shed on 2 October 1964 shows local 'Jubilee' No 45675 Hardy, Lancaster-allocated 'Crab' No 42926 and Fowler 2-6-4T No 42394, which was a recent transfer to the shed from Swansea. It received works attention before its arrival and did very little work before its withdrawal; it must have been in excellent condition when it succumbed.

I owe a great deal to the people at Holbeck shed, headed by shedmaster Mr Ted Geeson, who gave me so much help and information and happily organised the movement of locomotives around the yard for me to get pictures. The 'Jones Goods' No 103 was returning north from filming duties on the Bedford-Bletchley line — when the film Those Magnificent Men in their Flying Machines was shot. I am pleased to be able to include this picture of some of the shed staff, who were good enough to run the locomotive up and down the yard for me to take cine and pose it for pictures. The gentleman second from left is Mr White, one of the shed's foremen. I was the only person present to record this unique visit; how times have changed since 25 May 1964.

At the beginning of the year, there were still eight of the Hawksworth 'County' class in service, but by the end of the year they had all been withdrawn. The last eight all finished their days at Swindon shed (82C) where No 1013 County of Dorset was photographed on 26 April 1964. It is looking well cared for, although it only had another three months to go before withdrawal and I suspect it was seeing very little use. In my opinion, the 'Counties' were good looking locomotives when fitted with single chimneys, but the double chimney, as shown here, was far from handsome. The locomotive only saw 18 years of service.

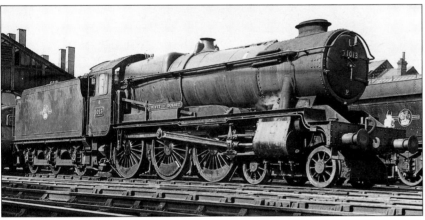

No 46229 Duchess of Hamilton was withdrawn during February 1964 with a recorded mileage of 1,533,846. Little did I appreciate at the time the significance of its purchase by Billy Butlin for display at his Minehead holiday camp. The locomotive emerged from Crewe Works painted in this somewhat inaccurate livery, but nevertheless it looked very smart indeed. I was visiting Crewe North for some reason on 18 April 1964 and found the locomotive inside the shed ready to be taken to Minehead. After photographing it inside, we persuaded the foreman to move it outside for pictures. Unfortunately, the ropes which had been placed between the cab and tender to stop people getting into the cab were pulled extremely tight, so when the locomotive was pulled onto a slight curve something had to give. The result was that the handrails got slightly bent; needless to say this caused considerable panic and I still don't know how the shed sorted the problem out. Note the 'Warship' diesel to the right of the picture; I am afraid that in those days I didn't even give it a second glance and so I have no knowledge of its number.

The facilities at the ex-Somerset & Dorset shed at Bath Green Park were not among the most modern in the country. Ex-S&D 2-8-0 No 53807, which I believe was the last one in service, had just worked a 'Home Counties' tour over the Mendips on 7 June 1964 with 0-6-0 '4F' No 44558, another locomotive which spent all its days on the S&D. The tour then left Bath behind 'Castle' No 7023 Penrice Castle, which was the only time a member of this class visited Green Park station.

The Lakeside branch closed on 6 September 1965 and the Metropolitan-Vickers Class 28 Co-Bos, which were based at Barrow at the end of their short careers, occasionally visited the branch. On 22 August 1964 No D5708, which lasted until September 1968, is pictured waiting to depart at the head of a rake of non-corridor coaches. Platform 1, at 745ft in length, was much longer than Platform 2. Note the camping coach in the siding. Happily, this section of the line reopened on 2 May 1973 in preservation, an event which is recorded on p127.

There were many variations of the Class O4 2-8-0, following the rebuilding of many examples. No 63914 was rebuilt as a Class O4/8 in July 1955 and was withdrawn during the month in which this photograph was taken. It was a Saturday, and so it might have been withdrawn over the weekend after this freight duty, seen near the old Great Central shed at Staveley on 9 May 1964. No 63914 was built in September 1919 and so gave 45 years of service.

Numerically, No 63913 is only one different from the locomotive illustrated on the preceding page, but being a non-rebuilt 'O4/1', its external appearance is very different. For me, these were fine looking machines, which performed the task for which they were built extremely well. This is another view at Staveley shed on 9 May 1964. The locomotive was withdrawn in June 1965.

'Jubilee' No 45694 Bellerophon spent over 20 years allocated to Holbeck shed, but by 1964, when there was little work for the class at Holbeck, it was transferred to Wakefield and then Low Moor. At weekends, it could be found along with long-time stablemate at Holbeck, No 45565 Victoria, working specials from the West Riding to Blackpool, but during the week there was little work and so it was often employed on the pick-up freight from Laisterdyke to Shipley over the ex-Great Northern route. On a lovely summer's evening, 7 July 1964, it is seen pulling away from Shipley Junction with a light freight. The friendly Low Moor crews at the time were happy to give footplate trips to local enthusiasts on this working. The ex-GNR somersault signal was one of the last of the type to survive in the West Riding; services over the line ceased three months later.

Together with the Class J27 0-6-0s, the 'Q6s' were the backbone of the freight services in the northeast for around 40 years. Looking unusually clean on 8 February 1964, No 63429 of Blaydon shed waits to enter Blyth North yard with a freight. Happily, both a Class J27 and a Class Q6 have been preserved by the North Eastern Locomotive Preservation Group and can be seen on the North Yorkshire Moors Railway.

Probably the most unusual locomotive ever to visit Hillhouse shed, Huddersfield, was a dirty Great Western 'Grange' No 6858 Woolston Grange. The locomotive had taken over what I believe was the summer only Poole-Bradford train at Oxford, which it would then have normally worked to Leicester or even Nottingham. For some reason on 15 August 1964 it got past Nottingham and Sheffield Victoria and headed for Penistone. I happened to be at home on this Saturday and was having tea when my friend in control phoned and said there was a 'Grange' passing Penistone and to get myself to Huddersfield immediately. Realising this was not 1 April, I departed and arrived at the shed at virtually the same time as the locomotive, as it had been removed as a result of hitting the platform edge at Honley. The damage can be seen on the cylinder cover. I managed a couple of pictures before an agitated foreman appeared and told me where to go in no uncertain terms. The locomotive remained hidden in the shed for two weeks, before being hauled back to Crewe dead as an out of gauge load.

The original Great Northern Railway terminus in Bradford was Adolphus Street, but passenger services were withdrawn in January 1867 with the opening of the new Exchange station. It remained open, however, for a further 105 years as a goods shed. The station was approached down a steep gradient and matters got totally out of control in early November when Ivatt 2-6-0 No 43072 ran away down the grade, ran through the goods yard wall and dropped 25ft into the street, narrowly missing a passing motorist. This was the scene a few days later, on 11 November 1964, when the scrap metal men arrived to cut up the locomotive and tender on site.

Carlisle Kingmoor shed is the furthest north that a 'Merchant Navy' has travelled. No 35028 Clan Line has traversed the Settle & Carlisle in preservation, but on 13 June 1964 the Railway Correspondence & Travel Society managed to organise a visit by No 35012 United States Line to Leeds with a trip over Shap northbound and back via the Settle & Carlisle. The locomotive arrived at Leeds Holbeck complete with a Nine Elms crew; in fact no less than the famous Bert Hooker and his fireman Ken Seaby. Those that were fortunate enough to travel on the 'Solway Ranger' will never forget the day out. The climb to Shap from Carnforth, where we had reversed off the Leeds line, took only 30min for the 26 miles from a standing start. Speed was just over 80mph at Tebay and was still above 60 at Scout Green, when we were brought to a dead stand at Shap Wells for a freight backing into the loop at the summit. On the return the 17.5 miles from Appleby to Ais Gill were covered at an average speed of just under 60mph. I was lucky enough to be on the footplate and I remember the Leeds conductor telling the crew to take water at the troughs at Garsdale; this was not a great deal of use as the locomotive was not fitted with a scoop! This caused considerable anxiety between Settle Junction and Hellifield, as the crew thought we would have to drop the fire; however, we just made it to Hellifield. As a tribute to Bert Hooker, who died recently, I include the picture of him and Ken at Leeds before departure; I trust that Ken is still fit and well.

Rebuilt 'Scot' No 46160 Queen Victoria's Rifleman was turned out on 28 November 1964 looking extremely smart for the Warwickshire Railway Society special return working from Carlisle. The northbound train ran via Shap and had been booked for a 'Britannia', but this had failed, to be replaced by a dirty Kingmoor Class 5 No 45013, which put up an excellent performance at the last minute. The picture was taken alongside Kingmoor shed and withdrawn 'Patriot' No 45526 can be seen on the right. Note the yellow cabside stripe, indicating that the locomotive was banned from working south of Crewe over the electrified lines.

1 9 6 5

On 11 June the last scheduled steam working left London Paddington behind No 7029 *Clun Castle* for Banbury. This was followed on 27 November by a commemorative 'Farewell to Steam' special, again hauled by *Clun Castle*. And so steam traction ended on the Western Region. The external state of some of the ex-Great Western locomotives in the latter years was terrible; very often they ran without nameplates and cab numberplates. Personally, I don't think there is a more depressing sight on the railways than a really run-down and dirty ex-GWR locomotive.

In addition to the demise of the ex-GWR classes that had survived, the end of the year also saw the withdrawal of the last of the rebuilt 'Royal Scots' and 'Patriots'. Both classes had already been banned from operating south from Crewe over the electrified lines.

Line closures still continued, resulting in many railtours being run for last visits. As the selection of photographs for the year shows, there was more happening than one could cover; nevertheless I tried hard and obtained a great variety of subjects. Once again, I concentrated on the old and vanishing scenes, rather than recording what was new; this is a policy that I have regretted more than once since.

The Stephenson Locomotive Society in the West Midlands organised some excellent railtours over the years, due to the efforts of W. A. Camwell, Pat Whitehouse and others. A tour was run on 23 May 1965, when unrebuilt 'Battle of Britain' No 34051 Winston Churchill *hauled a working from Birmingham Snow Hill to Salisbury. 'Merchant Navy' No 35017* Belgian Marine *then gave us a spirited run to Exeter Central, followed by a leisurely run along the GWR main line to Westbury. At this point No 7029* Clun Castle *took over for the trip back to Birmingham. A water stop was made on the outward journey at Leamington Spa, where I took the opportunity to get off and grab this photograph. The locomotive is now part of the National Collection; however, as there are some 20 members of the class preserved, in either rebuilt or unrebuilt form, it is unlikely to be a high priority for restoration to working order.*

The handsome and very capable Fowler 2-6-4Ts were getting very few in number by this time, but the Manchester University Railway Society managed to get this very well turned out example, No 42343, to head its 'Staffordshire Potter' tour on 13 March 1965. The train is seen pulling away from Kidsgrove off the Crewe line and heading towards Stoke. Later in the tour the train visited Congleton. The last examples of the class ended their days in the Leeds area, but they will always be remembered for their banking duties up Shap when allocated to Tebay shed.

This class of BR 2-6-2Ts seemed to elude me, even though a few of the type came to one of my local sheds, Low Moor, when new for a brief spell. No 84028 spent some time at Skipton and one of its duties was working the Barnoldswick branch, a line which closed on 27 September 1965. The closure of the line was no doubt one factor in the locomotive's withdrawal in the following December. It is pictured on 2 March 1965 on the turntable at Skipton.

This was a tour organised on 28 February 1965 by the Locomotive Club of Great Britain. Its purpose was to visit with steam the old Southern branch lines to the east of Exeter. These included Lyme Regis, Seaton, Sidmouth and Exmouth, before returning to Exeter and a fast run back to London behind 'Merchant Navy' No 35022 Holland America Line. After running round at Tipton St Johns, the train is ready to head for Exmouth with Ivatt 2-6-2T No 41206 piloting ex-GWR 0-6-0PT No 4666. Passenger services ceased on these lines, with the exception of the Exmouth branch, on 28 February 1965.

The last train over the Scarborough-Whitby line was the 'Whitby Moors Rail Tour' on 6 March 1965. It was double-headed by preserved Class K4 2-6-0 No 3442 The Great Marquess and 'K1' No 62005 (also now preserved). The train was captured crossing the impressive Larpool Viaduct, south of Whitby, just as an eight-car DMU headed along the line towards Grosmont. The fine structure still stands and I had reason, some 18 months ago, to try and retake this view; however, there were so many trees in the way that I couldn't work out where I had been standing when I took this view as it had been very much a last-minute effort since we had been following the train from Scarborough with extreme difficulty.

West Coast main line diversions over the Settle & Carlisle have been going on for a long time. On 4 April 1965 diversions were in force, and the Sunday Birmingham-Glasgow Central service, pictured crossing Ribblehead Viaduct, was headed by No D384. This location, with all the publicity surrounding the Settle & Carlisle in recent years, must now be one of the most famous railway locations in Britain. The viaduct was built between 1870 and 1875 and is 440yd long, 100ft high and has 24 arches. It is, however, not the highest on the route; that honour belongs to Smardale, which is 130ft high.

This beautiful viaduct at Hownes Ghyll is two miles south of Consett. It was built in 1858 by the Stockton & Darlington Railway and designed by Thomas Bouch. The material used in its construction was firebricks. It has 10 spans each of 50ft, with a total length of 730ft and a height of 150ft above the ground. The train illustrated was a special on 10 April 1965 run by the West Riding branch of the Railway Correspondence & Travel Society, which travelled to Waskerley, a line which closed completely on 2 August 1965. The passengers transferred to the DMU, which must have been the only one to use the line, at Consett, having travelled behind Class 9F No 92097. I expect that the trees will have grown now to such an extent that the viaduct will be totally obscured.

I don't know if the double chimney made a big difference to the performance of 'Jubilee' No 45596 Bahamas, *but for me it ruined the locomotive's appearance. No 45596 finished its working career at Stockport Edgeley shed and was frequently seen in the Leeds area. On 22 April 1965 it was in the LNWR yard at Copley Hill, Leeds, ready to leave with a freight for Lancashire. Only five of the class were fitted with double chimneys, starting with No 5684 in 1937, when it received a Kylchap double blastpipe and chimney; this was only retained for a year due to excessive spark throwing. No 45742 had a plain double exhaust chimney for 15 years, but reverted to a single chimney later; as a result, it was odd that as late as 1961 No 45596 should emerge from Crewe Works with a double blastpipe and chimney, which have been retained into preservation.*

After the closure of Copley Hill, Leeds, shed, the remaining steam duties on the Doncaster line were covered by Holbeck locomotives. This resulted in the regular appearance of Stanier Class 5s and 'Jubilees' at Doncaster. One of these duties was the 4.50pm stopping service from Leeds and on 28 June 1965 No 45574, originally named India, *approaches the site of Beeston station. Beeston had closed on 1 March 1953.*

The Derwent Valley Light Railway ceased passenger services in 1926, but freight continued on the line until May 1968, when the southern part of the line closed. On 9 January 1965, on what proved to be an extremely cold outing, the Railway Correspondence & Travel Society organised this passenger train, headed by diesel shunter No D2111, for a journey along the line. The train has just passed the station at Wheldrake; notice the very distinctive station building.

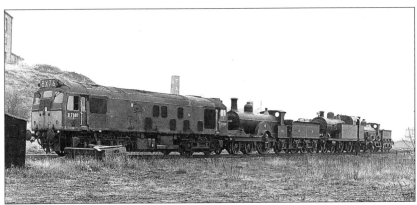

On a very dull 17 March 1965, this interesting train passed north along the Aire Valley. The Midland Spinner 4-2-2, the ex-London, Tilbury & Southend 4-4-2T Thundersley and the ex-MR 0-6-0 No 158A were en route from Derby for storage in Hellifield shed, hauled by No D7597. A brief pause was made, courtesy of the signalman whom I knew very well, just to check that nothing was running hot at Shipley. It is interesting to see the state of the locomotives in comparison to the condition they are in today. A similar train, with Class B1 No 61329, later hauled 'V2' Green Arrow and ex-Great Eastern 'J17' No 1217 to Hellifield for storage.

The West Riding branch of the Railway Correspondence & Travel Society was fortunate in being able to use the preserved Class K4 No 3442 The Great Marquess, then owned by Lord Garnock, on a number of specials. On 10 April 1965 it was used for a visit to the Weardale branch, going as far as St John's Chapel, and is pictured here passing Frosterley. The old stationmaster's house is today a fine private residence.

The Lancaster-Morecambe/Heysham electrics operated on an isolated system. The units were converted LNWR stock, which had been originally built to operate on the Willesden-Earls Court service, but were converted for the Morecambe line in 1953 and continued in service until the route was withdrawn on 1 January 1966. Driving trailer car No 29021 is on the rear of the train as it leaves Lancaster Green Ayre for Lancaster Castle on 9 October 1965. The steam locomotive shed was just to the left of the photograph.

On the Isle of Wight, services to Ventnor ceased on 18 April 1966; this closure included Wroxhall station viewed here on 3 October 1965. This was a day when the Locomotive Club of Great Britain was running a special along the line using two well-cleaned locomotives. The service train was being worked by No W28 Ashey, which was heading for Ventnor. There were 23 of the Class O2 0-4-4Ts operating on the island at this time, all of which were allocated to Ryde shed. Steam operation on the island ceased in 1966.

The Beyer Peacock-built 'Hymeks' (later Class 35) appeared in the Bournemouth area during the summer months. No D7015 is pictured passing through the woods between Bournemouth Central and Branksome on a down train on 31 August 1965. Built in December 1961, the locomotive only survived until June 1972; this was a very short career, by no means unusual for members of this class. Fortunately, four of the type are preserved and can be seen at work.

The Western Region had control of the Somerset & Dorset line in the last few years of operation and, as part of its plans to close the route, the WR diverted the 'Pines Express' away from the line, running the train via Oxford and Basingstoke to Bournemouth. It was still steam-hauled in 1965, but soon went over to Class 47 haulage. With a set of clean maroon stock, but a very dirty 'Merchant Navy' (No 35003 Royal Mail), the down train crosses Brockenhurst Common on the final stages of its journey on 9 September 1965. The locomotive would have worked from Oxford. The branch line to Lymington can be seen in the background.

The BRCW Type 3s (later Class 33) were sharing many duties with steam in 1965, especially during the summer months. On 29 August 1965, No D6565 (later No 33047) is ready to leave Bournemouth West station with an up train. The station closed on 4 October 1965, only a few weeks after this picture was taken. A dual carriageway is now built over the spot on which I was standing to take the photograph.

In the days when the Glasgow-Aberdeen expresses travelled via Forfar and departed from the north end of Perth station, Aberdeen Ferryhill (61B)-based Stanier Class 5 No 44703 pulls out of the station on its journey north on 13 August 1965. I was rather disappointed that this train didn't have a Gresley 'A4' on it, as I had gone to Perth for a few days to record these workings. The Aberdeen expresses were rerouted via Dundee in 1967.

By 1965 the 'Manors' were no longer working the ex-Cambrian lines on a regular basis. No 7802 Bradley Manor was a 'Cambrian Coast Express' locomotive for many years and, although not in the condition it used to be in when based at Aberystwyth, it had received some attention before working this Stephenson Locomotive Society Special to Oswestry on 17 January 1965. The special had been run in connection with the last day of services on the Llanfyllin branch. The train then travelled to Bettisfield, on the old Cambrian line to Whitchurch, which also lost its services on that date. The locomotive was later one of nine of the class to be preserved.

This was the 'Rebuilt Scot Commemorative' railtour, which ran on 13 February 1965 from Crewe to Carlisle via the Settle & Carlisle and returned via Shap. It was intended that this would be the last working for a rebuilt 'Scot', but as things turned out the locomotive lasted for nearly another year. The original locomotive selected for the tour was No 46160 Queen's Westminster Rifleman, but this had failed and so No 46115 Scots Guardsman was a last minute substitution. Credit must go to Crewe North shed for getting the locomotive looking so good. On what was a reasonable day for February in the dales, the train is shown approaching Ribblehead station on the climb to Blea Moor; the line on the right served the quarry at Ribblehead.

1966

This was a year when some well-loved lines closed. For me the closure of the Somerset & Dorset was a sad loss. It was a line that I had only known well for a matter of five years, but it always seemed to have an individual identity, probably because of the class of 2-8-0s which never worked anywhere else and the very stable allocation of locomotives after the war. It was the only line to have the superb Standard Class 9Fs diagrammed for passenger work and the gradients on the line were always guaranteed to produce combinations of locomotives not seen elsewhere in the country; for example, where else could you see 'West Country' Pacifics and ex-LMS Class 2P 4-4-0s operating in tandem? For others the final closure of the Great Central as a through route must have been a great loss; the last of the main lines to be built, it had lasted only 70 years. Another very individual system to see the withdrawal of its remaining steam locomotives was the isolated network on the Isle of Wight. Elsewhere Glasgow St Enoch and Buchanan Street stations closed as did many once famous steam sheds, whilst the Eastern Region Pacifics — Classes A1, A2, A3 and A4 — all worked their last trains. I was able to cover some of these 'lasts', although I had photographed most of them in previous years.

Personally, another milestone in the year was the fact that I made my first trip abroad purely to photograph steam. The trip was to Germany and, whilst I found the German Pacifics impressive, they were not quite like a graceful 'A3' for looks. Five of us went in my Volvo car and covered around 2,000 miles in five days; and what did it cost per head — well under £30 each all in!

5 March 1966 was the last weekend of the Somerset & Dorset line and this explains why I was at Templecombe. Little attention was paid to the passing 'Warships' on the Exeter–Waterloo services, but I did have the sense to point my camera at No D818 Glory which was in maroon livery as it arrived with an up working. The locomotive, like the rest of the class, had a relatively short career, only managing 13 years whilst others managed just 10. They were eventually replaced with Class 33s on the route.

There were spare Type 3 (Class 33s) around on Sundays, so the 'Bournemouth Belle' used to have diesel power on that day but was steam-hauled for the rest of the week. This did not please me at the time, as I wanted yet another dirty 'Merchant Navy' or 'West Country' on the train to increase my already fairly comprehensive collection of steam on the train during the 1960s. I am now glad I made the effort to get the Class 33s on my frequent visits to Bournemouth. On 31 July 1966 the train was photographed between Bournemouth Central and Branksome, with Nos D6549 and D6548 at the head. These later became Nos 33031 and 33030 respectively. The former was withdrawn in 1991, but happily at the time of writing the latter is still in service.

The final specials were already running over the Somerset & Dorset in January 1966, although the end did not come until March. One January special, on the 2nd of the month, was hauled by Southern 'U' class 2-6-0 No 31639 piloting 'West Country' No 34015 Exmouth, the latter representing a class which was used regularly over the route. The crowds gathered around the locomotives during a water stop at Evercreech Junction before the climb, mainly at 1 in 50, to the summit at Masbury.

During the last weeks before closure, Stanier 8Fs put in occasional appearances on passenger work. I suppose it was a question of using anything that was fit to run. On the last day of services, 5 March 1966, No 48760 was heading the 8.25am from Bath to Templecombe. It emerges from the morning mist as it approaches Midsomer Norton on the 1 in 50 climb from Radstock. As if by magic, the locomotives which ran the last specials on the Sunday, and which looked like this on Saturday, appeared commendably clean.

The services from Evercreech Junction to Glastonbury and Street lasted until the end of services over the main line from Bournemouth to Bath. The only passengers around at midday on 1 January 1966 for the train back to Evercreech Junction were enthusiasts. Ivatt 2-6-2T No 41290 was at the head of the train and had been turned at Glastonbury — apparently, a suggestion that I had made to the crew did not fall on deaf ears.

An immaculate green-liveried Class 40 No D279 pauses at Leeds City on the 10.20am Newcastle-Liverpool express on 2 June 1966. Gone were the days when a locomotive change took place at Leeds on these workings, when a Pacific or 'V2' would be replaced by a rebuilt 'Patriot' or 'Britannia', which would be piloted by a Class 5, 'Jubilee', 'Patriot', 'Royal Scot' or 'Britannia'. The displaced locomotive would head back on the return working which departed Liverpool at around 5pm. The Class 46s tended to be the regular motive power for these trains at this time and for many years to come.

The road bridge just to the north of Normanton station was an excellent vantage point; on the north side was the locomotive shed and this view to the south shows the box and station. Normanton, once a very important location on the Midland main line and an extremely busy centre for passenger and freight traffic, has gradually declined over the past 40 years to the point where the station is now reduced to the usual bus shelter with two through lines and the yards have all been closed. On a busy Saturday afternoon, 2 July 1966, 'Peak' No D87 passes nonstop with an express for Leeds, whilst Stanier '8F' No 48202 heads south with a freight. The shed closed on 2 October 1967, although some servicing continued until 1 January 1968; back in 1933, however, there were around 120 locomotives allocated to the shed.

The shed at York, coded 50A with its large turntables, was excellent for photography. There always seemed to be so much more light inside this shed than most others. It was still open for steam on 22 October 1966, although there was very little work for its locomotives. An interesting variety of motive power was lined up around the main turntable. From left to right can be seen Standard Class 3MT No 77012, alongside Carlisle Kingmoor Class 5 No 45363; a locally based '9F' No 92006, which had been used on Somerset & Dorset passenger workings in previous years; 'A4' No 60019 Bittern, which had been recently preserved and looks very clean in comparison with the rest; 'V2' No 60831, the last of the class to be withdrawn some 30 years after No 4772 had been allocated to the shed new; and finally WD 2-8-0 No 90348.

An up express from Bournemouth to Waterloo approaches Pokesdown station down the 1 in 99 gradient on 23 July 1966. The train is headed by 'West Country' No 34017 Ilfracombe, which still has its nameplate intact although the crest is missing. The locomotive was new in December 1945, being rebuilt in October 1958 and withdrawn in July 1967.

The Heaton-Red Bank (Newcastle-Manchester) empty van train pulls out of the loop at Neville Hill West ready to cross the Pennines on 3 July 1966. The train was probably in excess of 20 vehicles, but adequate motive power was provided by Stockport-based 'Britannia' No 70015 Apollo *piloting Newton Heath Class 5 No 45200. At the time, this was probably the most interesting steam working in the area as it was nearly always double-headed and could produce almost anything. I think that my most interesting combination was a Llandudno Junction Class 5 piloting a Gateshead 'A4' as far as Leeds. When new in June 1951* Apollo *was allocated to the Western Region; note the lack of handrails on the smoke deflector — this was a feature of WR 'Britannias'.*

A sad sight as Class A4 No 60010 Dominion of Canada *is hauled partially dismantled by Standard Class 4MT No 75019 out of the yard at Neville Hill West on 27 April 1966 en route from Darlington Works to Crewe Works, where the 'A4' was put into good external condition before being shipped on MV* Beaveroak *from Royal Victoria Dock, London, to Montreal in Canada.*

Prior to the locomotive being bought for preservation, a footplate ride was organised for the potential purchaser Pat Whitehouse on Holbeck 'Jubilee' No 45593 Kolhapur *to check its condition. The train selected was the afternoon Leeds-Wavertree vans on 19 September 1966. The train called at Mirfield en route to do some shunting. In those days the station had an overall roof in comparison with the terrible bus shelters that exist today. The locomotive had been well cleaned and the sale was agreed. Since preservation, No 45593 has been very active on preserved lines, appearing in many liveries and assuming false identities. It has also made a few trips on the main line. Note here the yellow stripe on the cab side, indicating that the locomotive was banned south of Crewe after the 25kV electrification.*

Since preserved steam returned to the main line, Southern Pacifics have appeared all over England and on trips into Wales; I don't think that they have yet ventured into Scotland. In 1966, on the other hand, the sight of a 'Merchant Navy' in the north of the country was still extremely rare, but on 20 November No 35026 *Lamport & Holt Line* worked a special from Manchester up the Hope Valley to Sheffield, Doncaster, York and Newcastle. The sanders were working well as the train passes Chinley East Junction. At this time the junction appears to be in the process of removal, but it was reinstated a few years later. No marks for picking out the track inspector, complete with trilby hat, pipe and regulation raincoat. Other occasions when the class visited the north included a trip over the Settle & Carlisle in June 1964 when No 35012 headed the 'Solway Ranger' and on 25 June 1966 when No 35026 took over from *Flying Scotsman* at Doncaster on the 'Aberdonian'.

On a frosty 3 December, Holbeck 'Jubilee' No 45593 *Kolhapur* passes Portsmouth on the climb to Copy Pit with a special from the Leeds area. The train eventually ran over the East Lancashire line all the way through to Bacup.

1967

*T*he year seemed to be one mad dash around the country trying to record everything that was finishing — either steam services or line closures. The end of steam on the Southern eventually came on 9 July. Specials were run for the event, but they were not as well patronised as had been hoped. I expect that this was due to the fact that steam enthusiasts had been enjoying quite incredible performances by the 'Merchant Navies' and the light Pacifics for several months, where speeds around and above the 100mph mark were achieved, so a formal (and, I believe, expensive) last day farewell did not seem attractive. The 'Pines Express' also ceased on 4 March; by this date the famous train was running via Basingstoke and Oxford. However, for me the true 'Pines' ceased when it was diverted away from the Somerset & Dorset.

Other significant trains and lines which disappeared were the Cromford & High Peak, the 'Cambrian Coast Express' and, for me the most important, the end of steam at Leeds Holbeck and other local sheds. This, of course, marked the end of the 'Jubilees', which had enjoyed a last fling every Saturday over the Settle & Carlisle and even managed a final working on the Royal train.

Little diesel photography was done, except when I came across it when out looking for steam. In diesel traction terms, No DP2 came to a premature end when it hit a cement train at Thirsk but, as its career ended, so the first of the future Class 50s, No D400, appeared in October.

Many other 'lasts' occurred during the year; some I managed to record, others I missed. Despite all this activity in the UK, I also visited Austria, Portugal and Czechoslovakia; the last named had some of the finest and most advanced steam locomotives in the world.

In the Yorkshire area, most of the main line passenger workings had gone over to diesel traction, except for the summer Saturday extras. This is emphasised by the open space visible behind the 'Yorkshire Pullman' on 29 April 1967 where Copley Hill shed in Leeds had once been sited. The carriage sidings were still in use at this date and continued until Leeds Central closed two days later on 1 May. Type 4 No D1103 (later No 47520) operated on the East Coast main line for many years. This location was a favourite one for enthusiasts to watch trains in Leeds, as they could see trains arriving and departing on the ex-LNWR lines from the Huddersfield direction. A large factory now stands on the shed site and the main line is electrified.

The line out of Bradford Exchange (as it was called in 1967) climbed at 1 in 50 to Bowling Junction and heavy trains were always banked. Class 40 No D396 is receiving assistance from a 2-6-4T on 9 June 1967 as it passes the junction with the Saturdays Only service from Bradford to Blackpool. Waiting to take the Bradford avoiding line to Laisterdyke is Class 37 No D6861 (later renumbered 37161 and now No 37899) on a freight. The Type 3 is provided with a brake tender at the front. There has been no booked freight over this route for many years and the avoiding line has been closed and lifted.

30 April 1967 was the last day of the Cromford & High Peak Railway and the Stephenson Locomotive Society organised a brakevan special over the line. The highlight of all tours on this route was the ascent of the 1 in 14 Hopton Bank. Two Class J94 0-6-0Ts, Nos 68012 and 68006, had been working the line for several years since the demise of the ex-North London 0-6-0Ts. The two locomotives failed to get up the bank the first time with, I believe, six brakevans, and had to return and split the train. The pair are working flat out here about halfway up the incline; they made it to the top on this attempt. As you can see, the road, which ran parallel to the line was blocked by cars, as there were crowds of people to witness the last ascent.

It was to be over a year before the Keighley & Worth Valley started running services but permission was obtained to run this special on 13 April 1967 with then resident Class J72 0-6-0T Joem to celebrate the centenary of the line. The train is pictured at Keighley station just before departure.

Six Brush Type 4s — Nos D1921-D1926 — were allocated to Eastleigh in this period to assist the fast disappearing Southern Pacifics on the main line duties. No D1923 was on Bournemouth shed (71B) along with 'Merchant Navy' No 35013 Blue Funnel and BR Standard Class 5MT No 73092 on 26 March 1967. At this time, steam still had over three months to run. The Class 47 later became No 47246, then 47644 and is currently No 47756 in the RES fleet (now part of English, Welsh & Scottish). The shed site at Bournemouth has now become the inevitable car park. As I spent Christmas at Bournemouth in the 1960s, I normally made a point of taking some fresh air on Christmas Day with a walk around the shed rather than along the seafront.

There were strange happenings going on in Leeds in August. Ex-GWR No 7029 Clun Castle arrived in the area for clearance tests prior to working specials from Peterborough up the East Coast main line to Newcastle and over the Settle & Carlisle. The locomotive also ran a special over Shap. After travelling around the area pushing an inspection coach, the locomotive arrived during the evening of 21 August 1967 at Holbeck shed for servicing, where it is seen on the ash pit. Notice it is not carrying a cabside number or nameplates. The shed closed to steam the following month.

The District Motive Power Superintendent of the Leeds area, a certain Mr T. Greaves, was a steam enthusiast at heart and the local enthusiasts and others had much to thank him for, for keeping the Holbeck 'Jubilees' going throughout the year and using them over the Settle & Carlisle every weekend. A visit by HRH Prince Philip to the region north of Harrogate occurred on 30 May 1967 and to everybody's surprise 'Jubilee' No 45562 Alberta was diagrammed to haul the train in the Leeds area, with Class 5 No 45428 as the stand-by locomotive. I believe that the Class 5, which was in plain black BR livery, was actually painted with red boiler bands, but the authorities banned this and they were removed. There is a story that the Duke of Edinburgh, when leaving the train, stopped to have a word with the driver and enquired what sort of locomotive the 'Jubilee' was and was given the very appropriate reply that it was a 'Sandringham'! This must have been the last steam-hauled Royal train on BR on which a member of the Royal Family was on board. The train travelled to Ripon where the locomotive ran round; it is pictured here at Wormald Green.

The Bradford portion of the King's Cross-Leeds trains was used for crew training on the local Class 24s and 25s. The regular power were the Low Moor-based Fairburn 2-6-4Ts. On 16 June 1967, the 11.55 from Bradford Exchange to King's Cross has Class 25 No D5180 (later No 25030) as pilot to No 42145. The pair are passing through the deep cutting at St Dunstans on the 1 in 50 gradient. The line to the left used to form a triangle with the old Great Northern route to Keighley or Halifax via Queensbury.

After almost three years of working the Aberdeen-Glasgow expresses, Class A4 No 60019 Bittern was withdrawn from Aberdeen Ferryhill in September 1966. It passed into preservation immediately and was then based at York shed, from where it operated some enthusiast specials. One of these was the Railway Correspondence & Travel Society West Riding Branch railtour from Leeds to Glasgow on 17 July 1967. After a brief stop at Beattock station to pick up a pilotman for wrong line working from Greskine to the summit, the train is seen leaving Beattock yard. The special returned via the Glasgow & South Western main line. The locomotive was repainted in blue livery and ran a few excursions around 1972, but has not been used since. The old steam shed can be seen just to the right of the signalbox.

The final steam-hauled 'Cambrian Coast Express' ran on 4 March 1967. Standard Class 4MT No 75033 was adorned with the proper headboard and shedplate 89C for Machynlleth. A group of enthusiasts had spent a good deal of the night cleaning the locomotive, which as a result looked very smart. The train is pictured ready to leave Aberystwyth having been photographed by the local newspaper. The return working was also steam-hauled, by No 75006; this was one of the class fitted with a double chimney.

Steam and diesel co-existed side by side at Holbeck shed, Leeds. This picture was taken on 27 August 1967, about a month before the remaining steam sheds closed in the West Riding. A Fairburn tank and two Stanier Class 5s — which possibly never worked again — are seen together with two Type 2s, Nos D7578 and D7588; the latter two became Nos 25228 and 25238 and lasted in service until March 1984 and October 1980 respectively.

A Locomotive Club of Great Britain special visited the Swanage branch on 7 May 1967. It was top-and-tailed by 'West Country' Pacific No 34023 Blackmore Vale (now preserved) and Standard 2-6-4T No 80011, in poor external condition. One can now virtually repeat the picture today, as the preserved Swanage Railway is operating classmate No 80104 and Battle of Britain Light Pacific No 34072 '257 Squadron'.

No 45697 Achilles *was one of the Holbeck 'Jubilees' that lasted until the closure of the West Riding steam sheds. Class mates* Alberta *and* Kolhapur *tended to receive all the attention as they were regularly diagrammed for the Saturdays Only Leeds-Carlisle trains. By this time,* Achilles *was in plain green livery but running with a lined black tender. On 15 March it was working the 12.55pm Stourton-Carlisle freight and is pictured just setting off from Skipton South after a crew change.*

By 1967 Patricroft shed in Manchester had a large allocation of Standard Class 5MTs, probably far more than were needed. They were regularly rostered for the Saturdays Only extras across the Pennines to Leeds, No 73039 makes an impressive sight as it storms across Saddleworth Viaduct heading for Standedge Tunnel on 27 May 1967. The locomotive spent its last two years at Patricroft before being withdrawn in July 1967. To the right of the locomotive and between the two walls used to be the branch to Delph; the push-pull train was known locally as the 'Delph Donkey'.

Whilst putting a slide show together a few months ago on the Settle & Carlisle line, I calculated that over the last 40 years I must have made at least 300 visits to the line, most of them south of Ais Gill. Many have been memorable trips, but the one that really stands out was on 4 November 1967, when, on a very cold and frosty morning, about five freights went north from Settle Junction, headed by a Standard '9F', some Class 5s and, in this case, an incredibly dirty Class 8F. The exhausts from the trains on this cold clear morning were magnificent, especially on the lower end of the climb where the sanders were working. Most of the photography was done with my cine camera, but I did take this black and white shot of No 48074 coming off Ribblehead Viaduct. What I don't understand is why I didn't take a colour slide and why only one monochrome exposure, as the train was only doing about 20mph. I am afraid that this remains a complete mystery.

All the ex-Crosti-boilered Class 9F 2-10-0s were still active up to November 1967 except for No 92028, which had been withdrawn in October 1966. With the exception of No 92027, the remainder were allocated to Birkenhead and were therefore frequent visitors to Leeds on the Stanlow-Hunslet oil trains, which travelled via Standedge. Their progress from Mirfield to Marsden was usually very slow and, if one chased in the car, it was quite usual to get at least seven pictures in the 12 miles. No 92022 is working hard past Gledholt Junction, about a mile west of Huddersfield, on 8 July 1967; it would probably be about 20min before it reached Marsden.

1 9 6 8

This was the year that I and countless other enthusiasts had been dreading — the end of steam on BR. For me and thousands of others this meant a real change in our lives. I attended the last rites at Preston and witnessed the departure of Class 5 No 45212 on the 20.48 to Blackpool and travelled behind No 45318 on the very last scheduled train, the 21.15 Preston-Liverpool Exchange service. I gave up trying to take pictures, as the crowds virtually made it impossible and just watched the unforgettable scene, after which I made my way to Lostock Hall shed, with many others, to do a little last minute cleaning of the locomotives booked for the specials on the Sunday and also take some pictures. I think that there were five specials around Lancashire and I tried to see them all. There was also, of course, the last official special the following week over the Settle & Carlisle with 'Britannia' No 70013 and Class 5s Nos 44781 and 44871.

The demise of main line steam in Britain marked the start of a long period of inactivity in this country, but I did make numerous trips abroad; I went to Germany in September 1968 and to Spain in October to keep me going.

Other things did happen during the year. The Keighley & Worth Valley opened on 29 June, whilst the Bluebell celebrated the purchase of the line's freehold from BR. 'Jubilee' No 5596 *Bahamas* was overhauled at Hunslet, Leeds, at a cost of £5,000 and many locomotives were secured for preservation.

The year, however, started with tragedy, as on 6 January Class 81 No E3009 hit a transporter on a level crossing at Hixton killing 11 people. More positive news was the appearance of the 4,000hp No HS4000 *Kestrel*, which left the Brush Works for Derby; this was a very impressive looking machine. The rebuilt Euston station was opened by HM the Queen. A new era had begun as far as I was concerned.

The state of the yard and the ash pits at Rose Grove shed got steadily worse as the months progressed during the year. This picture of local Stanier '8F' No 48257 on 17 February 1968 illustrates the point very well; the pit looks as if it hadn't been emptied for weeks and, with all the loose coals and implements left around, it must have been quite dangerous at night. The locomotive still had a few months of operation before withdrawal.

Four months after the previous picture had been taken, on 1 June 1968, '8F' No 48257 was looking a little better externally, with a 24B shedplate, due to the efforts of local enthusiasts. The shed foreman had been persuaded to diagram the locomotive for the Saturday afternoon Colne-Red Bank vans service to Manchester, a fact which was much appreciated. I managed to follow the train through the Saturday afternoon traffic, such as it was in 1968, and obtained several pictures, including this one taken at the delightfully named station of Church & Oswaldtwistle. The station is still open, although the buildings have vanished to be replaced by the usual bus shelters.

The end had already come in February for these two damaged Stanier '8Fs' as they catch some sunlight that had managed to penetrate through the shed windows at Rose Grove on 17 February 1968. The floor inside the shed appeared to be quite clean compared to the yard, but that was probably because all the locomotives inside had been withdrawn.

The last day of normal — such as it was — steam operation had arrived and I, and at least 25 others, spent the Saturday evening and the early hours of Sunday at Lostock Hall, cleaning the locomotives that were due to work the specials on the Sunday. At 01.00 on 4 August 1968, Class 5 No 45017 looks presentable. The locomotive was booked to work a Stephenson Locomotive Society special with No 44874 from Manchester to Todmorden and then over the Copy Pit line. On the climb to Copy Pit, after the train had passed Portsmouth, the drivers really opened the pair up; I have never heard such a noise from two Class 5s — it is something I'll never forget.

On 1 June 1968 Standard Class 4MT No 75019 was working the Grassington branch; this had become the locomotive's regular duty, in the company of two others. As the year progressed the locomotive got cleaner and cleaner, courtesy of local enthusiasts. My thanks are due to the driver and fireman for the exhaust, as the train was slowing down for the level crossing at Rylstone, which was operated by the train crews. The previous day, the locomotive had worked a ballast train from Swinden Quarry to Appleby, which I am sure was the last steam-hauled freight over the Settle & Carlisle. Unfortunately, it ran during the mid-morning, which made the light to Blea Moor extremely difficult from Settle Junction. The locomotive was withdrawn from Carnforth in August.

The months prior to the end of steam saw many specials running around the Lancashire and Yorkshire area. Normal motive power was provided by Stanier Class 5s with a few '8Fs' and BR Standard '4MTs' or '5MTs' also participating. 'Britannia' No 70013 Oliver Cromwell was also frequently seen. One of these specials is illustrated here. Class 5 No 45110 (now preserved) pilots sister No 44949 on the climb to Peak Forest past Great Rocks on 20 April 1968, having travelled via the old LNWR route from Stockport to Buxton.

The Blackburn-Bolton line over Sough Summit was included in many of the last steam trips. On 20 April 1968 two of Manchester Patricroft's Class 5MTs, Nos 73069 and 73134 — the latter a Caprotti version — pass Spring Vale. No 73069 was destined to become the last active member of the class.

Wilpshire Bank on the Hellifield-Blackburn line has seen a wide variety of locomotives since the return of main line steam; this ranges from a Scottish 'J36' 0-6-0 to 'Merchant Navy' Pacifics and others. In the latter days of steam, it was mainly Stanier Class 5s and '8Fs', together with '9Fs' and 'Britannias', all on freight turns. Passenger services over the route had ceased on 1 September 1962, but were reinstated as far as Clitheroe on 30 May 1994. On 20 April 1968 Class 5s Nos 45342 and 45156 — the latter carrying replica The Ayrshire Yeomanry nameplates — pass the closed Wilpshire station. A new station has been provided here, but this is sited half a mile towards Blackburn. No 45156 was one of only four of the Stanier Class 5s to be named.

No book such as this would be complete without a picture of the famous 'Fifteen Guinea' special on 11 August 1968; although this train was considered overpriced at the time it was, nonetheless, full. I took this rather ordinary picture of the train, hauled by 'Britannia' No 70013 Oliver Cromwell, approaching Ribblehead station, with the idea of catching it again at Blea Moor. The next picture shows why I didn't make it. Immediately after the train reached Carlisle No 70013 headed south light engine to Norfolk and into preservation at Bressingham. It has remained there ever since.

By the time I got this close to Ais Gill, having abandoned the car, the special must have been well past Appleby, so no picture of the train. There has never been such a traffic jam as this at Ais Gill; it still gets busy when steam specials operate but never like this. I did, however, manage to get a lot of cine film of the local, and rather agitated, police trying to sort out the chaos.

As one door closed, so another opened. BR steam had just about ended when the Keighley & Worth Valley sprang into life on 22 June 1968 with its opening specials. The assembled crowd listened to the speeches at Keighley before the departure of the reopening special headed by Ivatt 2-6-2T No 41241 in red livery and 'USA' 0-6-0T No 72 in light brown. Having a preserved railway so near to home provided many enjoyable hours and hundreds of photographs. Unfortunately, however, it must have considerably delayed the return of my interest in the BR scene, a fact which I very much regret.

I don't quite know why I was at Manchester on 24 August — perhaps I was expecting to see some steam — but I did take this picture of lined green Class 76 No E26053 *Perseus* waiting to leave for Sheffield Victoria. I was looking at the locomotive on the opposite platform when the driver of No E26053 popped his head out of the window and asked me if I wanted to join him to Sheffield. Naturally, I couldn't refuse such an offer, so enjoyed a very interesting journey over Woodhead. I particularly remember the driver pointing out to me the speed trap at the end of Dinting Viaduct and how bad the ride was at speed; I can only assume that the Class 77 Co-Co design rode much better.

Yet another last steam special, this time with '8F' No 48652 in charge. It was running, on 27 April 1968, from Bolton via Bury and Castleton to Rochdale. A photographic stop was made at Broadfield, which is now part of the East Lancashire Railway's extension, so I may not have to wait too long before I see another '8F' and other locomotives at this location again.

The Longmoor Military Railway had been renowned for its excellent open days for some years. I was quite prepared to travel big distances to see steam, so a couple of friends and I set off early one morning for a day out at Longmoor. The star of the show, as always, was the immaculately turned out WD 2-10-0 No 600 *Gordon*, which is now preserved on the Severn Valley. It is shown leaving Longmoor on 28 September 1968 for Bordon. It was a pity that this excellent system was not preserved after it finally closed.

1969

Selecting pictures for the years after 1977 has been extremely difficult, as I can only use about 1% of what I took during the year. However, for 1969, the selection is very easy, as the four photographs used are about a third of my output during the year in the UK. I obviously hadn't come to terms with the end of steam, so trips to Ireland, Germany and Portugal were made to record steam overseas. I hardly dare think of the opportunities that I missed on the diesel scene over here.

In terms of events, closures were still occurring with regularity; of these, one of the most notable was the closure of Manchester Exchange and Manchester Central. The weather caused considerable disruption to the Woodhead line, with snow, and to the Great Western line at Dawlish with gales and high seas. *Flying Scotsman* departed for the United States on 19 September for a much longer visit than originally planned, whilst, earlier in the year, the seven Class 77 Co-Co electrics from the Woodhead route were sold to the Netherlands; two of the latter have subsequently returned home and one is also preserved in the Netherlands.

Personally, 1969 was not an exciting year; the lack of railway activity must have meant my garden received more than its fair share of attention!

No 46115 Scots Guardsman *was the last rebuilt 'Royal Scot' to be withdrawn, succumbing on 1 January 1966 from Carlisle Kingmoor shed. The locomotive was also the first, in August 1947, to receive smoke deflectors. Following preservation, it arrived at Haworth for safe keeping, but being too big for use on the branch at that time, it soon departed for Dinting, where it arrived on 28 May 1969. It was eventually returned to main line running. It is seen at Haworth on 4 February 1969.*

Possibly one of the most bizarre events to have occurred on a preserved line was when a company decided to demonstrate the durability of its product by the use of the Keighley and Worth Valley's Class 5 No 5212. The locomotive was duly wallpapered and, whilst in steam, was sprayed with a water cannon to see if the glue/paper would survive the treatment. I don't know what conclusions were drawn from the exercise, but it made a memorable sight; the colour slide is even more dramatic! It is shown alongside Haworth shed on 6 February 1969.

To mark the closure of the 'Waverley' route from Carlisle to Edinburgh, the West Riding branch of the Railway Correspondence & Travel Society ran a special on the last day, 5 January 1969, hauled by Class 55 'Deltic' No 9007 Pinza. Obtaining a 'Deltic' for a railtour in 1969 was quite a feat in itself, as they were seldom released from their main line duties. A spirited run was made over the Settle & Carlisle, a fact which was not appreciated by the dining car crew who were endeavouring to serve soup at the time, as we passed through the Eden Valley and up the fells at a considerable speed. A photo stop was made at Riccarton Junction on the way out; there was a covering of snow at this wild and desolate place. Our tour returned without trouble, but the last train, the sleeper from Edinburgh to St Pancras, encountered considerable opposition to the closure from local people, who I believe, blockaded the level crossing at Newcastleton.

There were grand plans to preserve the line, but these died a not unexpected death; but currently there are serious plans to reopen the southern section from Carlisle to Kielder Forest for MoD and forestry purposes.

Dent Cutting is usually the first place to get blocked by snow on the Settle & Carlisle line. On 15 February 1969 there was plenty of snow about, but it was not likely to cause any major problem to the railway. Class 25 No D5186 trundles north at the head of a short freight; a few minutes earlier a Class 50 had headed south hauling two brakevans.

1 9 7 0

The period from 1970 to 1975 was undoubtedly my most unproductive; the number of outings to places in the country other than the Keighley & Worth Valley could be counted on the fingers of one hand. I had several trips abroad, but at home it was just too easy to go to the K&WVR and take hundreds of pictures. I have hardly looked at them since and am unlikely to do so in the future.

Another possible reason for the lack of activity was the fact that I moved house; this was an experience not to be forgotten — so much so that we are still in the same house 28 years on!

It should have been the time for going to Devon and Cornwall — to record the diesel-hydraulics — or to Scotland to see events north of the Border — such as the triple-headers on the 'Royal Highlander'. However, the fact remains that I did virtually nothing, not even recording the local scene on my own doorstep. It took me a long time to come to terms with the fact that steam had finished on BR and I also found that my camera equipment, whilst

adequate for stopping an '8F' 2-8-0 on a coal train at 25mph, just wasn't up to dealing with 90mph modern traction. This was a problem I didn't resolve for another six years. The small selection of pictures for these years is an accurate reflection, I am afraid, of this lack of activity.

Despite this, things were happening on BR and elsewhere. These included the destruction by fire of the Britannia Bridge across the Menai Straits, resulting in 16 locomotives being stranded on Anglesey until they were taken off by ship to Bangor. Scrap locomotives were leaving Barry for preservation and the Severn Valley Railway got underway. Passenger services on the Woodhead route ceased in January and in May the local services over the Settle & Carlisle route were withdrawn. On the other hand, virtually all the diesel classes introduced as a result of the Modernisation Plan were still running, even if a few were not performing as well as had been intended. It was definitely a year of missed opportunities.

There was snow on the Settle & Carlisle in February, so I made the effort to go and see what was on offer. One of the last Class 25s to be built, at Derby in March 1967, No D7673 approaches Ribblehead station on 14 February 1971 with a mixed northbound freight. The line heading out of the picture to the right was into Ribblehead Quarry, which was producing ballast for BR at the time and continued to do so for at least a further 12 years. On 2 May, local passenger services over the route were withdrawn, resulting in the closure of many stations on the line, including Ribblehead. It was to be another 16 years until they were reopened.

The Class 50s looked very drab in the plain blue livery, but when working properly were a vast improvement in terms of performance over the Class 40s on the West Coast main line. No D405 is passing through the cutting at Shap Summit in fine style on 7 March 1970 with the down 'Royal Scot'. Note the semaphore signal in the background; this was operated by the box at the summit.

The Woodhead route lost its passenger services on 3 January 1970, but on 14 March Manchester United were playing an important game at Sheffield. This resulted, if I remember correctly, in five specials. The first was double-headed by two Class 25s, the second by a Class 40, the third by Class 50 No D414, the fourth by a 'Peak' and one other. There was also a freightliner with a Class 47 at the head and three coal trains — quite a variety in only three hours on a Saturday morning! The picture shows the Class 50 just east of Torside heading for Woodhead. As far as I am aware, this was the only occasion that a Class 50 worked a passenger train over the line. The reservoirs in the background appear to be full; this is in contrast to recent years when they have often been empty.

Fortunately the preservation movement in general has painted its ex-BR locomotives in authentic liveries, save for some 'Thomas the Tank Engine' events when the extra income no doubt justifies the temporary liveries adopted. There are exceptions, however, such as this at Steamtown, Carnforth, when the now very much loved Class 5 No 5407 appeared in a spurious Furness Railway red, as shown here. I also have a colour slide of the locomotive and, I suppose had it been authentic, then it would have been all right, but somehow I couldn't quite come to terms with it. The date is 19 September 1970.

The filming of The Railway Children on the Keighley & Worth Valley Railway must have been the primary event that put the railway on the tourist map and gave it the publicity and financial boost it needed in its early days. Since then the line has never really looked back and must now rank as one of the best, if not the best, preserved branch line in the country. The Lancashire & Yorkshire Barton Wright 0-6-0 is seen in Mytholmes Cutting on 8 June 1970 at the head of the specially painted coaches. If you look carefully in the picture at the embankment above the locomotive you can see a tree, which is attached to runners in the ground; at the appropriate time this slipped down the embankment together with a lot of soil and stones thrown from the top of the cutting to produce the landslip in the film. The locomotive is currently under restoration and it is hoped to see it in action again in the near future.

The preserved Gresley 'N2' was at the K&WVR in its early preservation days and, after a great deal of effort, was restored to working order. It worked on the line in 1969 and 1970, but had to be withdrawn earlier than had been hoped due to the state of its tubes. It was painted in LNER livery and numbered 4744. Currently working on the Great Central Railway and is painted in full BR lined livery as No 69523. It is pictured here ready to leave Keighley for Oxenhope on 31 March 1970.

The little L&YR Pug No 51218 was the first locomotive to reach the Keighley & Worth Valley Railway when it arrived on 7 January 1965. It was used to haul items up the line once they had reached Keighley. The locomotive has subsequently visited many sites in preservation and, on 28 August 1970, it was being loaded in Ingrow Yard en route to Harewood House. It is currently in full working order and on its travels once again.

1971

*T*his was a remarkable year, but not for what I achieved photographically on BR but for what I didn't. I find it hard to believe, that I didn't take a single black and white photograph of a main line diesel and only six colour slides of them; how times changed over the next few years, when over 1,000 of each became the norm. I wasn't exactly doing nothing, as I had two trips to Germany and undertook my first visit to South Africa, but most weekends were spent at the Worth Valley, although I did accomplish trips to the North Yorkshire Moors and the Severn Valley.

The main event of the year was undoubtedly the return of steam to the main line on 2 October, an event which was to prove so important in how my photographic activities were to be directed over the next 15 years. I regret the fact that I allowed it to dominate my efforts so much; looking back, I feel my time would have been far better spent on the main line diesel classes that were around at the time, rather than accumulating vast mileages in the car for very few pictures. Hindsight is, however, a wonderful thing as I have said many times.

On the BR scene there were not many changes: the Class 27s started on the Glasgow-Edinburgh push-pull trains, the 'Baby Deltics' departed, work started on the West Coast electrification between Weaver Junction and Glasgow and the impressive Brush Type 5 diesel No HS4000 *Kestrel* was sold to Russia.

The Midland Class 1F 0-6-0T No 1708 was based on the Keighley & Worth Valley Railway at this time and was returned to traffic, but only for a very few occasions. As far as I can remember, it did not work a train on its own. It is pictured arriving at Oakworth station on 18 April 1971 piloting the railway's Ivatt 2-6-2T No 41241. At this time, the latter was painted in the distinctive lined red livery. The '1F' left the railway shortly afterwards, but returned for a limited period during 1997.

This picture will remind enthusiasts of the condition in which some locomotives arrived at the preserved railways from the Barry scrapyard. Standard Class 4MT No 80002 was sold to the K&WVR in March 1969 for £2,700; the price included delivery from Eastfield to Keighley. It was returned to working order relatively quickly and worked for a year or two before having to be withdrawn for major repairs. These repairs took nearly 15 years, but the locomotive is currently back in working order on the line. It was to be a matter of 10 years before City of Wells *was restored by a small band of dedicated Worth Valley members to main line condition; it later became one of the most popular main line locomotives with enthusiasts and achieved some very remarkable performances. It is currently undergoing another major overhaul. The pair are seen at Ingrow Yard on 31 October 1971.*

3 October 1971 was the day that steam enthusiasts had dreamed of, but few believed it would ever happen and perhaps wives and girlfriends wished that it had never happened. The most famous of Great Western 'Kings', No 6000 King George V, returned to the main line, largely due to the efforts of the Managing Director of H. P. Bulmers at Hereford, Peter Prior, when it hauled a Pullman special from Hereford over Llanwerhangel to the outskirts of Newport, through the Severn Tunnel and onward to Oxford and thence Tyseley. The public and enthusiasts turned out in their thousands to see the great event and for many a new chapter in their lives had commenced. No main line steam had run on BR since August 1968 except for a few trips with Flying Scotsman. I remember that day vividly; we covered 527 miles in the day, leaving at 06.00 and arriving home at 18.00. The picture shows the locomotive and train climbing the gradient out of the Severn Tunnel towards Pilning.

There were a considerable number of projects taking place on the K&WVR around this time. The shed at Oxenhope was built, the loop at Damems was being installed and the extension to the headshunt at Oxenhope was also being constructed. Visiting LMS Class 5 No 5025 is at Oxenhope on 1 May 1971 with the earthworks in the foreground and a good crowd on the platform. The Class 5 eventually moved to the Strathspey Railway at Aviemore, where it has been based ever since. Just to the left of the shed can be seen an ex-Sheffield Corporation double-deck tram, which was stored at Oxenhope for some time whilst a suitable home was found; it is currently based at Beamish.

A visit to the North Yorkshire Moors Railway on 23 October 1971 found the preserved Class P3 ('J27') No 2392 in action. The locomotive makes a fine sight in its North Eastern livery as it climbs the bank past Darnholme en route to Goathland. The locomotive became the property of the North Eastern Locomotive Preservation Group (NELPG) on 13 November 1967 for the princely sum of £1,400 and has spent most of its time since then on the NYMR, with occasional visits to other lines.

1 9 7 2

The selection of pictures which I have included for this year suggests I was extremely inactive. This is partly true, but for some reason I did very little black and white work, preferring to take colour slides. This may have been because I was not happy with my old 2¼in square camera, which was not producing the quality I wanted. Had this been a colour album I could have included pictures in Scotland, the last day of the Keswick branch and one of the rare outings of preserved 'A4' No 60019 *Bittern* in blue livery.

I remember vividly the hostile reaction from my friends in the area when I returned from Devon and showed 'Warships' and 'Westerns' at our slide shows; they had expected to see preserved steam on the local lines and considered my efforts a waste of time. Needless to say, nearly all of them have now spent years photographing the current scene.

On the Southern Region it was the end of two famous trains: the 'Golden Arrow' ran for the last time on 30 November and the 'Brighton Belle' went out in fine style with a champagne meal served on the last train on 30 April. For the last-named it was the end of a 90-year era.

The prototype gas-turbine four-car set emerged from Derby Works and the Advanced Passenger Train (APT-E) put in an appearance. Electric trains — but not yet passenger services — started running between Weaver Junction and Warrington.

On a sadder note, the Swanage branch closed, although this has subsequently been restored, as did the Penrith-Keswick line. Better news was that 20 locomotives left Barry for preservation and a further 20 were awaiting the conclusion of final negotiations.

Had it not been for a family holiday in Devon, the number of Class 52 'Western' photographs in my collection would be very small. The class was still very active during 1972 and I made some effort to get pictures. On 29 August 1972 an unidentified member of the class leaves Teignmouth with an up express. This location must have produced more photographs over the years than any other in the country; nevertheless, it is still a fine spot and even now it is very pleasant on a good summer's day to watch the trains pass along the sea wall.

By August 1972, there were only about a dozen active Class 42 'Warships', all the Class 43s having been withdrawn by this time. The Class 45s and 47s had replaced the diesel-hydraulics and I only managed to photograph a few in action. One of these few is No D814 Dragon working a down stock train along the sea wall on 29 August 1972. The locomotive was only to survive for a further three months after the date of this photograph.

A down Paddington-Plymouth train leaves Dawlish in the late afternoon of 2 September 1972. I believe the locomotive was No D1009 Western Invader, which had over four years to go before withdrawal. The next train produced a Class 35 'Hymek', which was the only one of the class I saw during the week; for some reason I only took a colour slide of it.

No D1019 Western Challenger was relegated on this day, 1 September 1972, to a down freight. It is pictured passing Dawlish on its journey west. This particular locomotive was withdrawn in May 1973 after only 10 years of active service.

Still in green livery, Class 31 No 5843 hauls a failed DMU along the sea wall towards Exeter on 31 August 1972. The locomotive later became No 31309 and was named Cricklewood *between May 1987 and December 1989. It was withdrawn in April 1991 and cut up at Booth-Roe at Rotherham.*

An interesting line-up of stored locomotives pictured outside the new shed at Ingrow on the Keighley & Worth Valley Railway on 4 April 1972. Gresley 'N2' No 4744, in LNER livery, stands in front of the National Collection's 2-6-0 Crab No 42700; the latter is in all-black. The Crab came to the line in 1968 and then worked some pre-Christmas trains, but it had very few days in service thereafter. It is now being restored on the East Lancashire Railway at Bury. At the front is Manning Wardle 0-6-0ST Sir Berkeley, *which was built in 1891 for use by the contractors building the Great Central main line between London and Sheffield. It has been steamed occasionally since it arrived in 1965.*

K&WVR Class 4F No 3924 and visiting Class 5 No 5025 make a fine sight in their matching liveries as they head a train up the Worth Valley just below Oakworth on 9 April 1972. No 3924 was the first locomotive to leave Barry scrapyard in September 1968 and the first ex-Barry locomotive to be successfully steamed (in June 1970).

1 9 7 3

With pictures taken as far apart as Kyle of Lochalsh and Teignmouth, it would suggest there was probably plenty of action in between these points. Unfortunately, this was not the case; the trip to Kyle was for the purpose of organising an outing for members of the West Riding branch of the Railway Correspondence & Travel Society and it was another family summer holiday in Devon. Preserved steam was appearing on a regular basis with new locomotives, so much time was devoted to these trains, but of course more time was spent on the Keighley & Worth Valley. In amongst this activity, both Turkey and Germany were visited, the former in particular producing fine pictures.

On BR the prototype InterCity 125 started trials, culminating in a record speed for this country of 143mph, which was also a record for diesel traction. The Advanced Passenger Train (APT-E) was being tested on the Old Dalby test track and reached 125mph, whilst on the main lines more 100mph running was being allowed on the East Coast main line.

The first of the Class 87 electrics appeared in advance of the completion of the West Coast electrification scheme from Weaver Junction to Glasgow and 'Deltic' No 9010 was recorded as having covered two million miles since it entered service in July 1961. It had achieved in 11 years a feat that some Gresley 'A3' Pacifics only managed after some 40 years.

On the whole, it was a quiet year.

This was my first visit to Kyle of Lochalsh as, unfortunately, I never managed to get there in steam days. Class 24 No 5121 worked the morning train from Inverness on which I travelled and, after shunting and running round, is shown ready to depart for Inverness in the afternoon. It was an Inverness-based locomotive at the time, but was withdrawn in December 1976 after only 16 years of service. Class 26 No 5345 (later No 26045) was passed at Achnasheen on the outward journey and this locomotive survived much longer. 10 March 1973 was a superb day, which was in sharp contrast to some of my later visits when the weather has been so bad that the Isle of Skye, clearly visible here, could not be seen from this point.

'Jubilee' No 45596 Bahamas was built by the North British Locomotive Co at its Queens Park Works in January 1935. It was fitted with the double chimney as late as 1961, being the fifth member of the class to receive this treatment. The others were Nos 45553, 45684, 45722 and 45742. Only No 45742 retained the modification for any length of time. No 45596 was withdrawn from Stockport Edgeley shed in July 1966 and was purchased by the Bahamas Locomotive Society and eventually based at Dinting. It visited the Hunslet Locomotive Works at Leeds for an overhaul and emerged in working order, painted in what was supposed to be LMS red livery, but I seem to remember that it looked a little pink. It ran a few main line steam tours during the early 1970s, one of which was this run on 17 June 1973 which took the locomotive to Sheffield via the Hope Valley line; it is shown passing Chinley East Junction after the long climb from New Mills. The locomotive is now in the correct BR Brunswick green livery and is based at Ingrow on the Keighley & Worth Valley Railway. It has made many main line trips during the 1990s and has performed very well. In addition, it has visited many preserved railways.

The driver applies power to Class 47 No 1674 Samson as the locomotive heads west past Dawlish Warren on a down express from Paddington on 25 August 1973. The locomotive entered service in April 1965. It received its TOPS number, 47088, in February 1974 and was subsequently renumbered 47653 and then 47808, which number it still retains while working Virgin Cross Country services. One nameplate was missing by September 1978 and the other had vanished by February 1985.

2 May 1973 was the official opening for the Lakeside & Haverthwaite Railway. Every locomotive that could work, did so; this included the two Fairburn 2-6-4Ts Nos 42073 and 42085, Bagnall 0-6-0ST Princess and 0-4-0ST Caliban. Also appearing was Class 5 No 44806 painted in BR lined green livery. The last mentioned is shown here arriving at Lakeside with a train in the afternoon. The Bishop of Wakefield, better known in railway circles as Eric Treacy, added sparkle to the opening ceremony, which he performed with Mrs Treacy, and a thoroughly good day was had by all who were fortunate enough to attend.

Class A4 Pacific No 4498 Sir Nigel Gresley was hauling specials on the main line during the year. On 6 October 1973 it was working from Carlisle to Newcastle on the 'Tynesider' and is pictured near Naworth. No 4498 was withdrawn by BR in February 1966 from the Scottish Region, at which time it was based at Aberdeen Ferryhill. It was then immediately bought by the A4 Locomotive Society. It went to Crewe Works for overhaul and was back in service again by 1 April 1967 when it made its first run in preservation from Crewe to Carlisle, returning via the Settle & Carlisle. After the steam ban was relaxed in 1971, No 4498 soon returned to main line duties and has been a regular performer ever since. It is now painted in the very attractive BR lined blue livery.

At the time, 22 September 1973, this must have been one of the more unlikely combinations to run on the main line. Gresley Class A3 No 4472 Flying Scotsman double-headed Great Western No 6000 King George V on the 'Atlantic Venturer Express'. As can be seen, the H. P. Bulmer Pullmans were providing some of the coaching stock. The bell, which had been fitted to No 4472 for its trip to America, was still in place. The pair are seen near Llanverhangel Summit heading north. The train returned with the 'King', whilst Flying Scotsman continued north light engine from Shrewsbury.

Swedish State Railways (SJ — Statens Jarnvager) took delivery of this WD 2-8-0, built by Vulcan Foundry at Newton-le-Willows in 1945 and initially sent to the Netherlands. It was stored in Sweden after 1958, becoming part of the strategic reserve until it was purchased by a group of Worth Valley members. It arrived at the railway in January 1973 after a difficult journey from Hull Docks. It was virtually in working order and was soon to be seen in action on the line. It worked for a year or two before being taken out of traffic and stored. After 20 years it is being restored, but as a UK version rather than in the condition it used to be in Sweden. It will be numbered 90733, this being the next number after the 732 British examples. It is pictured on 24 November 1973 storming out of Keighley up the bank piloting Ivatt 2-6-2T No 41241, which at the time was painted in a distinctive K&WVR red livery. As can be seen in the picture the WD was SJ No 1931 and was in plain black livery. It is the only example of the 2-8-0 version of the Austerity WD locomotives in the country.

Another picture of the popular Class 52 'Westerns', this time No D1057 Western Chieftain heading a down express along the sea wall at Teignmouth on 22 August 1973. The driver seems to be enjoying a breath of sea air on what was a hot summer's day. Some of the class were already withdrawn by this date, but No D1057 still had another three years of service to go.

1 9 7 4

My activities during the year were minimal, except for turning out for a few main line steam specials, the best of which was *Sir Nigel Gresley's* outing from Edinburgh to Aberdeen and return. Even if I was doing very little, except for an excellent trip to Turkey, progress was still occurring on BR and undoubtedly the most significant event was on 6 May, when through services with electric traction commenced on the West Coast main line with Class 87 locomotives between London and Glasgow. Schedules were reduced to 5hr 5min for the 401 miles. This, in turn, released the Class 50s to the Western Region, where they made a poor start with many failures; the transfer did, however, accelerate the decline of the Class 52 'Westerns'.

The HST prototype accumulated 100,000 miles mainly on the East Coast main line north of York and was then transferred to the Western Region prior to the introduction of the production trains to this region.

Preserved steam operation continued to expand, with 1,000 route miles being passed for main line operation. 'Merchant Navy' No 35028 *Clan Line* made its first main line run in preservation, whilst on the private lines, the Severn Valley Railway extended its services from Highley to Bewdley and the first service on the Kent & East Sussex, between Tenterden and Rolvenden, ran on 2 February.

On the whole, it was a quiet year, but 1975 was to be very different.

Most of the steam tours to Aberdeen have been performed by Class A4 No 60009 Union of South Africa, *but on 22 June 1974 Sir Nigel Gresley ventured north to the Granite City. The 'A4' made a spirited departure from Aberdeen on the return trip to Edinburgh. Unfortunately, the exhaust blotted out most of the fine signal gantry, the inclusion of which was the object of selecting the location in the first place.*

One of my favourite local locations is Paddock Cutting, about 1.5 miles up the bank from Huddersfield towards Marsden. As the photograph shows, there used to be four tracks at this point, three passing through the bridge and the fourth through the small tunnel. The cutting is only about 400yd long, but even in such a short distance one can produce a wide variety of pictures. The '1M67' headcode on Class 46 No 46047 indicates that the train is the 10.02 Newcastle-Liverpool service. The Gateshead-allocated Class 46s were the regular power around this time for these trans-Pennine expresses. The locomotive went new to Gateshead in October 1962 from where it was withdrawn in September 1984.

Class 2MT 2-6-0 No 78022 became the first of the preserved members of the class to be returned to working order. It was withdrawn in September 1966 from Lostock Hall shed and found its way to Barry scrapyard, where it is shown in this photograph taken on 10 December 1974. It became the 67th locomotive to be rescued from the dump and arrived on the Keighley & Worth Valley on 11 June 1975. Restoration was a long time coming, but at the end of 1992 it was steamed for the first time and it has now become a regular performer on the line.

No D0226 was one of two prototypes built by English Electric Ltd at its Vulcan Foundry works in 1956. They were 500hp machines and were designed for transfer freight work, being more powerful and faster than the BR 0-6-0s (the Class 08s). No D0226 was a diesel-electric whilst sister No D0227 was a diesel-hydraulic. Extensive trials were undertaken, the locomotives being employed at Liverpool, Doncaster, Sheffield, Stratford, Bristol and Swindon. After a three-year loan to BR, No D0226 was stored for six years, occasionally being used at the Vulcan Foundry for shunting. In March 1966 English Electric passed it to the Keighley & Worth Valley on permanent loan. No D0227 was, however, scrapped. No D0226 is not seen in photographs very often, but on 14 July 1974 it was on a permanent way train at Damems loop together with Stanier Class 5 No 5025 and another resident diesel shunter, a Peckett donated to the line by Austins steel stockists of Dewsbury.

On 29 September 1974, Gresley 'A3' No 4472 Flying Scotsman ran a special from Newcastle via the coast road to York, although the journey over the East Coast main line was Class 47 hauled, before heading off to Scarborough. It made a spirited start out of Newcastle across the High Level bridge over the River Tyne. The bridge was designed by Robert Stephenson and opened in September 1849. It is 1,312ft long and 120ft above high water level.

1975

This was the year that I finally seemed to recover from the end of steam and I started in earnest to photograph railways in this country again. I don't know what it was that really got things going again, although the Stockton & Darlington celebrations may have had something to do with it. Alternatively, I suspect that it was the purchase of a large format Pentax 6x7 camera, which allowed me to produce pictures of the quality that I was looking for. Whatever it was, it didn't come a day too soon; I bitterly regretted my period of inactivity as I had missed so much of interest in the previous seven years — lines and locomotive classes which I never really covered properly. Anyway, hindsight is a wonderful thing ...

Obviously, the Stockton & Darlington celebrations were the highlight of the year and, as always with big events such as this, the arrivals and departures of the various locomotives were as interesting as the event itself. It was a fantastic gathering, and I am afraid the almost daily outing to the northeast over about a three-week period clocked up a prodigious mileage on the car and left very little time for work.

The other significant event, which followed hard on the heels of the S&D 150, was the opening of the National Railway Museum on 27 September by HRH Prince Philip. Fortunately I had been able to photograph some of the movements of exhibits to the museum and the preparations inside; 23 years on, these make interesting pictures.

On BR, the prototype InterCity 125 entered service on the Western Region on 3 November after extensive trials. Swindon Works was busy refurbishing Southern Region 'BEP' and 'CEP' EMUs, whilst Horwich Works overhauled Class B1 4-6-0 No 61306 ready for S&D 150. The Class 35 'Hymeks' vanished from the scene, Nos 7011, 7017, 7018 and 7022 being the last in service. BR also introduced the Total Operations Processing System, better known by the acronym TOPS, which is still in use. Controlled from Marylebone, the system was connected to 155 out-stations. Almost a quarter of a century on, the system is scheduled for replacement by English, Welsh & Scottish Railways in the near future. It has, however, stood the test of time well, having been bought originally from the USA, where the Southern Pacific Railroad had developed it.

Less positive news was the number of serious accidents during the year. These involved electric traction at Watford Junction and at Nuneaton. There was also the tragic incident at Moorgate on London Underground, when 42 people were killed.

Personally, although I achieved a great deal in this country, I also managed another good trip to Turkey in the early part of the year.

After six years of service, primarily on the West Coast main line, the Class 50s were transferred to the Western Region. No 50028, in its drab overall blue livery and before being named Tiger *in May 1978, catches the evening light on 5 September 1975 as it hauls an up express from Plymouth to Paddington at Cowley Bridge Junction, just east of Exeter. The locomotives were not greeted with much enthusiasm by the WR crews, or operating department for that matter, as the class had a high failure rate which took some time to sort out. No 50028 was withdrawn in January 1991 and cut up at Old Oak Common later that year.*

A sight to gladden the hearts of Class 52 'Western' enthusiasts in 1975: No D1056 Western Sultan passes through the centre road at Totnes ready for the ascent of Rattery Bank at the head of a down Paddington-Plymouth service on 12 August 1975, as No D1068 Western Reliance waits to follow it on its way back to Plymouth Laira depot. In the bay platform, on an engineers' train, is Class 46 No 46004, which was locally based at this time. Both 'Westerns' still had over a year left, whilst No 46004 lasted until 1983.

An immaculate Class 45/1, No 45143 5th Royal Inniskilling Dragoon Guards, is shown at the head of the up 'Thames-Clyde' express (headcode 1M86) on 28 July 1975. It is passing the site of the former Lancashire & Yorkshire steam shed at Wakefield, which was originally coded 25A under London Midland ownership and then became 56A when transferred to the North Eastern Region. The Glasgow-St Pancras expresses were rerouted away from the old Midland main line out of Leeds and on to the ex-Great Northern route through Wakefield Westgate, then via Wakefield Kirkgate and on to rejoin the Midland main line at Walton Junction.

This fine view was obtained from above the eastern portal of Morley Tunnel; it is 3,369yd long and is the summit of the climb out of Leeds. In the days when the trans-Pennine Liverpool-Newcastle expresses were loaded to 10 coaches, an unidentified Class 46 is shown about to enter the tunnel on 11 June 1975. This train is far removed from the two- or three-car Class 158s which now cross the Pennines on this route at least three times every hour.

The number of green-liveried locomotives was rapidly dwindling by 1975, but Class 40 No 40052, which was clearly in need of a repaint, is at the head of an up express on 24 May 1975 as it passes through Princes Street Gardens, Edinburgh

The unique ex-Lancashire & Yorkshire Barton Wright Class 25 0-6-0, built in 1887, has been on the Keighley & Worth Valley Railway since March 1965. It was withdrawn by BR in May 1959 as No 52044 and was then stored at Ranskill in Nottinghamshire, until it moved to Haworth. It has had short periods of activity on the line and became famous for its part in the film The Railway Children. *Sporting a Wakefield shedplate in plain black livery, the locomotive is making a spectacular departure from Keighley on 22 March 1975 together with Ivatt 2-6-2T No 41241, which was in red livery. Why one of the crew on the Ivatt was dressed in a chef's uniform, complete with hat, is unknown.*

Inside the National Railway Museum work was progressing well on 17 September 1975 for the opening 10 days later by HRH Prince Philip. The sectioned 'Merchant Navy' No 35029 Ellerman Line *was on the turntable prior to being moved into position; where it is slightly raised and the wheels can be turned by an electric motor to show all the moving parts. It is a superb exhibit, which must have explained to hundreds and thousands of visitors how a steam locomotive works. Also in the picture is* Mallard, Evening Star, *the Midland Compound,* Hardwick *and several others under wraps. The magnificent collection of nameplates had also been installed on the back wall.*

The sectioned 'Merchant Navy' No 35029 Ellerman Line is pictured in the yard outside the museum on 17 September prior to being transferred inside.

I hope that it isn't unfair to the Chapelon SNCF Pacific to describe this as 'beauty and the beast', but I am afraid that this is how it appears to me. In 1975 Steamtown at Carnforth was host not only to this Class 231K French Pacific, but also a German ex-oil-fired Class 01. '9F' No 92220 was visiting with a railtour whilst based on the Keighley & Worth Valley Railway and a fine line-up of preserved locomotives was assembled outside the depot. Great Western 'Castle' No 4079 Pendennis Castle was then based at Steamtown. It worked a limited number of specials in preservation after being withdrawn in May 1964. It was eventually sold to the Hammersley Iron Co and shipped to Australia in May 1977 after working a final special, the 'Great Western Envoy'. The date is 31 May 1975.

'Modified Hall' No 6960 Raveningham Hall had more than one attempt to get itself from York to the Stockton & Darlington celebrations at Shildon. I believe a tender axlebox ran hot and the locomotive was banished to the sidings at Northallerton, where it is seen on 26 August 1975 receiving attention, as Class 40 No 40154 passes by on a down grain train returning to the northeast of Scotland. The 'Hall' eventually made it to Shildon and operated the shuttle service between Shildon Works and the main cavalcade viewing site.

Inside Shildon Works, the exhibits for the Stockton & Darlington cavalcade were well laid out for the visitors. There were 35 locomotives in the display, which involved a considerable amount of shunting the night before, but all left the works for Heighington in the correct order without a hitch. The oldest locomotive in steam was the Wantage Tramway 0-4-0WT No 5, built in 1857; the newest was the prototype InterCity 125. It was an event that most people had never seen the like of before and few thought they would again — but the 150th anniversary of the Liverpool & Manchester in 1980 was still to come. The famous Great Northern Stirling Single dominates this picture taken on 28 August 1975; it was not in steam for the cavalcade, but has steamed on several occasions since.

It was good to see the new InterCity 125 (or High Speed Train [HST]) included in the Stockton & Darlington 150 cavalcade, because the success of this train was to shape the future of express train travel in this country, just as some of the other exhibits had done in the past. At the Millennium, the InterCity 125s will still be operating many of our express services — and that's 25 years after the date of the cavalcade. Taking a break from its trials on the Western Region, the unit is shown as exhibit No 34 in the procession on 31 August 1975. Fortunately the design of the cab front was modified for the production models.

Some of the exhibits returned home almost immediately after the cavalcade, whilst the rest were marshalled in the yard north of Darlington station, where the old steam shed used to be, awaiting their paths home. This incredible view, taken from the bridge to the north of the station on 31 August 1975, shows the scene in the evening after the cavalcade. There were 400,000 people at the exhibition and cavalcade. In an age where accountants now seem to rule the world, I doubt if we will ever see such a gathering again, although some of the preserved railways do hold extremely fine 'gala' events.

Another visit was made to Turkey, which proved to be the last for almost 20 years. At home the first of the Romanian-assembled Class 56s arrived at Harwich from Zeebrugge. The Class 312 EMUs started work on the London Midland Region and the first production InterCity 125s started trials on 7 January. By 4 October, the Western Region was operating 32 services per day with these units. The Settle & Carlisle line reached its centenary, but steam was still banned on the route and, as portrayed in the photographs, the famous 'Thames-Clyde' express was withdrawn, as was the 'Tees-Tyne Pullman' on the East Coast main line.

A wide variety of locomotives operated the year's steam specials and I managed to photograph *Hardwick*, the Midland Compound, *Princess Elizabeth*, *Evening Star*, *Flying Scotsman*, 'B1' No 1306 and Class 5 No 4767 — not a bad selection.

My travels covered a wide area, with the East Coast main line receiving a fair amount of attention both in the north and in the south. I also had a couple of visits to the Edinburgh area and continued to record the local trans-Pennine service. The year was not quite as hectic as 1975, but I still obtained a good selection of photographs.

The services at Huntingdon in the late 1990s bear little resemblance to those in 1976. On 16 October 1976 a couple of Craven-built Class 105 DMUs were working the outer commuter services. The track layout was completely reorganised for electrification; the island platform was removed and the tracks quadrupled. Today, the commuter services are in the hands of the fast Class 317 EMUs, whilst Class 91s and InterCity 125s cover the GNER services.

A general view of King's Cross before electrification as seen from above Gas Works Tunnel on 10 July 1976. Gateshead-allocated Class 46 No 46038 is leaving on a relief train to Newcastle. The fuelling bay is on the right and St Pancras station dominates the background. Looking at the track layout, it makes me appreciate how difficult it was at busy times to cope with light engine movements to and from the yard.

I visited the site of the old Tinsley yard a few weeks ago and the sight of the derelict land made it very difficult to believe that this big marshalling yard, which opened in October 1955, used to have almost 60 miles of track and was capable of handling 275 trains every 24hr. These figures mean that the yard was planned to have an arrival or departure every five or six minutes — quite a thought. The hump shunting illustrated here was worked by three Class 13s; each of these was formed by combining two Class 08s permanently as master and slave units. The hump shunting eventually ceased in October 1984. No 13003 is shown on the hump on 6 October 1976, having just pushed a wagon over; two other '08s', used for general shunting, are in the background.

Class B1 4-6-0 No 61306 was built by the North British Locomotive Co in April 1948. It was never an LNER locomotive and so the livery illustrated here is not accurate. It was overhauled at Horwich Works in April 1975 and took part in the Stockton & Darlington 150 celebrations. It had been allocated to the North Eastern Region during its working life, starting at Hull Botanic Gardens and finishing at Low Moor, Bradford, from where it was withdrawn in September 1967 when steam finished in the area. It had the honour of working the last steam-hauled 'Yorkshire Pullman' from Bradford to Leeds. It worked several main line trips in 1975 and 1976, but seldom on its own. Here, on 15 May 1976, it is seen reaching the summit of Giggleswick Bank returning to its then home base of Steamtown, Carnforth.

King George V *was the locomotive that powered the first steam-hauled train on the main line after the lifting of the ban in 1971. It operated for many years before being retired and placed in Swindon Museum, its place having been taken by No 6024* King Edward I *and soon by No 6023* King Edward II. *Its normal sphere of operation was the north/west route between Chester and Hereford, although No 6024 has subsequently operated over a much wider area. This panned shot, one of the very few that I have ever managed to get sharp (unlike some photographers who seem to find the skill easy), was taken as it headed for Shrewsbury near Ruabon on 2 October 1976.*

Back in the days when the Inverness trains were dominated by the Type 2 Class 26s, Nos 26022 and 26038 were in charge of the 13.35 service from Edinburgh on 19 April 1976. The pair is seen just restarting after a stop at Haymarket. Some of the class lasted well into the 1990s, and some received the large logo Railfreight livery and sector symbols. Fortunately, the class is well represented in preservation.

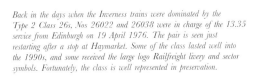

There was engineering work on the East Coast main line south of Peterborough on 7 November 1976 and so the 13.00 King's Cross-Edinburgh train was diverted via Cambridge. Finsbury Park 'Deltic' No 55001 St Paddy *was in charge and is seen catching the afternoon light as it rounds the curve at Shepreth Junction, near Cambridge. Together with No 55020* Nimbus, *St Paddy was the first member of the class to be withdrawn (in January 1980).*

Saturday 31 July 1976 provided an interesting morning between Huddersfield and Marsden. I was photographing the extra summer Saturday trains and had just taken Class 46 No 46055 on the regular 10.02 Newcastle-Liverpool service, when I noticed on my way back to the car that the train had stopped about one mile down the track. Upon investigation, I discovered that the locomotive had suddenly failed. I stayed around and after about 20min Class 40 No 40154 arrived complete with train — which I believe was the Newcastle-Manchester service — and buffered up to the failure. I thought this would test the starting capability of the Class 40, as the whole ensemble represented two locomotives and 19 coaches. The driver said that the weight shouldn't prove a problem and he was right. No 40154 set off on the 1 in 105 gradient without difficulty, pushing and pulling its train at least as far as Stalybridge. It is pictured just as it was setting off, between Golcar and Marsden.

It was extremely rare to be able to photograph a 'Western' and a 'Deltic' together in BR days, but on the preservation scene today it quite often happens. On the 20 November 1976 No 1023 Western Fusilier worked a special from King's Cross and was stabled just outside the National Railway Museum. I waited patiently, as the crowds inspected it, for the 11.00 from King's Cross to Edinburgh, hoping that the motive power would not be a Class 47. As can be seen, No 55001 St Paddy turned up, much to my delight. The 'Western' became part of the National Collection the following year.

Class 23 ('Baby Deltic') No D5901 is shown at Doncaster Works on 3 October 1976 awaiting scrapping. It had spent a considerable time at the Derby Research Centre since being withdrawn in December 1969. Built in 1959, it had managed only 10 years of service before withdrawal, and much of that time, for one reason or another, saw the locomotive out of service. The Class 23s were not successful and none survived into preservation.

It is only in the summer months that the sun gets round far enough to allow photography from the north side between Huddersfield and Marsden. On 2 June 1976 Class 40 No 40148 catches the evening light as it heads down the bank near Longwood at the head of the 18.00 from Manchester to Newcastle. This location shows several of the mills in the Colne Valley as well as some of the local terraced housing along the side of the A62 road across the Pennines.

Another piece of history was made on 2 May 1976 when the last through 'Thames-Clyde' express ran between Glasgow and St Pancras. A Nottingham-Glasgow service over the Settle & Carlisle was introduced, presumably to replace it but, during the run-down of the line, even this service was rerouted via the Hope Valley and the West Coast main line. Class 45 No 45073 was in charge of the last up train and is seen passing the south end of Hellifield. West Coast diversions were in operation on the same day, so the line southwards to Blackburn on the left was very busy.

1977

The year started for me in India and New Year's Eve at the end of the year was celebrated in Calcutta, where a very good evening was had courtesy of the Chief Mechanical Engineer of the Western Railway and his family. In between, there was a fair amount of activity in Britain. The end of the very popular Class 52 'Westerns' came as a sad blow to many enthusiasts. In the last months of their working careers every move was followed and there were railtours virtually every weekend. The withdrawal of the 'Westerns' was the start of the near fanatical following which accompanied the demise of diesel classes in the years to come; this was an aspect which never really happened to such an extent with steam, when it was more a case of following the steam workings rather than an individual class. There were exceptions to this rule, for example the 'A4s' on the Glasgow-Aberdeen route or the Bulleid Pacifics on the Southern, but these were rare. Five members of Class 52 remained in service in February 1977 and all eventually passed into preservation.

Another farewell was to *Pendennis Castle*, which left Avonmouth Docks for a new life with the Hammersley Iron Co in Australia. This departure upset many enthusiasts, particularly as, some 20 years later, the locomotive is still in the antipodes. Better news was the presence of more steam on the main line with several new routes and the opening of more preserved lines, including the Mid-Hants, the Nene Valley and the West Somerset.

On the main line, the first Doncaster-built Class 56s appeared and naming of locomotives came back into fashion with lists published for both Classes 50 and 87. The first InterCity 125 set for the East Coast main line was handed over on 7 September, with Heaton depot opening on 7 November. Plans for the remodelling of King's Cross were published and work soon commenced. Liverpool Exchange, however, closed after an active life of 127 years.

I spent a lot of time on the East Coast main line trying to catch up with the 'Deltic' pictures I had missed during the early 1970s as well as fitting in some preserved steam. As usual it was another very active year.

Prior to the modernisation of the signalling on the East Coast main line around Doncaster, there was a superb collection of semaphores at Black Carr Junction, where the Lincoln line headed east. A Craven Class 105 DMU has been given a clear road towards Doncaster whilst working a service from Lincoln on 5 February 1977. There was also a fine bird sanctuary just to the east of the main line at this point, which provided plenty of interest when there were no trains around.

When I worked in Leeds around this period, I would very often have an extended lunch hour on a sunny day at Horbury, just east of Healey Mills. One could expect to see at least 10 trains during an hour and, with six overbridges within 1.5 miles, there was plenty of variety as far as photographs were concerned. Horbury Cutting is an impressive location, and until the 1920s this section of track was in a tunnel; however, when the L&YR quadrupled the track, it was opened out. It was not unusual to have two trains coming out of Healey Mills side by side, but I never quite managed to get them positioned just as I would have liked them. This was a near miss, as unfortunately Class 37 No 37031 overtook Class 40 No 40154 just a little too early on 22 April 1977. There are now only two tracks again, but the level of traffic seems to have been rising recently.

There was still an excellent selection of signal gantries at Brent Junction, Cricklewood on 21 May 1977 and the Class 45/1s remained in charge of virtually all the long distance services out of St Pancras. No 45116 passes under the North Circular Road as it heads for the capital.

The electrification of the Bournemouth line was completed in March 1967 and 19 Class 33s were converted for push-pull operation between Bournemouth Central and Weymouth over the non-electrified section. New equipment included multiple-unit control gear and buck-eye couplings. Two four-car 'TC' sets were used, with the locomotive at the west end, so that, on up workings, the 'TC' sets could be coupled directly to the waiting 'REP' unit at Bournemouth Central. The system worked well after some teething problems with the electric stock. The climb out of Weymouth and Parkstone Bank were the only gradients of note on the route and here we see No 33101 pushing its train, with ex-works 'TC' No 411 leading, up the bank through the woods between Parkstone station and Branksome — a particularly photogenic section of line — on 16 April 1977.

Marsh Lane Cutting to the east of Leeds City station is impressive, with several bridges across it. It has four tracks at the west end and five at the east. Unfortunately, it has a tendency to be a dumping ground for all the rubbish in the area, as can be seen in the bottom left of this photograph, taken on 10 July 1977. Class A4 Pacific No 4498 Sir Nigel Gresley emerges from under one of the high bridges as it heads east towards York on the 'Dick Turpin' special.

The 'Granite City' of Aberdeen had many superb signal gantries, especially on the exit to the south of the station. All were still in place when I visited in September on a free ticket from BR, which I had won in a photographic competition they had organised. Class 08 No 08505 is shown shunting empty Royal Mail coaches near Ferryhill depot on 3 September 1977; the coaches were being prepared for their return working southwards.

An impressive line-up just to the south of Aberdeen station on 2 September 1977 shows Class 40 No 40077 heading for Ferryhill depot, while Class 47 No 47141 departs with the 13.35 working to Glasgow Queen Street as No 47072 waits to leave on an up freightliner. The freightliner services ceased with the closure of the local yard in 1987. No 47141 was originally No D1733, which was the first locomotive painted in the blue livery to match the XP64 coaches. It later became No 47614 and finally No 47853; at the time of writing it is still in service with Virgin Cross Country.

A rare opportunity to photograph two preserved blue 'A4s' together occurred on 27 April 1977. No 4498 Sir Nigel Gresley was visiting the National Railway Museum and the chance was taken to bring Mallard out into the open and pose the two locomotives together. Sir Nigel Gresley's daughter was invited to the museum for the occasion.

To commemorate the Silver Jubilee of HM the Queen, the 07.45 King's Cross-Edinburgh service and the 15.00 return working were named after the event and provided with a special headboard. The first train ran on 8 June and Finsbury Park turned out an immaculate No 55012 Crepello, with No 55022 Royal Scots Grey of Haymarket on the return. Unfortunately, the headboard did not always appear on the train, especially when a Class 47 was in charge. However, on 7 July 1977 it was in position on No 55015 Tulyar as the train passed nonstop through Doncaster on the down working. Alongside, No 40084 was awaiting a path in the up direction. Doncaster Works, known as 'The Plant', is in the background. No 55015 is now preserved by the Deltic Preservation Society and based at the Midland Railway Centre, Butterley.

This view is near Wath Junction on the former Great Central line, just to the east of Wath marshalling yard; this was the limit of the electrified Woodhead route. Class 37 No 37120, now No 37887, is heading a rake of coal empties for the South Yorkshire coalfield. On the skyline is Manvers Colliery and coking works, which closed in 1980. Today the skyline is clear of industrial buildings and the trackbed is being converted into a road. The present line from Sheffield to Leeds still passes over at the same point as it heads towards Moorthorpe.

1 9 7 8

*Y*et again, the first two weeks of the year found me in India, followed by a visit to Pakistan in November, where British-built inside-cylinder 4-4-0s and 0-6-0s were still very active.

Back in Britain, we had some special treats, such as the Great Northern Atlantic No 990 *Henry Oakley* working on the Keighley & Worth Valley Railway and rebuilt 'Royal Scot' No 6115 *Scots Guardsman* out on the main line. In addition, the Settle & Carlisle was passed for the operation of steam specials.

On the main line, six InterCity 125 sets went into service on the King's Cross-Edinburgh service, whilst the 'Yorkshire Pullman' and the 'Hull Pullman' were withdrawn from 5 May. A 10-year agreement was signed with Foster Yeoman for the haulage of stone trains using double-headed Class 37s. The Merseyrail system celebrated its centenary and the first of the Class 507 units arrived on the Wirral. In

Birmingham, the cross-city Class 116 DMUs were an instant success on the Longbridge-Four Oaks service.

In preservation, the Strathspey Railway opened on 22 July and Standard Class 7MT Pacific No 70000 *Britannia* was finally steamed again, after seven years of hard work.

On a sadder note, the Bishop of Wakefield, better known as the Right Reverend Eric Treacy MBE, died whilst photographing *Evening Star* at Appleby. He was undoubtedly one of the best of British photographers, and he had a great influence on my photography and, no doubt, on that of many others. Whilst he was in Halifax, he became a great friend of my family. My attendance at Halifax parish church on a regular basis might have had something to do with the chats we used to have in the vestry after the service, where, for some reason, I always seemed to have a photograph or two with me about which I would seek his advice.

The long-awaited return of steam to the Settle & Carlisle line finally came on 25 March 1978 with a trip hauled by the National Railway Museum's 'V2' No 4771 Green Arrow. The weather along the Aire Valley was dull, but, by the time the train was climbing up Ribblesdale, it had turned rather nasty, as it so often does. Green Arrow was making a spectacular climb in the snowstorm as it approached Helwith Bridge, with the steam almost blocking out the driver's vision. It was a memorable event and the start of a new era in main line steam running.

The Calder Valley, towards the west, becomes very narrow, especially between Hebden Bridge and Todmorden. As the picture shows, there is very little room for the road, railway, river and canal (which is out of the frame). In 1978 it was difficult getting a locomotive-hauled passenger train heading east along the valley, as all the regular services were DMUs and freight was erratic. Fortunately, on 15 April 1978, this special from Daisy Hill (Burnley) to Scarborough provided an opportunity to take this photograph. The locomotive is Class 40 No 40030, which is seen passing Charlestown. I had been driving along the main road for years and always thought that there was a suitable location for photography here, but had never made the effort. It was possible to drive within a few hundred yards of the spot, but now the bushes have grown alongside the track and it makes the shot difficult to take.

St Pancras is possibly the finest station in the country. This view, taken at the north end on 6 May 1978, shows the overall roof to good effect. Class 45/1 No 45102 is leaving on the 17.16 service to Nottingham. The type had a virtual monopoly of main line service from St Pancras until the InterCity 125s arrived some four years later.

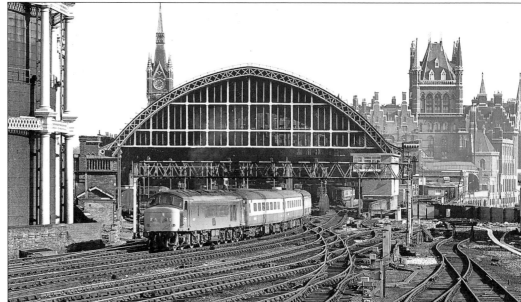

At Liverpool Street on 6 May 1978 Class 37s were still working some of the expresses to Norwich. No 37012 makes a vigorous start on what I believe was the 14.00 departure. Many of the Great Eastern Class 37s eventually made their way to the West Highland line in 1982, where they ran until they were displaced by Class 37/4s. No 37012 was named Loch Rannoch in March 1982, until the name was transferred to No 37408 in 1986.

Thornaby station had obviously seen better days before this photograph was taken on 24 May 1978; nevertheless, it remained a substantial building. I happened to visit it again in 1996 and was surprised to find the large platform area still in place but all signs of the buildings had gone, with the covered accommodation formed only of the inevitable bus shelter. A Class 101 Metro-Cammell DMU calls whilst working a Middlesbrough-Darlington service.

In contrast to St Pancras and Liverpool Street, Broad Street station has been consigned to the history books. Its fate was decided in 1975, when the British Railways Board decided to rebuild Liverpool Street and incorporate those services which had previously terminated at Broad Street. There was the inevitable controversy, which meant that part of the original Liverpool Street survived, but eventually Broad Street was demolished and the site used for the present Broadgate commercial development. The Class 501s were dedicated to the Broad Street-Richmond service and to Watford-Euston locals. A total of 57 of these three-car sets were built at Eastleigh. The last were withdrawn in 1985. This picture, taken on 6 May 1978, shows two of the units in Broad Street; both are in the plain blue livery. The station eventually closed on 3 June 1986.

Prior to the modernisation of the layout and resignalling, Chester was controlled by some impressive signalboxes. To the west was No 6, controlling the meeting of the main lines with those that came round the triangle from Birkenhead. The two tracks on the left were those used by the Great Western trains to Shrewsbury, whilst those on the immediate right of the box were the North Wales lines. The twin bore tunnels can be seen in the background. A Class 108 DMU is passing underneath with a working from Shrewsbury on 15 July 1978. It must have been an extremely dirty signal box to work in steam days, with locomotives passing underneath.

The present day scene at Bingley Junction, Shipley, is very different to that shown in this photograph taken on 19 April 1978. Eventually a third platform was installed on the down line of the Guiseley Junction-Bingley Junction side of the triangle. This was used by both up and down trains, an arrangement which was difficult to operate. A second platform was installed on the up side as part of the Aire Valley electrification scheme. Class 45 No 45007 passes round the very sharp curve as it heads north on the 10.20 Nottingham-Glasgow service. Passengers from Shipley wishing to catch this train would have had to take a local service to Skipton and change. Guiseley Junction box can be seen in the distance.

Two extremely handsome steam locomotives appear on this page (ignoring, of course, the Austerity tank). The Keighley & Worth Valley Railway was extremely fortunate to be loaned the Ivatt Atlantic No 990 Henry Oakley for a limited period. It arrived on the railway on 20 May 1977 hauled by Evening Star, which then returned to York with the Hughes 'Crab' No 42700 in tow. No 990 was built at Doncaster in May 1898 and was later classified 'C2' by the LNER. The class was nicknamed 'Klondykes'. A total of 22 were built. No 990 was eventually withdrawn from Lincoln in October 1937 after covering 1,250,000 miles. It was placed in the original railway museum at York until 1953 when it was restored to running order and worked some specials. Of these the most famous was the 'Plant Centenarian', which was run to mark the centenary of Doncaster Works, when it piloted Class C1 Atlantic No 251. Following its arrival at Keighley it was soon being used, some 24 years after its last working. It is shown here on 18 March 1978 at Damems loop heading towards Haworth, piloting the ex-Stewarts & Lloyd 0-6-0ST Samson. This was not an ideal combination photographically. No 990 later returned to the museum and has not worked since.

Rebuilt 'Royal Scot' No 6115 Scots Guardsman was the last of the class to remain active on BR, being withdrawn from Kingmoor shed in January 1966. It was then acquired for preservation and moved to the Worth Valley Railway. The locomotive was too big at that time for the railway and so moved to the Dinting Railway Centre, where it was eventually returned to working order in 1978. Unfortunately, it only had a few outings on the main line: a test run on 21 September followed by this outing on 11 November 1978 over the Hope Valley line. The locomotive was built by the North British Locomotive Co in 1927 and rebuilt in August 1947, when it appeared in this livery with smoke deflectors — the first of the class to be fitted with them. Unfortunately, No 6115 seems to have become one of the forgotten locomotives in preservation. This photograph shows the locomotive climbing the bank from New Mills to Chinley Junction, between Buxworth and Chinley station — and what a fine sight it makes. The 9A shedplate refers to the code for Longsight, a shed to which No 6115 was allocated for many years after rebuilding.

This remarkable gathering took place in the early hours of Sunday 19 March 1978 at the north end of York station. I don't know how I found out about it — I suspect that I must have been given a message by a friend at the museum — but I duly arrived as it got light, fully expecting to have found the area sealed off. I met a local BR manager, whom I knew and who assumed I had been invited, and so I took advantage of the situation. As far as I am aware, I was one of very few enthusiasts present. The scene had been arranged for a BBC filming project and, after this was finished, I rushed around and got masses of photographs. By 10.00, the locomotives were back in the museum; the '08', No 08245, hauled Mallard and the GNR Atlantic and I believe that the 'Deltic', No 55013 Black Watch, hauled the Stirling single and the North Eastern 4-4-0. The InterCity 125, which was included in the line-up (No 254.009) returned, presumably, to Neville Hill.

The attractive section of the East Coast main line around Burnmouth, just north of Berwick-upon-Tweed, is shown to advantage in this picture of 'Deltic' No 55017 The Durham Light Infantry as it hurries south with the up 17.00 Edinburgh Waverley-King's Cross train on 2 June 1978. The locomotive is commendably clean for a Gateshead-allocated locomotive, as the depot was not exactly renowned for maintaining the external condition of the class over the years; this may have been a reflection that Gateshead locomotives spent more time in service than those allocated to Finsbury Park or Haymarket.

I don't know when I last visited Penzance prior to this occasion, 25 October 1978, but there were Great Western 'Granges' and 'Counties' present, so it was probably 20 years earlier. Times were very different in 1978, with Class 50s having taken over the majority of services following their transfer from the LMR. The 10.21 to Leeds is ready to depart with No 50049 Defiance in charge. The state of the paintwork is terrible; the washer at Laira seemed to remove the paint from locomotives at this time, rather than simply washing them. Many of the 'Westerns' were in a similar poor condition in their latter days. Happily, No 50049 is now preserved on the West Somerset Railway and its paintwork has improved dramatically in 20 years.

1 9 7 9

This was a year when the majority of my photographs were taken in the north of the country, even if the selection of pictures may suggest otherwise.

There were some interesting developments on the BR network. The Class 47/7 push-pull fitted locomotives arrived at Haymarket early in the year, but were used on general duties and crew training before services started on 22 October. Swindon Works started a large contract to refurbish many Southern Region EMUs, and crew training started on the Waterloo-Exeter route with the Class 50s.

Elsewhere, the Advanced Passenger Train (APT) ran trials between Glasgow and Carlisle, a speed of 160mph being achieved. Also in Scotland, the Argyll line in Glasgow was reopened. On a sadder note, Penmanshiel Tunnel collapsed during engineering work, resulting in fatalities. The collapse completely disorganised the route, with shuttle services operating between Dunbar and Edinburgh and trains terminating at Berwick from the south. Once the decision was made to abandon the tunnel, the diversionary route round the site was constructed with commendable speed.

Main line steam notched another first, with 'King' class 4-6-0 No 6000 *King George V* and other locomotives visiting Paddington, the first steam locomotives to venture to the GWR's London terminus since the end of main line steam.

For me, the year started in Pakistan, with a second visit in November; the British-built inside-cylinder 4-4-0s and 0-6-0s pictured in superb scenery made the not inconsiderable discomforts which I encountered worthwhile.

Swinden Quarry, which belongs to Tilcon, is now the end of the former branch line to Grassington from Embsay Junction, near Skipton. Passenger services to Grassington finished on 22 September 1930 but freight lasted until 11 August 1969, when the section north of Swinden closed. The quarry is still very active and has a long-term future, with daily trains to Hull, Leeds and other destinations. Class 60s have been the regular performers in recent years. Class 31s worked the trains for many years and on 30 April 1979 Nos 31226 and 31109 were at the quarry. The former was to come to a premature end in October 1988 when, with No 31202, it ran away at Cricklewood and landed on top of No 31202 on the North Circular Road.

After the 'Deltics' had lost most of their East Coast main line duties, they were used on secondary turns. As a result, the King's Cross-Cleethorpes service occasionally had Class 55 power; such was the case on 12 May 1979 when No 55009 Alycidon hauled the 17.46 from Cleethorpes. With Lincoln cathedral dominating the skyline, the train powers away from St Marks station at 19.02. Finsbury Park tended to use this diagram when the depot staff wanted to make sure that the locomotive would return to base, as there was no opportunity for anybody to 'borrow' it on this working. Alycidon is now preserved by the Deltic Preservation Society and is currently nearing the end of a major overhaul.

As this photograph was taken from the railway employee's club car park, I suspect that somebody had requested the crew to put on a bit of a show from 'V2' No 4771 Green Arrow as it passed on the North Eastern on 21 April 1979. I assure you that, on this occasion, I had had nothing to do with this, but I was happy to be able to record the spectacle. The window of a building in the top righthand corner is just visible through the exhaust and looks like a spaceship appearing through the gloom. No 4771 was quite a sight, but the display was not exactly the result of a textbook way of firing the engine.

The Class 104 DMUs, built in 1957/58 by Birmingham RCW, were the backbone of the
Buxton-Manchester commuter services for many years. A trio of sets are seen parked in Buxton station
on Sunday, 19 August 1979, waiting for their duties on the Monday morning.

Peak Forest is still a busy centre for stone traffic, as it has been for decades. In 1979, Classes 40
and 25 were the most usual power on the trains, and on 3 July 1979 No 40082 is pictured
shunting the Buxton Limestone Co yard. The layout of the yard to the north of the road bridge as
shown here has been altered subsequently. Passenger services over the former Midland main line from
Derby to Manchester ceased on 1 July 1968.

The Stalybridge buffet and bar has been well-
known to enthusiasts and passengers over the years
and its condition was a credit to the railway staff
and its owners. The Class 108, which has just
arrived from Stockport on 23 June 1979, blends
in well with the Victorian architecture.

This superb view can be obtained from above Brighton station, and shows the yard, main line and the line over the viaduct to Lewes. On 11 August 1979 Class 33s Nos 33023, 33052 and 33021 are stabled in the yard along with Class 73s Nos 73101 and 73104. The old locomotive shed used to be on the left of the photograph, whilst the derelict site on the right was once occupied by the famous locomotive works. A 12-car EMU arrives from London with a further unit approaching from the Lewes direction.

The trans-Pennine services from Hull during the period ran via Doncaster and the Hope Valley and nearly always consisted of four-car sets formed from Class 123 and 124. The magnificent roof over Hull Paragon station looks to be in need of attention; this it duly received shortly afterwards. When the Class 124s were introduced on the trans-Pennine service back in 1960, the workings travelled via Leeds and Standedge Tunnel to Liverpool. A Class 123 heads this set west out of the station on 12 July 1979.

Yarmouth used to have stations at Beach, South and Vauxhall; the last-named is now the only one to survive and even this is very much reduced in size compared to how it looked when this photograph was taken on 25 August 1979. A Class 03 shunter was based here and a stabling point existed to the right of the photograph. Locomotive-hauled trains still get to Yarmouth in the summer, but normal services are virtually always formed of Class 150/2 Sprinters. Twenty years ago, Class 31/1 No 31325 leaves with the 09.40 departure to Manchester. The surrounding area has, today, been altered completely.

The start of the new decade produced what I feel must have been one of the golden years for the enthusiast in the post-steam era. Apart from the diesel-hydraulics and the other less significant classes, the BR main line diesel fleet was virtually intact, although the 'Deltics' had been relegated to secondary duties on the East Coast main line but were still active on trans-Pennine services, as were the Class 40s and the Class 46s.

The steam preservation movement had a fantastic year, boosted by the celebrations at Rainhill — 'Rocket 150' — to commemorate the 150th anniversary of the opening of the Liverpool & Manchester Railway. This produced a gathering of locomotives, both steam and modern traction, the likes of which we are unlikely to see again. Whilst it was a great event, the movements of the stock to and from the event produced the most interest to the enthusiast. Locomotives were in steam on the main line that had not been seen (in preservation) before or since, even if they were not actually hauling trains in most cases. The most remarkable journey must have been accomplished by the little North British Class J36 0-6-0 *Maude*, which hauled two preserved coaches from Kilmarnock to Rainhill in one day, probably the longest single journey in its entire career; both the inward and outward journeys were made via the Settle & Carlisle.

Steam locomotives continued to leave Barry scrapyard; one of the escapees in 1980 was 'West Country' No 34027 *Taw Valley* which has become such an excellent performer on the main line during the 1990s.

Many other changes were going on; of these the most noticeable was the introduction of InterCity 125s on Paddington-West Country services. This released the Class 50s on to Waterloo-Exeter services and the Class 47/7s started on the Glasgow-Edinburgh push-pull trains.

I can only scratch the surface of what I covered during the year in the few pages available. I was so busy in this country that I didn't manage a trip abroad for railways — one of the very few years since 1966 that this happened.

Film consumption was excessive; around 103 black and white 120 films and 1,665 colour slides, not to mention some 50,000 miles in the car. These were clocked up on the company Vauxhall Cavalier, which took some explaining to my manager as it was double the average for the other company cars! It was a great start to the 1980s.

Whilst the Class 33s were replaced on Waterloo-Exeter services, they continued for some time on the Saturdays Only Brighton-Exeter trains. On 8 March 1980 No 33061 is pictured approaching Exeter Central with the 13.58 service nearing the end of the 1 in 37 climb from St David's. The sound, which was considerable, was evidently being enjoyed by an enthusiast in the leading coach.

It is a pity that I am not able to use my colour slide of this magnificent combination of the National Railway Museum's Midland Compound and ex-LNER 'V2' 2-6-2 No 4771 Green Arrow. They are passing through the cutting at Rodley, about five miles north of Leeds, on 3 May 1980 with a special — the 'Mancunian' — from York to Carnforth. I believe that this was being used to get the locomotives positioned prior to the 'Rocket 150' event. This was a location which I used extensively in the 1960s and 1970s. Originally there were four tracks, but the two fast lines were taken out of use in the mid-1960s. The location has now been ruined by the electrification of the Aire Valley route, not to mention the fact that the bushes have grown.

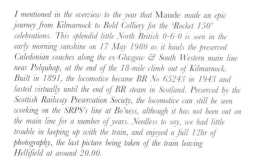

I mentioned in the overview to the year that Maude made an epic journey from Kilmarnock to Bold Colliery for the 'Rocket 150' celebrations. This splendid little North British 0-6-0 is seen in the early morning sunshine on 17 May 1980 as it hauls the preserved Caledonian coaches along the ex-Glasgow & South Western main line near Polquhap, at the end of the 18-mile climb out of Kilmarnock. Built in 1891, the locomotive became BR No 65243 in 1943 and lasted virtually until the end of BR steam in Scotland. Preserved by the Scottish Railway Preservation Society, the locomotive can still be seen working on the SRPS's line at Bo'ness, although it has not been out on the main line for a number of years. Needless to say, we had little trouble in keeping up with the train, and enjoyed a full 12hr of photography, the last picture being taken of the train leaving Hellifield at around 20.00.

I have witnessed a wide variety of motive power from the bridge at Mirfield alongside the old steam shed since I moved to Mirfield in 1971. The location — at 1.5 miles — also happens to be the nearest point to the railway from my house. This train, en route to the 'Rocket 150' celebrations at Bold Colliery, consisted of a number of exhibits from the National Railway Museum. These were Woodhead Class 76 No 26020 and various items of rolling stock. Also in the train was an ex-Welshpool & Llanfair 2ft 6in gauge 0-6-0T. Class 40 No 40075 provided the motive power on 21 May 1980. No 26020 is the only electric locomotive I have managed to photograph on my local line, although I understand that during a night in October 1997 a Class 90 was hauled through at the head of a diverted freightliner train. In the background can be seen a Class 110 Calder Valley DMU heading for Leeds on a local service.

A lucky photograph taken in Buxworth Cutting, near Chinley, on 29 May 1980, shows the now preserved Class 40 No 40145 on an ICI limestone train meeting Class 25 No 25217 hauling the ex-Midland Railway 4-2-2 No 673 and LMS Class 4F 0-6-0 No 4027, together with breakdown crane and coaches, on their way back to the Midland Railway Centre at Butterley after the 'Rocket 150' celebrations. The train travelled slowly, with regular stops to ensure that all was well, and so provided a good selection of photographs between Manchester Victoria and Chesterfield.

It came as quite a surprise to the enthusiast world when it was announced that steam was to be run over the Highland main line again from Perth to Aviemore, especially as the locomotive was to be Class A4 No 60009 Union of South Africa. There were many speed restrictions imposed, but nevertheless the train, on 27 June 1980, ran without apparent problems, although Scotrail banned the locomotive from taking its train over Slochd Summit, despite the fact that No 60009 had to go to Inverness to turn. The 'A4' passed Healey Mills-based Class 40 No 40197 at Newtonmore; the latter working the 09.30 service from Inverness to Edinburgh. I had not visited the Highland line, except for one brief journey north, for almost 23 years, and the day out made me realise the photographic potential, which I exploited during the 1980s.

Mention was made in the 1980 introduction to the fact that the 'Deltics' were now employed on secondary duties. The locomotives were based at York and during the summer were occasionally found on unusual workings. On 2 August 1980 No 55011, now nameless on one side but retaining The Royal Northumberland Fusilier on the other, is pictured ready to leave Scarborough on a 12.00 relief to Glasgow. The locomotive had been based at Gateshead for nearly 20 years prior to its transfer. A summer Saturday at Scarborough in 1980 produced a wide variety of motive power; on this day Class 31, 40, 45, 47 and 55 were present, as were various DMUs and the local Class 03 shunter for carriage movements. This side of the station has now been demolished.

Occasionally at weekends, the Class 43 InterCity 125s would be used for special workings. On what must have been the first visit of one of these units to Halifax, No 254.030 (formed with power cars No 43115/43114) pauses to pick up passengers for a shoppers' special on 18 October 1980 from Bradford to King's Cross. The train would have run from Halifax via the now closed — but possibly to reopen — Greetland Bank on to the Calder Valley line to Wakefield. The old Great Northern part of the station and the goods yard were on the left of the photograph. The latter had, by this time, lost all its tracks and today is used as the site of the 'Eureka' hands-on museum for children, a project which has received a great deal of support from HRH Prince Charles. The scene is a great contrast to my early days as an enthusiast, when I watched ex-GNR 'N1' 0-6-2Ts and 'J6' 0-6-0s working here alongside ex-L&YR 'A' class 0-6-0s.

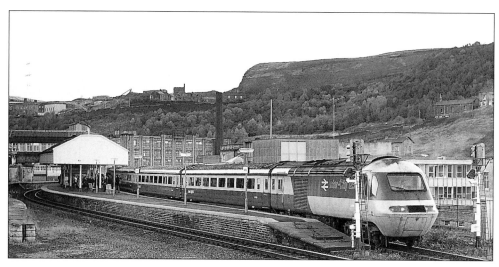

The Class 45/1 'Peaks' still had another three years to go in charge of the St Pancras services over the former Midland main line on 16 August 1980. No 45114 is pictured leaving Leicester London Road on the 13.12 Nottingham-St Pancras service. As can be seen, there were still plenty of semaphore signals in use around Leicester; these were to survive for a further five years, until the station and immediate vicinity was completely reorganised with the 'Leicester Gap' resignalling.

The Gateshead-based Class 46s were the backbone of trans-Pennine motive power for many years, with Classes 40 and 47 putting in occasional appearances. No 46052 is dwarfed by the then closed Tame Power Station, which used to be served by rail off the Micklehurst loop, On 23 August 1980, this photograph was taken from above Scout Tunnel at Mossley, which provided an excellent vantage point; sadly today it is now so overgrown that pictures are virtually impossible and the power station and buildings have long since vanished.

As mentioned earlier, the York-based 'Deltics' were frequent performers across the Pennines to Liverpool. As I was living at Mirfield, this was good news and allowed me to accumulate a huge collection of trans-Pennine 'Deltic' workings. The trains were not heavy, but on a calm day the locomotives could be heard several miles away as they sped up the bank out of Huddersfield to Standedge Tunnel. On a glorious autumn day, 18 October 1980, No 55017 The Durham Light Infantry is about to enter Paddock Cutting, approximately two miles west of Huddersfield, on the 13.05 Liverpool-York train. Milnsbridge Viaduct can be seen in the background. This was a very popular location for photographers at this time.

This is probably my favourite photograph of 1980. I think that this was because the chances of getting it right were virtually zero. On 1 November 1980, I had been waiting further up the Settle & Carlisle, near Horton in Ribblesdale, on a dismal day for Duchess of Hamilton, but had given up, only to find as I returned down the B6479, a road well-known to photographers, that the locomotive had stalled in Stainforth Cutting on the infamous autumn leaves. Banking assistance arrived in the form of Class 40 No 40134 after a considerable delay. I had just time to guess the exposure on 400ASA film as 1/30th at f5.6, which is very dark. I tried panning, which nearly always results in failure, but on this occasion worked and so I feel I produced my most dramatic picture of a Stanier Pacific. This all goes to show that you should never give up; film is relatively cheap in comparison to the cost of getting to locations.

1981

This again proved to be a very busy year, but largely centred around my home area rather than every corner of the country. My activities started in India during January, but upon my return I was soon into photographing as many 'Deltic' workings as possible, as it was clear that the class had not long to run. As will be seen from the selection of pictures, it was definitely the year of the 'Deltics' for me. When the class was new and painted in the attractive two-tone green livery, I didn't really like the type because they were replacing the ex-LNER Pacifics, which had been part of my life for so long. However, once steam had finished, the 'Deltics' grew on me, even in the rather drab blue livery and I spent more time photographing the class than any other main line diesel type. After the 'Deltics' finished their East Coast main line duties and started on the trans-Pennine services for the last few months, the chases across the M62 were happening during extended lunch hours several times per week, as I was working virtually next to the line at Eccles just to the west of Manchester.

Elsewhere in the country things were not standing still. The Woodhead route, with the 15V dc electrification, passed quietly into history on 20 July and I regret that I did not spend more time than I did recording it. The steam railtours were running well, with the 'Cumbrian Mountain Express' along with the newly introduced 'Welsh Marches' specials. There was a wide variety of motive power available after the activity at Rainhill the previous year and I photographed at least 13 different locomotives on the steam excursions.

The first revenue-earning trip with the Advanced Passenger Train (APT) took place but with little success. Plymouth Laira InterCity 125 depot opened, whilst the Class 47/7s were now working well on the Edinburgh-Glasgow push-pull services and the start of the electrification of the suburban services at the southern end of the Midland main line was underway.

Another very significant event was the tour carried out by the Class 140 Leyland railbus; it travelled to virtually every part of the country except the Southern Region. This vehicle was, of course, later developed into the fleet of Pacer units, which helped to retain services on many of the less well used lines.

Another reason for my activity being mainly local was that the summer extras across the Pennines via Standedge were still running with a wide variety of motive power.

The year finally finished with plenty of snow in the north, as well as other parts of the country, and the sun managed to shine as well, providing a limited opportunity in this country for that elusive combination of sun and snow.

It was a good year photographically, with the black and white consumption on the Pentax 6x7 once again exceeding 100 films, providing many hours in the darkroom, plus some 1,300 slides. The real highlight of my BR activities was my footplate ride from King's Cross to Retford on the 17.05 'Hull Executive', when we managed to better the 91.3mph average required to keep time, but by how much I think had better remain unrecorded.

The Lancashire & Yorkshire Trust's 0-6-0ST No 752 has not been steamed for around 16 years at the time of writing. Fortunately, with the help of the lottery and hard work by members of the trust, it is likely that it will be back in traffic by the end of 1998. It worked on a very limited basis during 1981 and 1982 on the Worth Valley Railway and is shown here, on 5 April 1981, piloting the resident Ivatt 2-6-2T No 41241 at the passing loop at Damems. No 752 is the only member of the class in preservation and has an interesting history. Built in May 1881 by Beyer Peacock, it was rebuilt as a saddle tank in 1896; passing to the LMS in 1923 it remained in service, as No 11456, until 1937 when it was sold to Parsonage Colliery at Leigh in Lancashire. It was eventually bought by the trust in 1967 and went to Yates Duxberry at Heaton Bridge, Bury. It took part in the 'Rocket 150' procession at Rainhill in 1980, after which it travelled by itself along the main line to Liverpool Road, Manchester for the museum's celebrations, remaining there for 12 months. It is currently at the Ian Riley works on the East Lancashire Railway having its boiler repaired.

After the 'Deltics' lost their main line duties on the East Coast main line to the InterCity 125s, they occasionally appeared on other duties. If one of the class worked a sleeper train from King's Cross to Edinburgh, it had little to do during the day and so Haymarket depot occasionally rostered one for an Edinburgh-Aberdeen working. This occurred on 20 April 1981 when No 55017 The Durham Light Infantry was booked for the 08.55 working, returning on the 12.40 from Aberdeen. I happened to be staying in Edinburgh for the Easter weekend and so was fortunate to get this picture of the train coming off the Forth Bridge at North Queensferry; needless to say, I was still around for the return working.

'Deltic' No 55009 Alycidon had the sad duty of working the last express for a Finsbury Park locomotive. The 'Park', as it was known, lost its allocation from 1 June 1981. The locomotive had been at the depot since new and, being the last one at the depot to visit Doncaster Works, was specially prepared for the occasion. The staff at the 'Park' will long be remembered for the way they never missed an opportunity to groom one of their 'racehorses' for an occasion. Looking superb with its white cab, the distinguishing feature of the 'Park' 'Deltics', No 55009 approaches Doncaster on the 16.05 King's Cross-York service on 31 May 1981, whilst the depot manager looks out of the rear cab to ensure that I was present to record the occasion. The special headboard was removed at Doncaster for safe-keeping. No 55009 remained in service until the last of the class were withdrawn in January 1982, hauling many specials around the country, before finally passing into the safe hands of the Deltic Preservation Society. After many years working on the North Yorkshire Moors Railway, it was withdrawn and sent to ICI Wilton, where it is currently nearing the end of an extensive overhaul by the team of dedicated society members.

This is New Holland Pier, situated at the end of a 500yd-long pier out into the Humber estuary. Opened in 1848, it was eventually used from around the time of World War 1 for the through service via the ferry from King's Cross to Hull. It was a fascinating location, but by the time this picture was taken on 12 April 1981, closure was only two months away as the opening of the new Humber road bridge made the ferry service redundant. The mixed livery two-car unit is ready to leave with a service to Cleethorpes. As a matter of interest, the pier still survives as does some of the track and the little signalbox; it is now used as a loading dock with a conveyor belt running over the track.

The headboard — the 'Wedding Belle' — tells the tale of this picture. On the wedding day — 29 May 1981 — of Prince Charles to Lady Diana Spencer, virtually the whole country was glued to the television set, except of course for steam enthusiasts and some photographers who preferred to use their extra day's holiday travelling behind or recording steam on the Settle & Carlisle line. No 850 Lord Nelson headed the train and put up another of its excellent performances on the climb from Appleby to the summit, but as the roads were virtually deserted, it was not difficult to follow. It is shown in this picture shutting off for a slack near New Biggen and immediately blowing off. I only knew the class during their last years on the Southern, when they were all based at Eastleigh shed and generally only on secondary duties, but I never witnessed them performing anything like as well as this locomotive did on the various routes it worked during its few years of active service in preservation. After many years in store, it is again being restored to working order by a group based at Eastleigh and I look forward to seeing and hearing it again, with its distinctive exhaust, on the main line — hopefully in a different livery.

The days of through freight over the Settle & Carlisle were rapidly drawing to a close by the summer of 1981. Dwarfed by Pen-y-ghent (which rises to 2,273ft), Class 47/0 No 47205 hauls a very heavy fertiliser train up the 1 in 100 gradient just north of Horton in Ribblesdale on 5 August 1981. The station opened on 1 May 1876 and became a victim of the line's rationalisation when it closed on 4 May 1970 with the withdrawal of local trains over the route. Happily, services were restored in July 1986 and currently there are seven trains in each direction on weekdays.

Photographs of 'Deltics' and 'Westerns' appear in their hundreds in railway magazines and books, but the West Coast electrics, particularly the early types (Classes 81 to 85) are seldom seen.

The Beyer Peacock-built Class 82s numbered only 10 in total and were built between 1960 and 1962. Two of the class were withdrawn in 1969 and 1971, whilst the others remained in regular use until 1981, after which they were put in and out of store. All but two of the class, Nos 82005 and 82008, were withdrawn by August 1983.

In the summer of 1981, the type had a regular duty from Crewe to Preston on a semi-fast train and No 82006 is shown on this working on 10 August 1981 near Farrington Junction heading north. One of the class, No 82008, has been preserved.

Blackburn has managed to retain, even in 1998, much of its old world charm, even after some 30 years since the last steam workings in the area, although I believe that there are currently plans to modernise the station area — no doubt with yet another shopping complex. Back on 22 October 1981 there was a wide variety of DMUs working in the area, and in this picture we can see a Craven-built Class 105 on a service to Colne. At the time, the unit was 24 years old. Of special interest is the fine clock, but also worthy of note is the superb model of the ship Viking in the glass case. This was the first turbine steamer on the Liverpool-Douglas (Isle of Man) service, on which it sailed from 1905 until 1954. No doubt there is a good reason why the model was on display at Blackburn — but I am unaware of it.

I have very few pictures in my collection of 'Deltics' being double-headed. This occasion, on 4 November 1981, caught me completely by surprise as I had gone to Batley to photograph No 55022 as I had seen it en route to Liverpool in the morning. The train was the 13.05 Liverpool-York service, a regular 'Deltic' working during the last months of 1981. The 'Peak' was No 45005, which had apparently been attached at Manchester Victoria, and, as can be seen, both locomotives were under power. The low winter light catches the train, and the terrace houses in the background, to advantage as it crosses the viaduct. Sadly the trees to the left have now grown to such an extent that it is almost impossible to take a photograph today from this viewpoint.

Every year, as winter approaches, photographers around the country dream of snow and sun, but seldom are their dreams realised. The end of 1981 was the exception, when a particularly cold period in mid-December covered the country with snow and caused considerable disruption. Fortunately, on 12 December 1981, the roads were clear enough for me to set forth up the Yorkshire Dales to see the Keighley & Worth Valley Railway's 'West Country' Pacific No 34092 City of Wells on the Carnforth-Hellifield line. Adorned with full 'Golden Arrow' regalia, the sight and sound remains as one of the most memorable preserved steam spectacles for me. The train was running very late and the light was fading fast as the locomotive stormed past Kettlebeck Bridge on its way south.

The flats at Ordsall Lane, Manchester, which have long since been demolished, provided an excellent vantage point to photograph trains. I seem to remember in 1981 that the flats were unoccupied and it wasn't a very wise move to go wandering around on your own draped in camera equipment. Nevertheless for a sight such as this I was prepared to take the risk. 'Deltic' No 55022 Royal Scots Grey heads its lightweight 13.05 Liverpool-York train through the snow on 17 December 1981. It was one of those days when you wanted to be at every location and I know that there were some superb photographs taken on the climb to Diggle, but at least I got an exclusive from the flats. This proved to be my penultimate 'Deltic' picture of the class in BR service, as I was not around for the final specials. I had certainly taken many worse shots of the class over the years, and very few that were better.

1 9 8 2

I was once again abroad at the beginning of the year, so was not able to witness the final workings of the 'Deltics' on 2 January 1982, when No 55022 *Royal Scots Grey* performed the final leg of the 'Deltic Scotsman Farewell' from Edinburgh to King's Cross.

This was the year when InterCity 125s took over more services, including those over the Midland main line and the northeast/southwest route. Of course, there were still a few locomotive-hauled diagrams, especially in the summer in the southwest, but it removed the 'Peaks' from the workings for which they will always be remembered.

Once again it appears that the majority of my photographic activities were in the north of England, with virtually nothing in Scotland. The preserved steam on the main line was mainly the 'Cumbrian Coast Express' and the 'Welsh Marches' workings, which provided a good variety of motive power. The 'King Arthur' *Sir Lamiel* was extremely active and the Keighley & Worth Valley's 'West Country' *City of Wells* appeared on the main line for the first time since withdrawal.

After the hysteria which followed the demise of the 'Deltics' had died down, the enthusiasts started to pay more attention to the Class 40s as it appeared that the class would not be around for many more years, so I made several trips to capture them on film in North Wales before it was too late. I also had several visits to the Midland main line to record the Class 45/1s.

Another event of note during the year was the inaugural trip of the 'Venice-Simplon Orient Express' (VSOE) on 28 May; the train continues to operate today, giving much pleasure to both enthusiasts and to the general public.

After 20 years steam was again heard on the Kyle of Lochalsh line, with a limited number of trips behind Aviemore-based Class 5 No 5025, although another 15 years were to pass before it happened again.

Whilst the 'Deltics' vanished off the main line, the first of the new Class 58s emerged from Doncaster Works on 9 December; this type was to dominate MGR working in the Midlands for many years.

This was another busy year, but not quite the hectic pace set in the previous two years. I still took 80 black and white films and a total of 1,560 transparencies (although a third were in India).

Locomotive-hauled passenger trains over the Copy Pit route between Hall Royd Junction and Stansfield Hall were not very frequent at this time, as the passenger service was withdrawn on 1 November 1965. Through services over the line were reinstated later. This viewpoint, just east of Portsmouth, shows the typical houses and mills of the area. The train is a special '5Z95' from Chesterfield to Blackpool on 12 April 1982. It is headed by Class 47/4 No 47425 (before it was named Holbeck in April 1986). The five-mile climb from Stansfield Hall to Copy Pit is mainly at either 1 in 65 or 1 in 80, but the 10-coach train represented no problem for the Class 47.

It was 2 May 1976 when Class 45/0 No 45073 passed this spot with the last through up 'Thames-Clyde Express' and the service was then altered to run from Glasgow to Nottingham. Two weeks after this picture was taken on 1 May 1982 these services finished and the route was reduced to about three trains a day in each direction headed by Class 31s and usually formed of four coaches. Class 45/0 No 45002 crosses the River Ribble at Helwith Bridge as it descends the bank from Blea Moor to Settle Junction with the 11.50 Glasgow Central-Nottingham service on a glorious sunny day.

The 'Peaks' had virtually monopolised Midland main line services for 20 years, but on 4 October 1982 InterCity 125s took over most of the diagrams. Class 45/1 No 45123 The Lancashire Fusilier, *named in October 1963 when it was numbered D52, powers through the cutting at Barrow-on-Soar, which it must have done hundreds of times before, at the head of the 14.00 Derby-St Pancras train.*

After they were displaced from the Midland main line, many of the Class 45/1s replaced Class 46s from trans-Pennine services; the latter class was rapidly withdrawn. The Class 45/1s retained this work until they were again displaced, this time by Class 47/4s at the end of the decade.

The highlight of the year as far as I was concerned in preserved steam terms was the transfer to the Great Central Railway of the National Railway Museum's Class G Great Northern Railway single No 1. Designed by Patrick Stirling, 37 of the class were built at Doncaster between 1870 and 1873. The last member of the class was withdrawn in 1914, No 1 having succumbed in 1907. Speeds around 85mph were regularly reached on the descent of Stoke Bank and when the class worked the Anglo-Scottish trains from King's Cross to York average speeds of 57mph were achieved.

No 1 was restored to operational condition in 1938 on the 50th anniversary of the 'Races to the North' and it was also used that year on the first Railway Correspondence & Travel Society special.

The locomotive is pictured passing Woodthorpe Lane, just south of Loughborough, on 9 May 1982 on one of its outings. These trips were always supervised by the late John Bellwood of the NRM, who can be seen on the footplate.

In the days when the fine signal gantries were still in operation at Exeter St David's, the 09.15 Birmingham-Paignton service is pictured approaching the station on August 1982 headed by Class 46 No 46029. The locomotive had only another four months left in traffic before withdrawal. The modernisation of the signalling at Exeter St David's was completed in May 1985.

The through services from Glasgow to Nottingham which had travelled via the Settle & Carlisle line were diverted via Preston and the Hope Valley after the introduction of the summer timetable on 15 May 1982. The service over the S&C was then reduced to three or four trains per day between Leeds and Carlisle and it appeared to be that these were timed to miss connections at Carlisle. Class 31s were the normal motive power with four coaches. The 15.37 from Carlisle to Leeds is headed by No 31126 on 2 September 1982 and is pictured approaching Bell Busk; the station here closed on 4 May 1959. These services were all part of a scheme by BR which was perceived at the time to make it appear that the line was not required and was totally uneconomic.

For many, 31 May 1982 will be remembered in York as the day when Pope John Paul II visited the great city. For railway enthusiasts it was the day when the greatest number of specials passed through the station for years. I cannot remember the number, but it must have been around 20 trains. A wide variety of motive power was used, with Class 31, 40, 45, 46 and 47 being represented as well as InterCity 125s. The trains appeared to be named 'Popex' specials and it was obvious that York could not accommodate them, so the trains continued to various points north and south of the city for stabling.

Unfortunately, it was not a good day for photographs, being extremely hazy in the Vale of York and I didn't stay to see the return workings, but headed off up the Settle & Carlisle to see a steam special headed by a 'Jubilee' and a Class 5 — probably the most authentic combination that the preservation movement could turn out for the line.

Class 40 No 40087 is caught passing the site of Bolton Percy station with the an ECS working having delivered its passengers to York.

The viaduct over the River Weaver at Frodsham is still an attractive location, although there are now only a few locomotive-hauled trains over it each day. Back in 1982 there were plenty of locomotive workings, one of which was this van train to Red Bank at Manchester, which on 21 August 1982 was headed by Class 40 No 40104. The ship in the picture, Cuddington, has been replaced by a more modern vessel, which can usually be seen moored alongside the warehouse.

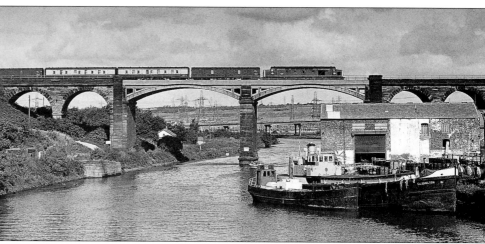

After around 30 years of being mainly restricted to the Southern Region, the diagramming of Class 33s to West Wales, Manchester, Crewe and North Wales was very welcome to enthusiasts. Up to the early 1980s, the only area where a Class 33 could meet a Class 86 was probably in the Willesden area, but here we see No 33006 leaving Crewe on the 16.02 service to Cardiff, whilst No 86230, which was then named The Duke of Wellington — a name very familiar to me in West Yorkshire as it was also carried by 'Royal Scot' No 46145, which was allocated to Holbeck shed, Leeds, for many years — The Duke of Wellington was one of the West Riding's local regiments.

The handsome 'King Arthur' class 4-6-0 No 777 Sir Lamiel makes a spectacular departure from Appleby as it leaves for the south and the long climb to Ais Gill summit with the up 'Cumbrian Mountain Pullman' on 4 December 1982. Owned by the National Railway Museum and restored by a group in Humberside, the locomotive gave an excellent account of itself over the Settle & Carlisle and other northern lines. Before being retired from the main line to the Great Central Railway it also travelled extensively over more familiar Southern Region haunts.

Time does not stand still and whilst the 'Deltics' died at Doncaster in January, the first Class 58 was handed over to Railfreight by BREL at 'The Plant' on 9 December 1982. The locomotive is shown breaking the banner before being parked for the handover ceremony alongside the rostrum. Some 16 years on, the class is still intact and giving excellent service to English, Welsh & Scottish. This was the first locomotive to wear the striking new Railfreight livery of grey with a large white arrow and red band on the frame.

One of the handsome Class 124 trans-Pennine units is shown in Manchester Piccadilly displaying its prominent logo on 23 November 1982; this was carried by a few of the class when they were working Manchester-Hull services via the Hope Valley. The sets were built at Swindon during 1959 and 1960 and were introduced to Liverpool-Hull trans-Pennine services in early 1961. They were originally provided with a buffet car and had a maximum speed of 75mph; however, since they had 460hp Leyland/Albion motors, the units were capable of fast hill climbing over the Pennines. It is sad that, amongst the many preserved DMUs, not one representative of this class survives.

A depressing sight for 'Deltic' enthusiasts as No 55004, formerly named Queen's Own Highlander, awaits its fate at Doncaster just over 12 months after withdrawal. I believe its last day in service was 28 October 1981 when it worked the 08.49 York-Liverpool returning on the 12.05 Liverpool-Newcastle. I managed to obtain two good pictures of it on the bank between Huddersfield and Marsden on that occasion.

1 9 8 3

*O*nce again, this year followed a very similar pattern for me to previous years, with a trip to India in January, but once back in the country it was another year of considerable activity, much of it directed towards the Class 40s, which were being gradually withdrawn. The amount of attention given to preserved steam on the main line was less, but there was the marvellous sight of the Midland Compound piloting 'Jubilee' *Leander* over the Settle & Carlisle in snow on 12 February.

Sir Nigel Gresley's famous Pacific No 4472 *Flying Scotsman* celebrated its diamond jubilee with trips over the East Coast main line and, elsewhere, a special steam service was introduced on Sundays to run from Paddington to Stratford-upon-Avon.

Of considerable importance on the East Coast main line was the opening of the Selby Diversion,

although traffic was restricted to 60mph until 1984 to allow the track to bed in properly. Also, of local interest in Yorkshire, was the handover of the Class 141 railbus sets.

Work started at Doncaster on the refurbishment of the Class 50s and in Scotland a programme to refurbish the Class 303 EMUs began, it being 23 years since the class was introduced as the 'Blue Trains'. The new Strathclyde PTE livery also appeared during the year.

On a more depressing note, the formal notice of withdrawal of passenger services over the Settle & Carlisle route was issued, but this immediately ran into legal problems.

Another very active year resulting in hours of darkroom work and cataloguing of slides. All this contributes to making the selection of photographs for 1983 particularly difficult to select.

Super power for the Preston Docks-Immingham tanks on 23 November 1983 as it passes Thornhill on the ex-Lancashire & Yorkshire main line just west of Healey Mills yard. The Class 47/4 No 47588 with silver roof had failed and a couple of Immingham-based Class 37/0s, Nos 37161 and 37166, had come to the rescue, although double-headed Class 37/0s were the normal motive power for the train. No 47588 is now part of the RES fleet (as No 47737 Resurgent), whilst the Class 37s are now Class 37/7s Nos 37899 and 37891 respectively.

Two years after the closure of the Woodhead route, BR was busy lifting the track. In July 1983 the section being lifted was that between Crowden and Torside. The works train, with the lifted track, is shown arriving back at Hadfield on 12 July 1983 headed by Class 25 No 25209 and Class 40 No 40104. There have been suggestions in the railway press recently that, in order to increase freight traffic across the Pennines from east to west, the possible reopening of the Woodhead route has been put forward as an option; however, the reports did stress that this was the least likely of the four being considered. The Class 40 No 40104 only remained in service for a further five months.

A busy scene at New Mills South Junction on 13 April 1983 as a Class 123 DMU on a trans-Pennine service from Hull to Manchester passes Class 40 No 40056 hauling a rake of withdrawn Class 76s (Nos 76008/28/09/01/36) on their last journey across the Pennines to C. F. Booth's scrapyard at Rotherham for disposal. All the Class 76s in the convoy had lasted until the closure of the line, except No 76001 which was withdrawn in November 1980. The Woodhead route closed to traffic on 20 July 1981 and, during 1983, there were a number of trains hauling withdrawn Class 76s across the Pennines via the Hope Valley route to Rotherham.

Saturday 2 April 1983 was yet another occasion when the services via the West Coast main line were diverted over the Settle & Carlisle line. I happened to be in the right place at the right time to capture this passing shot on Ribblehead Viaduct. The condition of the viaduct was put forward as one of the main reasons for the closure of the line, but you will notice in April 1983 that no scaffolding can be seen and that locomotive-hauled trains were allowed to pass over it. This was the only occasion I managed to get a picture of trains passing on the structure, which has 24 spans and is 440yd long and 100ft high.. The diverted trains were the 07.45 Euston-Glasgow service headed by Class 47/4 No 47518 whilst No 47444 University of Nottingham headed south on the Glasgow Central Euston service.

One of the 19 Class 503 sets, No 29146, which were ordered by the LMS in 1938 to supplement the 159 Class 502 cars on the Liverpool (Central) 650V dc system, calls at Bidston on 29 April 1983 on a Liverpool Central-West Kirby service. In the background is Bidston Dee Junction, whilst a Class 101 No M53930 waits with the connecting service to Wrexham Central over the former Great Central line.

This is the Leyland Experimental Vehicle (LEV), which was built by BR and British Leyland in 1978. It is basically a 'Railbus' built from two standard Leyland National bus bodies, mounted on a modified four-wheel wagon underframe. It was number RDB975874 and was put into service on several routes for evaluation. It is pictured passing one of South Yorkshire PTE's bus depots south of Sheffield Midland station on 16 July 1983 en route from Derby to the Keighley & Worth Valley Railway.

Whilst shunting in the Penmaenmawr Quarry sidings on 4 May 1983, Class 40 No 40150 had this headboard attached to commemorate the silver jubilee of the class. Note the old loading bunkers at this location in 1983; these were later completely modernised when the new North Wales coast road was constructed. The headboard was removed by the time that the train departed with its ballast wagons for Helsby Junction.

Dwarfed by the Glasgow high rise flats, Class 26 No 26031 descends the 1 in 41 bank to Glasgow Queen Street station with the empty stock train to form an evening express to the Highlands. When the railway opened in 1842 between Queen Street and Edinburgh Haymarket, the incline at Cowlairs was worked by cable and a stationary engine. Throughout the steam era most trains were banked up the gradient, Eastfield shed providing specially modified locomotives with uncouplers for the purpose. Now the incline has been modernised for bi-directional working and the modern trains no longer need assistance.

The new high-speed Selby Diversion opened for traffic on 3 October 1983, but with a 60mph restriction to allow the track to settle. With only a few days left before the traffic was diverted away from Selby, the down 09.30 King's Cross-Newcastle train passes through the centre roads on its way north on 20 September 1983 formed of InterCity 125 rake No 254035. The picture was taken from the swing bridge across the River Ouse. The present bridge was built in 1891 and has a fixed span of 110ft and a swing span of 130ft allowing 61ft of water for navigation. The bridge is operated from a signalbox position on top. It was raised 3ft 6in in 1960 for electrification of the East Coast main line, but this has never taken place through Selby. The centre roads at the station were removed several years ago.

This once very busy route, which was mainly freight, from Hall Royd Junction at Todmorden to Gannow Junction outside Burnley was selected by the BR Filming Unit to produce a film on the new liveried InterCity 125s. Traffic had dwindled to such an extent that by this date there was no booked traffic over the route, so this made it easy to get occupation for two days. A DMU apparently made a return trip about once every two weeks to make sure that the line was fit for use, because Preston signalbox covered the Calder Valley route as far east as Hebden Bridge as well as this line. The InterCity 125 rake selected was No 253.028 formed with power cars Nos 43126 and 43151 from the Western Region. The train, pictured in its unfamiliar surroundings on 25 September 1983, is crossing Lydgate Viaduct on the 1 in 65 gradient on the climb to Copy Pit. Many film sequences, including some from a helicopter, were taken over the weekend. A landslip closed the line for eight months in 1986, but fortunately it was reopened and there is now an hourly service from Bradford to Blackpool together with a limited amount of freight. The reopening to passenger services was originally supported by a building society when a merger meant that it had head offices in both Bradford and Burnley. The line was again temporarily closed for a month in January and February 1998 to allow for relaying of the track.

The National Railway Museum's Midland Compound No 1000 made one of its then relatively rare appearances on the main line along the Calder Valley from York to Manchester on 28 September 1983. The signalman waves the train on its way as it approaches the station at Hebden Bridge. No 1000 is currently on display at York, but has not been steamed for at least 12 years. The platforms at Hebden Bridge are staggered; the down one can be seen on the left.

Garsdale on the Settle & Carlisle route is supposed to be one of the wettest places in England, but on 2 April 1983 the rain had turned into a blizzard. This resulted in an extremely difficult journey home. A Carlisle-Leeds service passes nonstop through the deserted station. Garsdale was one of the many stations closed on the line on 4 May 1970 when stopping services were withdrawn, but fortunately 16 years later, on 14 July 1986, it was reopened along with others on the route. The meagre service running in 1983 was normally a Class 31 with coaches rather than a DMU.

Freightliner trains were an everyday sight along the North Wales coast in 1983. Class 40 No 40170, which was withdrawn in December 1983, heads a Trafford Park-Holyhead train through the arch at Conwy Castle on 21 April 1983. These freightliner services to and from Holyhead ceased in the early 1990s.

1 9 8 4

*I*I suppose I will remember 1984 as the year I rediscovered Scotland, at least as far as the West Highland was concerned. For years I had put off going to photograph the Class 27s, because in comparison with other parts of the country there were so few trains — not really a valid reason.

Although the services had not really increased, what I did discover was that by making Tyndrum one's base, one could start the day by photographing the Euston-Fort William sleeper near County March Summit and by operating in the triangle bounded by Fort William, Oban and Tyndrum I was able, by keeping moving, to get nearly 30 action shots during the day. I remember returning home from a four-day trip in the area in 1985 and finding we had put 2,200 miles on the clock. This was only possible in the period between Easter and Whitsuntide when the roads were quiet and there was little traffic around.

A trip to East Anglia was made to cover the main Liverpool Street-Norwich line whilst the Class 47/4s from Stratford were still in charge of these services and when the locomotives were kept in excellent external condition.

The 'Gatwick Express' service started on 14 May and I went to photograph the variety of liveries on the Class 73s working the trains. As can be seen in the selection of photographs, I covered a good part of the country rather than concentrating on local services as had been the case in the last few years.

Elsewhere, the Class 46s came to an end and all the Class 56s had entered traffic. Another important event was the return of steam to the Fort William-Mallaig line, an operation which has been repeated with great success during the summer months ever since, although there are occasional fire risk problems.

Of local interest was the introduction of the Class 141 railbuses in the West Riding, but this was not without some serious problems.

Looking back, it was an excellent year and I even managed a trip to China in December.

The driver of the loaded limestone train from Tunstead to ICI's plant at Northwich was making a cautious descent down the bank from Peak Forest on 27 April 1984. The mainly 1 in 90 gradient has witnessed more than one runaway over the years. The train is approaching New Mills South Junction and the locomotive is Class 40 No 40135, which is now preserved on the East Lancashire Railway. No 40135 received a major overhaul at Crewe Works in September 1979 and became one of the last of the class to be withdrawn. It was transferred to departmental stock, becoming No 97406 before being withdrawn in January 1985.

The Class 20s were still regular performers on the summer extra trains from the Midlands to Skegness at this time. They generated a lot of interest amongst enthusiasts and BR must have made a lot of extra income over the years. The 11.58 Saturdays Only service from Skegness to Leicester arrives at Loughborough with Nos 20113 and 20161 in charge on 30 June 1984. In the background is the Brush factory, which has been the main supplier of new locomotives built in this country in recent years. No 20161 was withdrawn in February 1988, but No 20113 lasted until September 1991.

The trees and bushes have been removed from the banking on the right of the picture prior to work starting on the Liverpool Street-Ipswich electrification. This opened up the location from above the tunnel at Ipswich to photographs and allowed this picture of a white-roofed Stratford-allocated Class 47/4 to be taken on 13 April 1984. The train is the 14.30 from Liverpool Street to Norwich. In the background is a power station and part of the docks, whilst the diesel depot stands on the site of the former steam shed (32B).

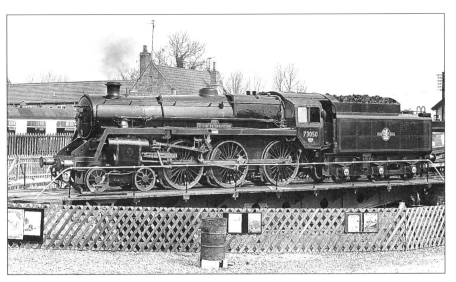

Originally allocated to the Somerset & Dorset, Standard Class 5MT No 73050 was new to Bath Green Park shed in June 1954, where it remained until August 1972. It was then allocated to Llanelly, Shrewsbury and Agecroft before finally arriving at Patricroft in October 1966. It was withdrawn in August 1968 and passed immediately into preservation. It could be seen parked alongside the main line to the north of Peterborough for many years, before being moved to the Nene Valley Railway, where it remains to this day. It is pictured on 20 April 1984 on the turntable at Wansford, painted in BR lined green livery.

The first 14 Class 58s were in traffic by the date of this photograph (9 May 1984), although it would be nearly another three years before the final member of the class, No 58050, was commissioned. All were based at Toton depot and spent their time on MGR coal traffic, mainly in the East Midlands. This picture at Bennerley was taken from the remains of the now 'listed' ex-Great Northern Railway viaduct, which crossed the Midland main line at this point, on the former Derby Friargate-Nottingham Victoria line. No 58004 is passing with a loaded MGR, probably heading for Toton yard, whilst a Class 56 waits to leave the sidings after being loaded at the site.

Whilst the Class 46s were all withdrawn by November 1984, the Class 45s were still active, mainly on trans-Pennine and northeast/southwest services, and were maintained at Toton. No 45133, now preserved at the Midland Railway Centre (Butterley), receives attention alongside sister No 45101 on 20 April 1984.

The Woodhead route across the Pennines was electrified in September 1954 at 1,500V dc. Following on from this was the electrification of the branch to Glossop and eight three-car EMUs (later Class 506) were built for the service. No 59401M passes Dinting station signalbox on 27 April 1984 on the direct service from Hadfield to Manchester Piccadilly. Normally, all trains travel via Glossop in both directions, but at peak periods there were a few direct trains. The class was maintained at Reddish depot, but when that closed in 1984 they were transferred to Longsight, which meant they had to be loco-hauled, usually by a Class 08 shunter, between Piccadilly and Longsight. The line was later converted to 25kV ac and these units replaced by Class 305s, which in turn have been replaced by Longsight-based Class 323s.

I had to have several attempts to get this picture of the almost simultaneous departures from Manchester Piccadilly of the 16.40 Pullman to London Euston and the 16.42 InterCity 125 to Plymouth. I eventually succeeded on 24 September 1984, when Class 86/2 No 86252 The Liverpool Daily Post starts to overtake InterCity 125 No 43180. The Pullman would travel via the Styal line to Crewe, whilst the InterCity 125 went via Stockport.

Steam workings on the ex-LNWR route over the Pennines have happened occasionally during the years since steam returned to the main line. On 9 June 1984 Class A4 No 4498 Sir Nigel Gresley hauled a special to York. It is pictured climbing the gradient from Thornhill Junction to the summit in Morley Tunnel passing Batley Carr. The headboard proclaims the train to be an outing from Clitheroe parish church.

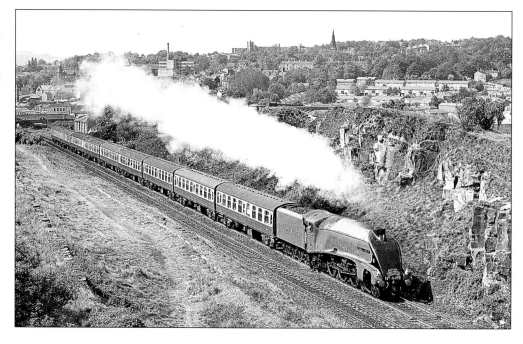

On 17 April 1984, the 06.05 Bristol-Newcastle InterCity 125 passes Broughton, near Ferrybridge, on the ex-Swinton & Knottingley Joint line, which was the direct route out of Sheffield towards York. The northeast/southwest InterCity services were subsequently rerouted via either Leeds or Doncaster, leaving this route to be served by only the local Sheffield-York Pacer units. The leading powercar on the train is No 43167.

The 'Gatwick Express' service commenced on 14 May, with a 15min frequency and a journey time of 30min. Some 14 years on, the service remains virtually the same with the Class 73s and the driver/guard luggage vans. No 73123 was painted in this special livery and is pictured passing through East Croydon on a down train on 26 August 1984. Certain locomotives were eventually dedicated to the service, becoming sub-Class 73/2.

The then thrice-weekly tank train to Oban is currently something of the past, but in 1984 it was '7B05' — the 13.30 from Mossend. On 2 May 1984 Class 37/0 No 37175, with its small Scottie dog logo, has just arrived at Oban station and is shunting the wagons into the sidings next to the ships. The elegant Austin Sheerline makes an interesting comparison with the Class 37, as both were built around the same time. The car was, I believe, owned by a railwayman and was well known around the station. The mainly wooden Callander & Oban station looks in reasonable condition, although it was demolished in April 1987, being deemed to be unsafe.

The days of the Class 25s on the Cambrian lines were drawing to a close by the end of 1984. The class had dominated the locomotive-hauled passenger workings for many years, especially at the head of the extra summer trains. Nos 25254 and 25298 are pictured leaving Newtown on 1 September 1984 with the 07.25 Saturdays Only service from Euston to Aberystwyth.

Dugald Drummond designed the very successful 'T9s' for the London & South Western Railway; No 120 appeared in August 1899. From 1922 the class was superheated and rebuilt with an extended smokebox, including No 120 (in May 1927). This made the locomotives' performance even better and they earned themselves the nickname of 'Greyhounds'. All were withdrawn by July 1961 with the exception of No 30120, which was overhauled at Eastleigh Works in March 1962 and restored to LSWR livery for hauling specials. It was then withdrawn in July 1963 and went into store until it became part of the National Collection. It was on loan to the Mid-Hants Railway in 1984 and painted in the very smart BR lined black livery. It is seen here on 27 October 1984 at Ropley.

1 9 8 5

*T*he mileage which I must have covered during this year, both at home and abroad, must have been enormous. There were several visits to Devon and Cornwall as a result of the 'GWR 150' events. The West Highland seems to have received a fair amount of attention, and London was visited on several days; the latter was an area which had received little attention from me over the years.

Interesting developments were taking place on British Rail; the involvement of the local Passenger Transport Executives (PTEs) encouraged new liveries, such as those in West Yorkshire, Greater Manchester and Tyne & Wear, plus a chocolate and cream livery applied to the new Class 142 Pacer units. The 'GWR 150' celebrations produced several special namings of InterCity 125s and Class 47s, with four of the latter being repainted in Great Western green. The highlight of these celebrations must have been the return of steam over the Devon banks and a trip across Saltash Bridge to Truro by *Clun Castle*.

Steam returned on a regular basis to Marylebone with specials to Stratford-upon-Avon, called the 'Thames-Avon Express', whilst in preservation the Bluebell Railway celebrated its first 25 years and the Mid-Hants started working through to Alton. To finish it all off, I had an extensive tour of South America just before the end of the year. My records show that I exposed over 50 36-exposure Kodachrome films during the year, not to mention a vast quantity of black and white film.

It was very rare to get a Class 31 on the trans-Pennine services via Standedge, but on 8 March 1985 No 31452 was obviously standing in for a Class 45 or a Class 47, and was at the head of the 12.05 Liverpool-Scarborough train. It was running 20min late when it passed Marsden before starting to descend the bank into Huddersfield.

Having left West Yorkshire earlier in the day without a hint of snow, it came as a great surprise to find this deep snow near Wrexham. Green-liveried Class 40 No D200 had taken over from an electric at Stafford on 16 February 1985 to work the 'Birkenhead Bandit' special. This dramatic picture was taken at Acrefair, at the east end of Cefn Viaduct. The tour travelled via Bidston and through Birkenhead Docks to Hooton, thence to Manchester. No D200 continued in service until May 1988 when it became part of the National Railway Museum's collection.

There were just about two months to go when this picture was taken before the Class 47/4s were to be replaced by the Class 86/2s on the Liverpool Street expresses as far as Ipswich. Silver-roofed Stratford-allocated No 47458 climbs the 1 in 70 Bethnal Green Bank on the 13.35 express to Cambridge on 19 March 1985. EMU No 315857 was running alongside the Class 47 on a Gidea Park service.

The first steam-hauled passenger train over the Devon banks since the end of BR steam was part of the 'GWR 150' celebrations. Unfortunately, the train did not run smoothly on the outward journey, but on the return Severn Valley-based locomotives Nos 4930 Hagley Hall *and No 7819* Hinton Manor *made a spectacular ascent of the 1 in 42 grade up Hemmerdon on 8 April 1985. The train is seen near Ivybridge. The 'Hall' had been sent overnight to replace No 6000* King George V, *which had failed the previous day.*

Since the end of steam in Scotland, there were very few opportunities to photograph steam heading south from Edinburgh before the electrification masts were erected. One of the rare opportunities came on 27 April 1985 when 'A4' No 60009 Union of South Africa *was working round the Edinburgh suburban line and I obtained this picture of the train leaving Calton Tunnel. This is my favourite shot of* Union of South Africa, *the smoke for once doing exactly the right thing.*

On a glorious summer's morning, the overnight 22.10 Euston-Fort William sleeper calls on time at Ardlui at 07.19. An immaculate Eastfield-allocated Class 37/0 No 37111 Loch Eil Outward Bound, *complete with large Scottie dog logo, is ready to leave before facing the eight-mile climb up Glen Falloch on the mostly 1 in 60 gradient. Behind the locomotive is ex-Class 25 No 25310, which in May 1983 had been converted into an Electric Train Heating unit (nicknamed 'Ethel') and numbered 97250. There were three of these conversions for use on the West Highland sleepers until the Class 37/4s took over. The date is 15 June 1985.*

The 1 in 45 off the platform end at Glasgow Queen Street for 1.5 miles to Cowlairs did not cause the Class 47/7s any problems on the push-pull workings to Edinburgh and Aberdeen. Painted in the smart Scotrail livery, with a matching set of coaches, No 47711 Greyfriars Bobby *passes the summit as it rapidly picks up speed on the 17.30 working to Edinburgh Waverley on 15 June 1985. This was one of 17 Class 47s converted for these services; they were eventually replaced by Class 158s with the Class 47/7s being transferred to Waterloo-Exeter services displacing the Class 50s.*

A picture to gladden the hearts of Class 20 enthusiasts: a loaded MGR heading west for Fiddlers Ferry Power Station, hauled by Nos 20196 and 20194, meets an empty train working with Nos 20192 and 20181 at Warrington Arpley. Warrington Bank Quay station on the West Coast main line can be seen above the bridge in the background.

Taunton had a great selection of signal gantries at both ends of the station until they were replaced by colour lights in the late 1980s. One of the now-preserved Class 50s, No 50008 Thunderer, with a black roof, enters the station heading the 10.25 Paddington-Paignton service on 22 August 1985. The locomotive was withdrawn in May 1992, after being restricted to special duties from February 1991; this work was mainly departmental. By October 1992 it was working on the East Lancashire Railway, but only rarely and it has not been active for some time.

In ex-works condition, Class 491 '4TC' No 410 stands out against the rather dirty EMU with which it was working as it leaves Woking on a down Waterloo-Bournemouth train on 10 March 1985. In the stabling point on this occasion were a variety of locomotives, consisting of Class 47/3 No 47319, Class 33/1 No 33117 (now preserved on the East Lancashire Railway), Class 73/1 No 73119 (still in plain blue livery), Class 47/0 No 47293 and Class 33/0 No 33062. The 34 rakes of non-powered '4TCs' were converted from Mk 1 coaches at York Works in 1966 for use with EMUs on services to Bournemouth; a further six sets followed in 1974. The '4TCs' could also operate with Classes 33 and 73 for use over non-electrified lines.

A wide variety of motive power is pictured lined up outside Toton depot on 17 April 1985. From left to right are Class 20 No 20086, Class 45/0 No 45042, Class 20s Nos 20065 and 20041, Class 58 No 58009, Class 56 No 56083, Class 45/1 No 45120 and Class 25 No 25185 (numbered D7535).

For the 150th anniversary of the Great Western Railway, the Western Region allowed steam across the Saltash Bridge for a trip to Truro. The locomotive was able to use the turntable at St Blazey depot to turn before the return working. No 7029 Clun Castle looked superb on 6 September 1985 in the bright morning sunlight as it crossed the bridge and rounded the curve at Defiance as it headed west. The last BR steam special to run in Cornwall was named the 'Cornishman' and it had run more than 20 years earlier, on 3 May 1964.

1986

Some significant events took place on the railways. Network SouthEast was launched on 10 June, with Chris Green at the helm. The new eye-catching livery was in stark contrast to the rather drab standard BR blue livery. Class 317 EMUs entered service in the Great Northern allowing the Class 312s to be transferred to the Great Eastern.

It was a hot summer, which resulted in a lot of InterCity 125 Class 43 power car failures; this caused considerable disruption. The unique Class 89 left Crewe Works for testing at Derby. Another event, minor at the time but of great significance later, was the arrival at Southampton Docks of the first of the General Motors-built Class 59s for Foster Yeoman. These locomotives have, no doubt, influenced English, Welsh & Scottish Railways to order the new Class 66s and 67s. Also of note was the reopening of stations on the Settle & Carlisle line and the reintroduction of locomotive-hauled trains on the Cambrian line to Pwllheli after Barmouth Bridge had had its woodwork renovated.

It was also a good year for steam enthusiasts, with the National Railway Museum's Class A4 *Mallard* and the Great Western *City of Truro* both working on the main line, not to mention the appearance of the London & North Western Coal Tank. In what must be the most ambitious restoration job achieved thus far in preservation, 1986 saw the return to steam of Standard Class 8P No 71000 *Duke of Gloucester*, a project which I must admit I never thought would materialise in its earlier days.

As can be seen from my selection of photographs, it was an extremely busy year. The year saw several visits to Scotland, including Inverness and the Kyle line (which I had not been to for 12 years), North Wales, primarily due to the activity of the Class 33s, and the London & South Western main line around Yeovil. There was still plenty going on with trans-Pennine services, both via the Hope Valley with the Class 31/4s on passenger workings and via Standedge with the 'Peaks' and Class 47s.

In addition to all the interesting activity in the UK, I also managed an excellent trip to Jordan and Syria.

The Sunday Leeds-Red Bank vans was a much photographed train by local enthusiasts over the years, as you were never quite sure what the motive power would be; this was an attribute that applied even in steam days. On a wintry 9 February 1986 Class 31 No 31290 was in charge. The train is seen passing Mirfield; the old steam shed, which still stands, is to the left of the picture. The viewpoint is from the north side; most photographs seem to be taken at this location from the south side.

Sprinters were introduced in 1984 and the following year two impressive-looking Class 151 prototypes appeared from Metro-Cammell. No 151002 is pictured on 29 April 1986 leaving Doncaster for Sheffield, although it was not in public service. The design was not put into production and the units were taken out of service and stored at Llandudno Junction carriage shed for many years. The pair still survive, but no work has been done on them.

Three Class 128 single-car units, headed by No 55993, leave Birmingham via Proof House Junction on 2 August 1986. Eight of the units were built in 1959 by the Gloucester RCW, each being fitted with a 460hp engine. At this time they were painted in blue with a red stripe and full yellow ends for use by Red Star Parcels.

Around this period there were regular engineering possessions on the West Coast main line in the Wigan area. This resulted in diversions via Lostock Junction when trains were hauled by pairs of Class 20s, with the train locomotive at the rear. On 29 June 1986, the diverted 08.22 Birmingham New Street-Blackpool arrives at Lostock Junction headed by Nos 20047 and 20210. Class 47/4 No 47537 Sir Gwynedd/County of Gwynedd, recently ex Crewe Works, is at the rear and will haul the train to Preston whilst the Class 20s will return to Wigan for their next duty.

It must have been at least 25 years since a London & North Western locomotive passed through the 5,344yd-long Standedge Tunnel, but on 1 August 1986 'Coal Tank' No 1054 travelled from the Keighley & Worth Valley Railway to its then home base at Dinting. Times have now changed and, after the closure of Dinting, the locomotive returned to the K&WVR. There used to be water troughs in the tunnel; these were situated just inside at this, the west end, and the water tank for the troughs was just to the right of the area featured in the picture. There were 300 'Coal Tanks' constructed between 1881 and 1896; No 1054 was the last member of the class to survive, becoming No 58926 on Nationalisation. It was withdrawn in 1958 and acquired by the National Trust and kept at Penrhyn Castle near Bangor.

Class 31s were regular performers on the Saturdays Only summer extras to the east coast. On 28 June 1986 the 10.50 Yarmouth-Birmingham train was headed by Nos 31463 and 31434 as it passed Manton Junction. The line in the foreground is the old Midland route to Corby and through to Kettering, which today sees little traffic but is used occassionally for diversions off the Midland main line.

Stratford-allocated Class 47/4s were regular performers on the through Harwich-Glasgow and return 'European' express, which often resulted in some of the well-kept locomotives appearing in the north. No 47582 County of Norfolk, in its distinctive Network South East livery, was having a break from its more normal duties on Liverpool Street-King's Lynn services on 10 September 1986, when it headed the up 'European' (10.20 ex-Glasgow) past Hasland. The famous crooked spire of Chesterfield parish church stands out on the skyline. The old steam shed, which used to have LMS Garrett locomotives allocated to it, was just south of this location.

Engineering works on the Western Region main line between Castle Cary and Exeter St David's resulted in diversions via the London & South Western main line. The diverted 09.40 Paddington-Plymouth calls briefly at Yeovil Pen Mill before proceeding to Yeovil Junction to join the main line on 5 April 1986. Class 50 No 50005 Collingwood heads the train and is in immaculate condition, having only left Doncaster Works after an overhaul earlier in the week.

The National Railway Museum returned Gresley's record-breaking Class A4 No 4468 Mallard to operational condition in good time for the celebrations to mark the 50th anniversary of its achieving 126mph down Stoke Bank in 1938. The locomotive worked several railtours and, on 8 July 1986, it had an outing to Hull; I photographed it from the Humber Bridge alongside the new dual carriageway heading into Hull; as can be seen the train attracted plenty of attention. No 4468 (as No 60022) was withdrawn in April 1963 and then visited Doncaster Works for restoration to original condition; quite how much, if any, mechanical work was undertaken at the time now seems, with the passage of the years, to be unknown. It was then displayed at the Museum of British Transport at Clapham until being moved to the new National Railway Museum at York. After being restored for the 50th anniversary it worked for a relatively short period before being placed back on display and has not been used for almost a decade. The class is, however, well represented on the main line by sister locomotives Sir Nigel Gresley and Union of South Africa, with Bittern possibly joining them in the future.

The superb signal gantries at the entrance to Inverness station, operated from Welch's Bridge signalbox (to the right of this picture), were on borrowed time by 1986 as the resignalling of the area was not far away. The 12.30 to Glasgow Queen Street approaches under clear signals on 18 April 1986 as it departs headed by Class 47/4 No 47528 (originally No D1111), which was named The Queen's Own Mercian Yeomanry *in November 1989. The locomotive depot is in the background to the right; this used to be the old Highland Railway Loch Gorm Works. Just visible on the extreme left is Loco Box signalbox whilst at the north end of the station was Rose Street signalbox.*

Great Western 'City' class No 3440 City of Truro *was another record-breaking locomotive from the National Collection that was in action during 1986. It is claimed that, back in May 1904, No 3440 reached a speed of 104mph descending Whiteball Bank on a Plymouth-London mail train. There are those that doubt this, but it seems to have been accepted over the years by railwaymen and enthusiasts. No 3440 was restored to working order at the Severn Valley Railway ready for the 'GWR 150' celebrations in 1985. It travelled widely on the BR system thereafter, often acting as pilot locomotive, but on 6 August 1986 it worked an eight-coach special from York to Scarborough and is shown at Falsgrave signalbox on the return working. The locomotive is currently on display in the museum.*

The luxury 'Royal Scotsman' train waits at Dingwall on 19 April 1986 for the 11.10 from Kyle of Lochalsh to arrive behind Class 37/4 No 37415, which was one of the seven refurbished locomotives allocated to Inverness that normally worked most of the trains north of the city. The steam heat boiler on Class 37/0 No 37262 Dounreay appears to be working well. The 'Royal Scotsman' would be stabled overnight on the Kyle line and return the following morning. Note the Highland stag logo on the locomotives; this was applied to locomotives allocated to Inverness.

The hourly service from Edinburgh to Dundee was still locomotive-hauled at this date, the normal motive power being Class 27. This made the main line through Fife well worth a visit as one could be kept occupied all day with the local trains plus occasional freights and InterCity 125s. Looking across the Firth of Forth, and down on Burntisland Harbour (which was nearly empty), on 5 July 1986, Class 27 No 27025 was photographed leaving the town on the 08.30 from Dundee to Edinburgh. The locomotive was withdrawn one year later and was scrapped at the famous yard of Vic Berry in Leicester.

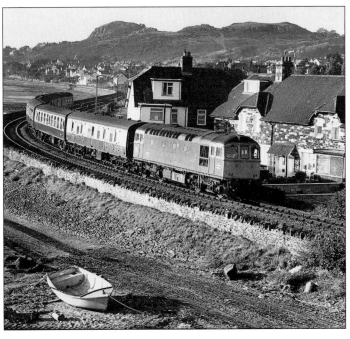

Class 33s were regularly diagrammed for work on the North Wales Coast line at this time on through workings from Cardiff. No 33032 catches the evening light as it enters the sharp curve on the approach to Llandudno Junction at the head of the 17.40 Llandudno-Crewe service on 19 September 1986. The locomotive was withdrawn six months later. At the time of writing, the branch to Llandudno has no locomotive workings except for the occasional special.

1987

Selecting pictures to represent the 1980s has not been easy, but 1987 has proved to be possibly the most difficult, as the selection shows that I was taking photographs as far north as Wick — and you can't get much further north than that on the railways — to Par in Cornwall and a lot of places in between. It must have been a good year for weather, as most of the 1,200 black and white photographs I took seem to have been taken in reasonable conditions. I finally made it back to Wick after 30 years and it was my first ever visit to Thurso. The Newport area in South Wales received plenty of attention, as the volume of traffic and variety of motive power made it very worthwhile. These trips all added up to at least 50,000 miles on the clock of the car for the year. The penalty for all this activity was that I only had a short railway trip to Ireland as well as a visit to Egypt, which produced only two railway photographs.

Some interesting events were happening on the railway network. An InterCity 125 broke the world speed record for diesel traction at 148mph; the electrification of the old Great Eastern main line to Norwich was completed; even a few fish trains were run again from Mallaig to Grimsby, but this was shortlived. New classes appeared, such as the Class 442 Wessex Electrics, whilst the first Class 90 left Crewe Works and the unique Class 89 worked revenue-earning trains. West Yorkshire PTE took delivery of its red-liveried Class 155s. The Queen opened the Docklands Light Railway on 30 July and Birmingham Snow Hill reopened. On the preservation front, the most significant event was the return of steam to the Cambrian line and, on 25 July, the opening of the East Lancashire Railway. It is quite amazing what the ELR has achieved in the 11 years since it reopened.

This was a very busy year, with some very pleasing results.

Looking very smart in the large logo blue livery, Class 50 No 50030 Repulse passes slowly through Par on 29 August 1987 with the Saturdays Only 17.17 Newquay-Plymouth train. The locomotive and stock had worked a Paddington-Newquay service earlier in the day. At the other end of the station is a chocolate and cream-liveried Pacer unit, which would have been providing the local service on the Newquay branch. No 50030 was later painted in Network SouthEast livery for working Waterloo-Exeter services.

Severn Tunnel Junction yard and depot were, as late as 1987, still busy centres for traffic. On 2 March 1987 there was plenty of activity, belying the fact that the yard was later to close. Class 33/0 No 33028, which was withdrawn in October 1988, approaches the station with the 10.07 Cardiff-Portsmouth train. In the background are several Class 37s and one Class 47, with a Class 31 to the left.

It is only in recent years that Class 37s have been seen on the Settle & Carlisle route on a regular basis. In 1987 they were extremely rare, so it came as a surprise when No 37135 appeared at the head of the diverted 07.30 Penzance-Aberdeen 'Cornishman' on 2 May 1987. I only happened to select this location by chance, so I was very pleased to have Eastfield-based No 37178 in the loop at Blea Moor on standby duties for the diversion. My only regret is that the sun went in just before the train arrived. I can't help wondering if the Class 37 had been provided by special request as there were plenty of Class 47s around.

The 07.12 loaded aluminium train from Blyth to Mallaig Junction was proving a challenge to Class 37/4 No 37403 Isle of Mull *on 1 April 1987 as it reaches the end of the climb up Glen Falloch — an ascent which is mostly 1 in 60 for some eight miles. The snow still lies around at the 2,000ft level on this clear but dull day. The locomotive has changed liveries frequently. Since the large logo blue livery seen here, it has been painted in Railfreight Distribution livery when it exchanged names with No 37424* Glendarroch. *It was then painted in BR green livery when it was again renamed, this time to* Ben Cruachan *and carried the number D6607 as well as No 37403. Quite a problem for historians in the years to come!*

This Class 104 DMU was painted in a special livery, becoming known locally as the 'Mexican Bean'. The main colour was reddish brown, with a white roof and white flashes. It was based at Oban and its only regular diagram was a Sunday evening service to Crianlarich and back — not what you would call intensive work. It was also, however, a useful standby in case any Class 37/4 failed on a passenger train since the nearest spare locomotive might be as far away as Eastfield. It is pictured on 31 March 1987, a Tuesday, in the yard at Oban, where no doubt it remained until the next Sunday. The wooden Callander & Oban station building was being demolished during this week. The skyline is dominated by the famous McCaig's Folly.

Bellerophon, built in 1874, is the oldest locomotive on the Keighley & Worth Valley Railway. On 12 April 1987 it was in action and having no difficulty climbing the bank out of Keighley. Built by Richard Evans & Co at Haydock Foundry for use on the company's own colliery lines, it eventually passed into the ownership of the National Coal Board, where it lasted until 1964. It was originally offered to the Liverpool Museum, but space was not available and so it found a new home on the K&WVR. It is a well tank, with outside cylinders, outside Gooch valve gear and piston valves. It is still in full working order and has made a limited number of visits to other preserved railways.

An extremely unusual combination on the 08.12 Holyhead-Newcastle service caught me by surprise on 7 February 1987. Class 37/0 No 37091 of Stratford (note the Cockney sparrow logo) had been attached in front of Class 47/7 No 47702 Saint Cuthbert, which was just out of Crewe Works and painted in the attractive Scotrail livery. No 47702 had been put on this train no doubt to return it north to its home base at Haymarket, but I believe that it suffered a broken window en route resulting in the Class 37 acting as pilot. I don't know how far the Class 37 worked, but I expect it was removed at Leeds or York. The train is just about to enter Paddock Cutting, near Huddersfield.

The amount of traffic in the Nottinghamshire coalfield has drastically reduced since the miners' dispute of the mid-1980s. One casualty of the decline was the depot at Shirebrook, as Worksop has proved to be a much better location to cover the area's remaining requirements. On 29 April 1987, Class 56 No 56018, painted in the grey Railfreight livery, heads east past the depot at Shirebrook with a loaded MGR train. Outside the depot are two Class 58s and another two Class 56s. Just behind the signalbox are a pair of Class 20s. The platforms of the former (ex-Midland Railway) station, which was known as Shirebrook West and which closed on 12 October 1964, can also be seen. Behind the bridge on which I was standing to take this photograph is a triangle which is, at the time of writing, still in use.

Frequent outings were made to the Cardiff-Newport-Severn Tunnel area during 1987, producing some very worthwhile results. One of the attractions of the area was that one was very likely to see the six Class 37/9s at work. On 4 August 1987 I managed to photograph No 37901 Mirrlees Pioneer emerging from Hillfield Tunnel at Newport with an up ballast train. Locomotives Nos 37901-37904 were fitted with a Mirrlees 6MB275T, 1,800hp engine, coupled to a Brush alternator, whilst Nos 37905 and 37906 had a 1800hp Ruston RK270T, coupled to a GEC alternator; the latter pair were also fitted with ballast weights. They were modified as testbeds pending the possible building of a Class 38, which never happened although information was gathered which proved useful on the later Class 60s.

It was 30 years ago since I was last in Wick, at a time when there were still ex-Caledonian Railway 4-4-0s on the shed as well as Stanier Class 5s. In 1987 the yard and the shed site were empty, with no tracks, although there were still run-round facilities and there was a siding. The station building only covered two coaches. The building was well looked after, with a pleasant mural of a Highland Railway steam locomotive inside; it can just be seen behind the second coach. Class 37s were the only class to be seen here by this date and No 37420 The Scottish Hosteller had worked the early morning train north from Inverness on 30 June 1987 and was ready to leave with '2H62', the 12.00 return working, which would, in the time honoured tradition, combine with the Thurso portion at Georgemas Junction. On my visits, the branch always seemed to be worked by No 37418 An Comunn Gaidhealach as it was named at the time; this locomotive has since been named East Lancashire Railway. Note the Highland stag logo on the cab side; this was a feature of Inverness-allocated engines.

1988

The lack of any railway trips abroad is usually because there was so much going on at home. So, apart from a family trip to Canada, the year's action was over here. Scotland received plenty of attention with at least four trips, and time was spent on the London & South Western line with the Class 73s on the Waterloo-Bournemouth route before the introduction of the Wessex Electrics.

Apart from *Mallard's* special working, very little time was devoted to steam during the year. The diesel preservation scene was well covered by the Severn Valley and Keighley & Worth Valley galas.

The Wessex Electrics — Class 442s — entered service through to Weymouth on 16 May 1988, although the first test train had run on 1 February. One of these units achieved a speed of 109mph, a record for 750V third-rail traction. More electric developments included the use of the unique Class 89 No 89001 on services to Leeds. The locomotive was also used on the special held to commemorate the 50th anniversary of *Mallard's* world steam record. The first Class 91s appeared on trials, culminating in a speed of 145mph being achieved by No 91002. Class 40 No D200 was finally withdrawn after 30 years' service and was placed in the National Railway Museum. The Class 45 'Peaks' were withdrawn, except for No 45106 which was painted green presumably to act as a replacement for No D200.

In preservation, the last, and 213th, locomotive left Barry scrapyard; it was an ex-GWR 2-8-0 No 2873. The Swanage Railway extended to Harman's Cross and 'Merchant Navy' No 35027 *Port Line* returned to steam on the Bluebell Railway.

All in all, another very busy and productive year.

Prior to the introduction of the Class 442 Wessex Electrics, the Class 73s were operating on the express Waterloo-Bournemouth services; this was, with the exception of the 'Gatwick Express' operation, probably the last opportunity to see these interesting locomotives on main line duties in any quantity. No 73126, in InterCity livery, leaves Southampton at 13.45 on 1 May 1988 with an up service for Waterloo.

After the electrification of the London-Norwich services on 11 May 1987, a small batch of Class 47/4s was retained at Stratford depot to work the trains to King's Lynn. This pool of locomotives were all painted in Network SouthEast livery and No 47573 was named The London Standard. The locomotive is seen approaching Downham Market on the 12.35 service from Liverpool Street to King's Lynn on 20 February 1988. After the electrification to King's Lynn was completed, the locomotives were transferred to the Western Region where they continued to give good service.

1988 was the 50th anniversary of Sir Nigel Gresley's 'A4' Pacific Mallard's world record run for a steam locomotive of 126mph down Stoke Bank. The locomotive had been returned to running order well before 1988 and was available for railtours during 1987 and 1988. One special duty, on 10 May 1988, was to haul the 'Pennine Postal Pullman', which was run to celebrate 150 years of the Travelling Post Office. The locomotive and the red Royal Mail vans made a colourful sight as they passed Marsden heading east towards Huddersfield.

By 1988, the Class 110 Calder Valley DMUs had been operating Trans-Pennine services through Halifax for 16 years. Locomotive-hauled passenger trains only appeared regularly over the route in summer months and when trains were diverted via Bradford due to engineering work between Leeds, Dewsbury and Heaton Lodge Junction. Freight trains through Halifax, even in 1988, were very few. On a day of diversions, 17 April 1988, the 10.00 Newcastle-Liverpool headed by No 47413 emerges from Beacon Hill Tunnel and will use the line between Dryclough Junction and Greetland; this route is now mothballed, although there is talk about it being reopened. The old Great Northern route to Bradford via Queensbury headed off to the left at this point.

A special was organised on 3 July 1988 to commemorate the 50th anniversary of Mallard's world steam record. The opportunity was taken to use Class 89 No 89001 on the train from King's Cross to Doncaster and return. The locomotive is in its first InterCity livery and is approaching Doncaster at Bridge junction. The crowds which greeted it and the departure of Mallard must have been several thousand; the multi-storey carpark at the north end of the station was solid with people on each level. After a brief career, the '89' went into preservation but re-emerged in full working order in 1997 to supplement the Class 91s on the GNER services between King's Cross, Leeds and Bradford.

One of my favourite diesel depots was Eastfield, particularly during the later 1980s, due to the good variety of locomotive classes and liveries. There are five different liveries in this photograph and four different classes of locomotive. The picture was taken at the north end on 4 September 1988 and the locomotives on view, from left to right, are Nos 47617, 47622, 26032, 47595, 26043, 37408, 20192 and 20138. Needless to say, I also recorded the scene in colour.

The service between Fort William and Mallaig must have been the only one in the country where trains were formed of a locomotive and two coaches in the winter timetable at this time. This picture was taken from high up the hillside to the west of Morar on 1 April 1988 and shows the 14.05 departure from Fort William. Class 37/4 No 37401 Mary Queen of Scots is at the head of the train.

In superb evening light, Class 37/4 No 37418 An Comunn Gaidhealach heads east on the 16.40 Kyle of Lochalsh-Inverness service on 24 September 1988, along the banks of Loch Carron, having just passed through the rock shelter situated between Attadale and Strome Ferry. I really needed the services of a small boat to get a better angle on this picture, but perched myself on a slippery rock at the water's edge; the inevitable happened as I started to return to the car and I narrowly avoided a good soaking as I fell. There was, fortunately, no damage to the cameras! The converted DMU observation car is next to the locomotive.

In 1988 the Keighley & Worth Valley Railway organised an excellent diesel gala, when the railway had two visiting 'Deltics', a Class 52 and a Class 24 from the East Lancashire Railway, and their own locomotives. The weather was fine for the event and on the Sunday morning, 6 November 1988, Class 52 Western Prince was double-heading with Class 55 Tulyar — possibly the first time that this combination had headed a train together. Glinting in the early morning light, the pair is seen approaching Haworth yard, heading for Keighley.

It was an early start from West Yorkshire to get myself down to Fairbourne in time for the 08.00 Pwllheli-Euston train on 21 May 1988, but with impeccable timing we arrived at this location just as the train was crossing Barmouth Bridge in the background. One of the six Class 37/4s based at Cardiff Canton and kept in immaculate condition for the Cambrian services, No 37429 Eisteddfod Genedlaethol, climbs the bank towards the rock shelter at Friog. Locomotive-hauled trains had returned to this line in 1986 after repairs to Barmouth Bridge. The locomotive was originally numbered D6600 when built in August 1965. It then became No 37300 in November 1973, and finally No 37429 in March 1986. Over the last four years it was a regular performer on North Wales coast services and is painted today in Regional Railways livery.

This picture was taken to show the Cheshire Lines/Great Central warehouse at Warrington rather than Class 31/4 No 31429 leaving Central station with the 12.45 Liverpool-Sheffield service on 9 April 1988.

It is, at the time of writing, an extremely rare event for a train to travel along the tramway to Weymouth Quay, although the line remains nominally operational. On 10 November 1988, Class 33/1 No 33114 Sultan makes very cautious progress with a Hertfordshire Rail Tours special. The BR staff had to 'bounce' several cars out of the way, a procedure which is quite normal since regular traffic ceased. It is quite amusing to see the faces of the motorists when they return to find their cars have moved a few yards but are still locked.

The Severn Valley Railway achieved a scoop for its diesel gala, when it managed to borrow one of the Foster Yeoman Class 59s, No 59001 Yeoman Endeavour. The first passenger working for the class is seen leaving Bridgnorth on 7 May 1988; since then the class has been extremely popular on railtours.

1 9 8 9

The number of photographs which I have allocated to this year indicates that it was extremely busy. Much more time was spent in the London area, primarily because I was doing a lot of work for Network SouthEast and managing to fit in other pictures for myself. The area had been badly neglected by me over the years, probably because I really prefer to be out on the West Highland or Settle & Carlisle lines rather than in the back streets of Clapham, even if you do get a lot more photographs at the latter location, but it did wonders for my collection of Class 50s on the Great Western and London & South Western routes. Preserved steam was almost totally ignored during the year.

The big news on British Rail was the reprieve of the Settle & Carlisle; the saga of this sorry episode in BR history has been well documented in many books. Elsewhere, steam did return to the attractive North Wales route and 'West Country' *Taw Valley* made the first of its many main line outings.

New liveries were unveiled for InterCity, Railfreight and Mainline, suddenly giving the railways a splash of colour after more than 20 years of standard blue.

Class 90s appeared on test runs, whilst the Class 91s were introduced on the Leeds-King's Cross trains, using InterCity 125 power cars as DVT units, which made for some extremely rapid departures from stations.

The first Class 158 started trials; this was a class which was to dominate the railway scene in the future from Inverness to Penzance. The first Class 60 was handed over by Brush Electrical Machines, whilst the Class 321s started operation on the Northampton line. It was a year that foreshadowed change, the results of which are still very much part of the daily railway scene today.

The first Class 37 was No D6700, which entered service in December 1960 at Stratford depot and, 38 years later, it is still in service. It became No 37119 under TOPS in February 1974 and then No 37350 in March 1988. It was specially repainted in the old BR green livery in 1988 and first appeared at Immingham, where it was used on the Scunthorpe ore trains. It then moved to the Western Region, where it is seen double-heading with classmate No 37371 approaching Slough on 28 March 1989 with an up oil train. It carried both its original (D6700) and current (37350) numbers.

Another locomotive which kept changing numbers was No 86507. It started life as No E3169 in June 1965, becoming No 86239 under TOPS. It was named L. S. Lowry in October 1980 and at which time it became No 86507. It is seen in immaculate Railfreight livery on 13 May 1989, heading the Larbert-Oakley tanks past Beckfoot. It later reverted to No 86239 under RES control, before coming to a premature end in a house garden following an accident at Rickerscote near Stafford.

There is plenty of Class 33 action in this view along the coast at Shakespeare Cliff Tunnel at Dover, as No 33012 emerges with a Channel Tunnel spoil train and Nos 33022 and 33204 head towards Folkestone, no doubt to collect another train. The class was involved extensively on this work and in the carrying of the concrete segments for the tunnel lining from the Isle of Grain in Kent. The date is 23 September 1989.

Diversions off the East Coast main line were in operation south of Newcastle on 19 February 1989 and the trains were travelling over the now mothballed Leamside branch. A Class 47 heads the 11.42 Newcastle-Liverpool train over the impressive Victoria Bridge across the River Wear.

Pictures of Class 47s in Lime Street Cutting, Liverpool, have hardly the same appeal as those magnificent studies taken by the Rev Eric Treacy many years ago of rebuilt 'Patriots' and 'Royal Scots'; for me, the latter are possibly some of the finest steam photographs taken in this country. No 47434 Pride of Huddersfield arrives with the 13.52 down Newcastle on 14 May 1989 looking smart in the large logo blue livery. No 47434 was a Gateshead locomotive at this time and was a regular performer on the Trans-Pennine trains — hence its appropriate name.

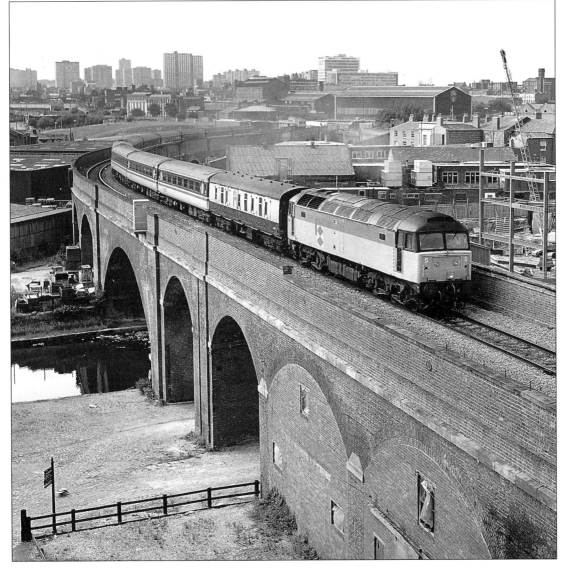

This picture was taken from the then disused viaduct which used to carry the tracks into Manchester Central station and which gave this excellent vantage point for trains travelling between Ordsall Lane and Castlefield Junction and on to Manchester Piccadilly. On a day of diversions, 23 July 1989, the up 10.10 Glasgow Central-Euston service has Railfreight Distribution Class 47 No 47187 in charge. Today, the viaduct is used by the trams of Manchester Metrolink.

The remains of the Ness Viaduct, immediately north of Inverness station are viewed on 8 July 1989. The viaduct collapsed on 7 February 1989, isolating some Class 37/4s and coaching stock on the north side. The bridge was completely rebuilt and Sprinter No 156458 was the first train to use the new structure on 9 May 1990. During the period of isolation, Class 37s were moved by road between Muir of Ord and Inverness when they were in need of major attention. Fortunately, nobody was injured as a result of the collapse.

The 17.30 Waterloo-Bournemouth service on 28 April 1989, comprising two five-car Class 442 Wessex EMUs, leaves Waterloo on its journey west. A Class 50, No 50043, can just be seen at one of the platforms amongst the many EMUs. This view was taken from the flats just outside the station; the Eurostar platforms are now situated to the left of the picture.

The first visit of a Class 86/2 to Leeds occurred on 18 February 1989 when No 86234 J. B. Priestley worked a 14-coach InterCity charter from King's Cross to Leeds, where green-liveried Class 45/1 No 45106 took over for the journey over the Settle & Carlisle. The immaculate locomotive is pictured passing InterCity 125 No 43038 as it sets off back to London light engine. The InterCity 125 was forming the 12.00 service to King's Cross.

A busy scene at the west end of Acton yard shows Class 56 No 56065, with the construction decals, on 28 April 1989 passing on a sand train, whilst No 56036 prepares to leave the yard on an empty stone train. In the distance is one of Foster Yeoman's Class 59s, No 59002 Alan J. Day. Acton yard, as one can see, is now only a fraction of the size it used to be.

One of the Class 31s used in the nuclear flask pool found itself working the Carlisle-Lancaster shuttles during the West Coast main line engineering work. The crews seemed to be enjoying a day out on the Class 31s as the speeds they were travelling appeared to be extremely fast. No 31120 just catches a flash of sunlight as it rounds the curve at Low Gill on its way south.

A powerful picture of the Mid-Hants Railway's unrebuilt 'West Country' Pacific No 34105 Swanage as it hauls a 'Santa Special' near Ropley on 26 November 1989.

This picture is not quite what it seems. Large logo grey Class 26 No 26010 is heading the 09.25 Glasgow Queen Street-Aberdeen service up Cowlairs Bank on 6 July 1989. This was a very pleasant surprise for me as it increased my collection of Class 26s on push-pull stock by 100%. If you look at the rear of the train you can just see Class 47/7 No 47701 Saint Andrew giving assistance, which explained why the Class 26 was going so well. Apparently at Cowlairs the train went round the triangle before heading north with Saint Andrew at the front, leaving the Class 26 to return to Eastfield depot. Definitely a case of being in the right place at the right time and with sunshine.

*I*t wasn't the snow which caused the problems this year, but the gales, well in excess of 100mph, which brought chaos to the south and west. More positively, however, the Channel Tunnel work continued and the underground meeting between the French and English bores took place on 30 October.

On the locomotive front, the first Class 59/1s arrived from Halifax, Nova Scotia (Canada), and Class 60 No 60005 worked the first revenue-earning train for the class. No 60024 was the first to be delivered with the modifications which had been required as a result of the testing programme.

On the preserved steam front, the main event was undoubtedly the return of BR Standard Class 8 Pacific No 71000 *Duke of Gloucester*, which surely must be the biggest miracle of the preservation world. *Flying Scotsman* returned to the main line after its visit to Australia, and other locomotives such as 'Princess Royal' No 46203 *Princess Margaret Rose*, '9F' No 92240, 'Q7' No 63460 and 'Battle of Britain' No 34072 *257 Squadron* all sprang into life.

There were celebrations for the centenary of the Forth Bridge, which was floodlit for the occasion, and the new bridge over the River Ness at Inverness was opened, after the old one had collapsed.

Class 158s entered service on the Glasgow-Aberdeen route, but not without problems, and the Portsmouth-Southampton electrification was completed.

I enjoyed a considerable amount of photography in the London area, but as usual there were trips to Scotland and the West Country. In addition, I managed an extensive tour of South America and also did my first photography of the Santa Fe in North America.

After a dull trip across the Settle & Carlisle, the sun eventually came out at the right moment as the National Railway Museum's Class V2 2-6-2 No 4771 Green Arrow *stormed out of Hellifield heading for Skipton on the up 'Cumbrian Mountain Express' on 22 September 1990.*

The down 'Bradford Executive' was not able to go to Bradford Forster Square due to electrification and rebuilding, so the train was hauled through to Skipton by the usual Class 47. The 19.45 Skipton-King's Cross service leaves on 11 June 1990 with No 47413 hauling Class 91 No 91011 with the Mk 4 stock. DVT No 82205 is at the rear.

Freight traffic on the West Highland Mallaig extension is currently history, but who knows what English, Welsh & Scottish may find on the line. On a Sunday morning, 4 March 1990, I discovered there was a Permanent Way train going out to the Arisaig area. It was too good an opportunity to miss, so I followed it out. Also running on the same day was the 'West Highlander' landcruise train, which passed the PW train at Arisaig station. This provided the now very rare opportunity to photograph two Class 37/4s, both facing west, on the line at the same time. Both are in Mainline livery: No 37406 The Saltire Society is on the left and No 37401 Mary Queen of Scots is on the landcruise.

By 1990 locomotive-hauled passenger trains between Leeds and Hull were rare, except for an empty stock train on a Sunday afternoon, which ran from Neville Hill carriage sidings to Hull, to form the 17.00 Hull-King's Cross service. Still in plain blue livery, which it retained until withdrawal in February 1991, Class 47 No 47418 passes through the Gascoigne Wood Colliery complex on 23 September 1990 as it heads east.

The Class 20 Society ran this excellent tour on 11 May 1990; it was memorable not only for where it went but also for the name — the 'Vladivostok Avoider'. Having travelled over the Pennines to Scarborough, then down the coast to Hull, it headed west before doing a circle around Castleford, north to York, then round the York circle to Leeds. Two large logo grey liveried Class 20s — Nos 20010 and 20132 — were used. The train is passing Goole with the cranes of the port dominating the skyline.

Bevercoates Colliery used to be a few miles southwest of Retford. In 1990 the mine was still very much in use, but it has since closed. A visit in 1997 found the whole site completely cleared of all equipment and a bare concrete space, except for a coal dump which was being cleared by train. Class 58 No 58016 is pulling an MGR through the loading hopper on 27 March 1990 before heading off to High Marnham Power Station.

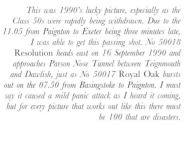

This was 1990's lucky picture, especially as the Class 50s were rapidly being withdrawn. Due to the 11.05 from Paignton to Exeter being three minutes late, I was able to get this passing shot. No 50018 Resolution heads east on 16 September 1990 and approaches Parson Nose Tunnel between Teignmouth and Dawlish, just as No 50017 Royal Oak bursts out on the 07.50 from Basingstoke to Paignton. I must say it caused a mild panic attack as I heard it coming, but for every picture that works out like this there must be 100 that are disasters.

The Class 309s were introduced on the Liverpool Street-Clacton services as far back as 1963 and were the most powerful EMUs on British Rail until the arrival of the Southern Region's '4REPs'. Set No 309611 is seen arriving at Clacton, something it must have done thousands of times before, on 16 June 1990 with the 10.00 service from Liverpool Street. Originally these units were fitted with the wrap-around front windows, but due to the trouble that these caused, they were replaced with flat panes. Most of the units are now withdrawn, but in the last few years Regional Railways North West have operated a few on Manchester-Stoke-Birmingham services.

One of the 10 Motor Luggage Van Class 419 single units, No 9010, is pictured in Jaffa Cake livery at London Bridge station on 15 March 1990. These units were built in 1959 at Eastleigh and were traditionally associated with boat trains to Dover and Folkestone; here, however, the unit is being used for Royal Mail purposes.

The Class 302s are now history on the London, Tilbury & Southend line, but back in 1990 they were still operational. Unit No 302212 has just left Grays en route to Tilbury Riverside on 29 March 1990; the station at Tilbury Riverside is now also history, having lost its passenger services and being converted to a freight terminal.

A busy scene at the south end of Colchester station on 16 June 1990 shows Class 37/0s Nos 37045 and 37009 passing the depot at the head of a rake of empty freightliner wagons, whilst Class 31/1s Nos 31196 and 31268 await their next turn of duty. Being a Saturday afternoon, several EMUs are parked in the yard.

1991

The early part of February produced some very bad weather as shown by my photograph of a Class 156 at Clay Cross. The new EMUs in the south did not seem to manage the snow very well and the Class 158s were disappearing from track circuit diagrams due to leaves on the track — not a very healthy state of affairs. Nevertheless, the Class 158s did take over the local Trans-Pennine services on 21 January 1991; this ended the locomotive-hauled passenger trains over the route, virtually ending, I am afraid, my interest in the line.

There were new classes appearing, such as the 'Networker' Class 465/0s and 465/2s, but only for testing, whereas the Class 91s started on the Edinburgh-King's Cross services on extremely fast schedules.

Rail Express Systems was launched at Crewe on 11 October, which resulted in their locomotives being painted in an attractive red livery. Another striking livery, although a one-off, was No 73101 in the Pullman livery.

The end finally came for Classes 81 and 85 electrics after around 30 years' service.

The preservation scene saw Class A2 No 60532 *Blue Peter* return to steam and steam specials worked to King's Lynn. Another interesting operation was the Folkestone Harbour branch, where 'West Country' No 34027 *Taw Valley* and Standard 2-6-4T No 80080 operated a shuttle service up and down the steep incline.

Although my selection of pictures does not portray the fact, I was visiting London, often twice a week, for work, and took a large number of pictures in the area, especially of the Class 50s on the London & South Western.

The most interesting special, I think, was that headed by the Class 50s over the Devon Banks and through to Newquay. Against the advice of the weather forecasters, I decided to make a day trip of it — about 750 miles — and every photograph in lovely sunshine. My thanks, on this occasion, go to my son for providing his company car and doing the driving.

Some extremely severe weather conditions hit the North and Midlands during early February, causing chaos to the roads and railways. I managed to travel down the M1 motorway to Clay Cross and have a few hours at the junction on 9 February, but it was impossible to identify the trains. I believe this Class 156 was working from Liverpool to East Anglia; it had just set off after having been stopped at the signals and it then headed off down the Erewash Valley line.

The railtour operators, in this case Hertfordshire, occasionally take InterCity 125s to some odd locations. This tour, on 26 January 1991, started at St Pancras and went, via Barnsley and Penistone, to the buffer stops at Swinden Quarry on the old Grassington branch. The train is just leaving for the return to Skipton, with power car No 43076 at the front and No 43064 bringing up the rear. I was surprised that the train was allowed into the quarry with passengers on board; several other tours had only got as far as the quarry limit.

By the middle of 1991 the new Class 60s had largely displaced the double-headed Class 37s on the ore trains from Hunterston to Ravenscraig. On a stormy 14 June 1991, I just managed to catch No 60050 Roseberry Topping in a gap in the clouds as it waited to set off from the terminal with a loaded train.

Only a matter of weeks before the Class 504 EMUs were withdrawn from the Manchester-Bury service, unit No 77178 stands inside Bury depot awaiting attention. The line was to be closed for conversion into part of the replacement Manchester Metrolink with the stations modernised for the new service. This fine building has since been saved and is now the main repair base for the East Lancashire Railway and is known as Buckley Wells. The date is 11 May 1991.

Prior to the introduction of the West Yorkshire PTE's three Class 321/9 EMUs, which have been dedicated to the Leeds-Doncaster service for several years, some surplus Class 307s were acquired from the Great Eastern area. Some were painted into the smart West Yorkshire PTE livery of red, whilst others, such as No 307130, remained in Network SouthEast colours. The train is the 16.14 from Doncaster to Leeds on 20 August 1991 and is seen approaching Bentley station, near Doncaster.

On 24 June 1991, the 13.10 Wilton-Southampton freightliner service passes through the now dormant coking plant and steelworks at Grangetown on Tees-side; the station can be seen at the rear of the train. The locomotive is No 47204 in Railfreight Distribution livery and the train was booked to call at Stourton freightliner terminal en route.

Class 60 No 60034 Carnedd Llewelyn was only four months old when I took this picture of it on 24 June 1991 passing Cargo Fleet at the head of the morning Lackenby-Corby steel train. The Class 60s had only just taken over these workings from Thornaby-based Class 37/5s, which had worked these trains since early in 1987.

Class 47/4 No 47594 was the first to receive the new Rail Express Systems (RES) livery and ran around with it long before the official launch in London. On 15 September 1991 it was hauling the diverted Liverpool-Euston trains and is pictured at the head of '1A13', the 10.58 from Liverpool, with a DVT immediately behind. The photograph was taken between Manchester Oxford Road and Piccadilly stations from the top floor of a multi-storey car park.

Diversion of West Coast main line trains to Liverpool and Scotland via Manchester on Sundays is not unusual; these workings result in the electric services being hauled by Class 47s. The old flats at Ordsall Lane, Salford, used to provide a superb viewpoint for the junction, but they have been demolished and so a step-ladder is now needed to see over the high road bridge to obtain photographs such as this. The modern skyline of Manchester stands out well as Class 47/4 No 47488 Rail Riders hauls InterCity Class 90 No 90020 on an express to Liverpool on 8 September 1991. No 90020 was later to become the first of the class to receive the new English, Welsh & Scottish livery.

There was trouble at Sheffield on Saturday 31 August 1991: the 09.57 Sheffield-Skegness service, headed by Class 47/9 No 47973 Derby Evening Telegraph, *set off from Midland station and failed after about half-a-mile, completely blocking the up line. The Leeds-Yarmouth train was already in the station ready to head south; its locomotive, No 47481, was detached to push the Skegness train up the loop to Millhouses. No 47481 returned towards Sheffield, but first had to head south to Dore to use the crossover. Photographically everything just fitted together as the delayed 07.50 Newcastle-Penzance service, headed by InterCity 125 No 43197, passed the failed train just as No 47481 set off back to Sheffield to collect its train. The Skegness train was eventually rescued by Class 31/4 No 31461, 1¼ hours after it had left Sheffield, just over a couple of miles away.*

A line-up of East Coast motive power at 07.30 on Saturday 21 September 1991 at King's Cross. From left to right are Class 91 No 91018, a Class 90 (believed to be No 90003 on a charter train) and InterCity 125 No 43050. All are in the InterCity swallow livery.

There were a few triple-headed specials during the years; some planned, others not. On this occasion, the piloting of the Pathfinder Class 50 tour over the South Devon banks on 23 November 1991 was not scheduled. Class 37/0 No 37142 had to be attached to the front of Nos 50015 Valiant and 50008 Thunderer from Newton Abbot to Plymouth; this was the result, I believe, of a faulty speedometer on Valiant. The train is shown sweeping round the curve at Langford Bridge, just past Aller Junction, prior to starting the climb up Dainton which, with only 11 coaches, would hardly cause any problem to the combination.

Regional Railways North organised special motive power for a couple of days between Christmas and the New Year on the morning Leeds-Carlisle train, plus several additional coaches. The trains were well filled and must have made a good profit. On 27 December 1991, Class 37/0s Nos 37083 and 37071 piloted Class 47/4 No 47479, which was in RES livery and named Track 29 at the time. The train is passing Bell Busk in pleasant winter sunshine.

My last picture of 1991, taken at Durran Hill, Carlisle, on 31 December, shows more of the special motive power used by Regional Railways North, this time on the 13.18 Carlisle-Leeds train. The train arrived with Class 56 No 56109 piloting the unique Regional Railways-liveried Class 47/4 No 47475. The '56' was exchanged for these immaculate Dutch-liveried Class 26s, Nos 26040 and 26011, for the return journey.

This was undoubtedly my luckiest picture of the year. The closing speed of the trains would be around 250mph. When I fired the shutter I didn't know if I had let them run into one another, or what the locomotive numbers were. To my surprise I got it about right and could read the numbers on both; I also managed a colour slide as well! It is odd how sometimes you get photographs of trains travelling more slowly much less sharp. Photographers seem to blame everything but themselves, as nine times out of ten it is nothing more than camera shake. InterCity 125 No 43049 Neville Hill heads south as Class 91 No 91031 Sir Henry Royce rushes north. The location is Bishop Wood, on the Selby Diversion, and the date is 27 December 1991.

1 9 9 2

*B*y comparison with some years, 1992 appeared to be relatively quiet; possibly the most important events were the introduction of the Class 165 'Networker Turbos' on the Marylebone-Banbury trains and the Class 465/0 delivered to Strawberry Hill depot for testing. New speed records were set up by Class 158s on the Glasgow-Edinburgh route and Class 91 No 91029 was let loose between Manchester and Euston, producing another record.

On the steam preservation side, Class A2 No 60532 *Blue Peter* was back on the main line in February and No 71000 *Duke of Gloucester* made its first ever visit to Paddington.

My own activities were mainly concentrated in Scotland, which included visits to Wick, Inverness (several times), Mallaig and the Ayrshire area, as well as the Class 26 tour to Oban. On a sad note, the end of the Class 50s on the London & South Western main line was celebrated with special workings on 24 May. More positive, however, and more surprising was the reappearance of the preserved Class 71 on the main line.

My foreign wanderings included a first visit to Cuba, but the less said about that the better; it was a disaster. Fortunately, the selection of photographs in this country was much more successful.

It was so dull and wet when I left Inverness that I almost turned back, and even when I arrived it was pouring down. Just as the train got to where the last coach is in the photograph, the clouds parted and out came the sun, just until the last coach had passed. It does happen this way very occasionally, but not very often. The 'Orcadian' is seen passing Luib Summit on 22 March 1992 heading back to London behind Class 37/4s Nos 37401 Mary Queen of Scots *and 37428* David Lloyd George.

The Class 26s were seldom seen on the Oban and West Highland lines, but a tour was organised on 12 July 1992 with Nos 26026 and 26025. Unfortunately, the latter failed for most of the journey, which made the train very late, resulting in these locomotives being changed at Dumbarton for Nos 26042 and 26036 for the return to Edinburgh. The train is shown at the head of Loch Awe.

Bradford Forster Square station has been altered out of all recognition. Since this photograph was taken, the background has been tidied up and industrial units built. Immaculate 'A2' Blue Peter leaves with a special for a trip on 28 March 1992 over the Settle & Carlisle line. The train arrived behind a Class 47.

An impressive line-up at Goathland on the North Yorkshire Moors Railway on 19 September 1992. On the left is 'Deltic' No 55015 Tulyar, which unfortunately had just caught fire and was removed from the train. The fire brigade was called, but the Deltic Preservation Society members had extinguished it by the time the brigade arrived 50min later. However, the locomotive had got quite hot and smoke can still be seen coming from it. Class 31/4 No 31439 North Yorkshire Moors Railway had appropriately worked a special to the line, as well as having a trip on the NYMR. Class 45/1 No 45133 was visiting from the Midland Railway Centre, and was ready to leave for Pickering.

The National Railway Museum's Class D11 'Director' No 62660 Butler Henderson had been at the Great Central Railway on loan for some time and was returned to York early in the year. It was specially painted in British Railways lined black livery for its last workings and, on its final day of operation (24 February 1992), it is pictured passing Woodthorpe Lane heading south. The scene is somewhat marred by the chalk message on the smokebox.

Hertfordshire Rail Tours ran the 'Dukeries Collier' to the Nottinghamshire coalfield on 27 June 1992. The special visited Thoresby Colliery, where the train was top-and-tailed by Class 20s Nos 20168 and 20059, together with Class 56 No 56024, which is shown leaving the loading bunker. This was, I believe, the first locomotive-hauled passenger train to visit the colliery.

The Wensleydale line originally ran through from Northallerton to Garsdale, but in 1964 it was cut back at Redmire, passenger services having ceased in 1959. The line had only another two weeks to go before closure when this picture was taken on 16 December 1992; the last working was a Hertfordshire Rail Tours special on 2 January 1993. There has been a very active society to try and get the line reopened; this has subsequently been achieved, not by the society, but by the Ministry of Defence, which uses the line to carry tanks to and from Catterick Camp. Trains now run on a regular basis, if somewhat infrequently and, after just over five years, there are to be railtours on the line again. Class 60s were the regular motive power for the daily train, and No 60030 Cir Mhor is pictured passing Leyburn station.

The new station at Ystrad Rhondda is located on the line to Treherbert, with services originating at Barry Island. On 16 February 1992 Pacer No 143621 leaves for Treherbert as Sprinter No 150261 heads off towards Barry Island.

The old Grassington branch now terminates at Swinden Quarry and has regular stone trains. Class 60s are now the usual motive power and on 30 July 1992 No 60095 Crib Goch was heading the 10.16 Tilcon train to Hull. It is pictured passing the site of Embsay Junction. The preserved Yorkshire Dales Railway terminates just to the right and it is possible that, sometime in the future, the junction may be reinstated.

The end of the Class 50s on the London & South Western main line finally came on 24 May 1992. Nos D400 in plain blue livery and No 50007 Sir Edward Elgar in green were paired together on the 09.28 Exeter-Waterloo service. The immaculate locomotives are shown storming out of Gillingham. The very last working, the 16.55 from Waterloo, also used these locomotives. No 50033 Glorious was to have hauled the 08.55 from Waterloo and the 14.28 return from Exeter, but it failed and Class 33s Nos 33002 and 33102 worked the trains instead.

The National Railway Museum's Class 71 No E5001 was put back into main line working order and was used on the 'Royal Wessex' special from Waterloo to the Bournemouth depot open day on 12 September 1992. Just in case of difficulties, Class 73/1 No 73132 was added to the train. The special is passing St Denys on the Sunday.

1 9 9 3

The year got off to a bad start with what was thought to be the last train to depart from Redmire on 2 January, but the track was left in position and negotiations started for the possible sale of the line. As we now know, the line has been reopened for Ministry of Defence traffic and the first railtour since reopening was due to run in March 1998. Another last was the final cement train on the Weardale line, which ran on 17 March; again efforts have been made to reopen the line, but currently nothing definite has happened.

It was announced that the BRML sites and Level 5 depots were to be put up for sale. This indirectly led to certain depots, such as Selhurst repainting Class 73/0 No 73003 (E6003) in green, and doing work not previously undertaken. The Old Oak Common 'Factory' did its last major overhaul in March, although it has continued in use since then.

On a more positive note, the first phase of the Robin Hood line, north from Nottingham, opened on 17 May, a major open day was held at Worcester, and the first through diesel train for 28 years ran between Whitby and Pickering.

In June, the first of the Eurostar Class 373s arrived at North Pole depot and testing commenced as the Channel Tunnel project headed towards completion.

There were some interesting workings on the network. Most surprising was the continuation of the use of Class 20s on some of the summer extras to Skegness and Class 26s were seen in Lancashire and Yorkshire before the class bowed out later in the year. A triple-headed Class 50 special, with each locomotive in a different livery plus the Pilkington train set, ran from Minehead to York, what a sight!

There was the much photographed accident at Maidstone, when Class 47/0 No 47288 landed on its side in the station.

The first Class 92 emerged from the Brush works at Loughborough and was hauled to the Technical Centre at Derby for the start of the class's lengthy, and possibly still incomplete, tests.

For me, it was a year of considerable activity, from Kyle of Lochalsh to the South Coast; the picture of the Class 60 piloting the Class 47 on a Settle & Carlisle diversion (as illustrated later) was probably the most unusual photograph I took during the year. There was no time for a trip abroad for railways.

There were West Coast main line diversions over the Settle & Carlisle during the weekend of 24/25 April 1993 and so I decided to spend the day between Blackburn and Hellifield for a change. I settled down near Whalley on 24 April to photograph a procession of Class 47/4s and 47/8s until the arrival of the 09.24 from Edinburgh to Birmingham, which had Class 60 No 60094 Tryfan at the head. I did not expect to see it return, but was delighted when the down 'Royal Scot' emerged from Gisburn Tunnel with No 60094 piloting Class 47/4 No 47973 Derby Evening Telegraph. I wonder if this is the only occasion on which the 'Royal Scot' has had Class 60 haulage?

An extremely successful open day was held at Worcester on Sunday 3 May 1993. Specials were run to the event, as were extra trips to Hereford and Gloucester with Class 20s. There was also a shuttle service from Worcester to Henwick on the Malvern line with 'Castle' class No 5029 Nunney Castle *with a diesel at the other end. The 'Castle' is shown crossing the River Severn, with Worcester Cathedral in the background, during the afternoon. Class 37/0 No 37114 was named* City of Worcester.

The Regional Railways livery is well represented in this picture taken to the east of Bolton station on 1 October 1993, as Class 101 Metro-Cammell unit No 101655 passes Class 31/4 No 31410 Granada Telethon *on an evening Manchester-Blackpool commuter working.*

An eight-car EMU crosses the River Arun as it heads west on the approach to Ford station in West Sussex on 19 October 1993. The train was a working from Victoria to the Sussex coast.

The superb scenery of the Aire Valley around Skipton is shown to advantage in this picture taken above Snaygill, about two miles south of Skipton station, on 15 May 1993. This was a special from Whitby to Carlisle, returning via the Settle & Carlisle, Leeds and York. Motive power was provided in the form of Class 31/4s Nos 31413 Severn Valley Railway (in its unique livery) and No 31427 behind. The following day the locomotives were transferred into the InterCity infrastructure pool, so passenger workings thereafter would be very infrequent. The line here is now electrified, with local workings formed of Class 308 units.

The previous year Scotrail repainted the two oldest Class 26s, built in 1958, into the original green livery at Eastfield depot and gave them their original numbers of D5300 and D5301. The pair were based at Inverness during the summer and were diagrammed to work the 12.35 Inverness-Kyle of Lochalsh and the 17.05 return working during the week. Unfortunately, my visit on 11 August 1993 coincided with a typically dismal Highland day, which ruined the colour photography and severely tested the black and white as well. The locomotives are at Kyle of Lochalsh ready to return to Inverness. No D5301 (ex-No 26001) was named Eastfield, after the famous Glasgow depot; the depot is now closed and completely demolished whilst both Class 26s have also been withdrawn and preserved.

The Saturday afternoon Stourton-Southampton freightliner, which can just be seen on the right, had not got through Moorthorpe Junction quickly enough and caused the King's Cross-Leeds express, hauled by Class 91 No 91015, to be stopped for a few minutes on 17 April 1993. In the background can be seen the Swinton & Knottingley line crossing the ex-Great Northern main line.

The Bedford-Bletchley line seems to exist in a time warp, but in spite of everything still manages to survive. The massive chimneys of the brick works at Stewartby dominate the skyline at Forders Siding as 'Bubble Car' Class 121 single unit No L127 passes through the weeds en route for Bedford in Network SouthEast livery on 18 June 1993.

This must have been one of the longest trips Class 26s had performed for many years. Dutch-liveried Nos 26003 and 26005 were selected to work a special from Manchester to Carlisle on 13 March 1993. From Carlisle the train travelled via Newcastle, Wakefield and the Calder Valley back to Manchester and thence to Carlisle. I believe a travelling fitter was on board just in case, but the pair passed Brighouse in fine style with their 12-coach train on time. The area behind the train was once occupied by the extensive goods yard and the main line used to be four tracks.

Class 47/8 No 47833 was selected for special treatment and sent to Llandore depot to be painted into something like the original green livery applied to the class. The shades were not the same as the original colours, but nevertheless it looked very smart, especially when at the head of the 'Venice-Simplon Orient Express', which it regularly worked. The train is passing Balm Road, south of Leeds, on 10 April 1993, after a trip over the Settle & Carlisle and was returning to York. Whilst in this livery the locomotive was named Captain Peter Manisty RN. It is now painted in Rail Express Systems red livery.

On 29 May 1993 there was engineering work at Acton Grange and West Coast main line services were diverted through St Helens, still with the electric locomotives attached. Class 47s hauled the trains over the non-electrified section. No 47488 Rail Riders is heading an up express with DVT No 82118 behind and Class 86/2 No 86252 The Liverpool Daily Post bringing up the rear. The train is just west of St Helens station and is surrounded by the Pilkington glass factories. The aerial ropeway on the left has since been dismantled.

You can probably count on the fingers of one hand the number of superb mornings like this that you get at Blaenau Ffestiniog in a year. Fortunately, this day coincided with the visit of the Hunslet Barclay weedkilling train along the branch to Trawsfynydd. I felt I was well rewarded by this picture after the very early start from Yorkshire to get the train, headed by Class 20/9 No 20902 Lorna crossing the viaduct out of the town at around 08.00. Sister locomotive No 20903 Alison was at the rear of the train. I have to admit that it was another perfect day when the last nuclear flask train ran on 8 August 1995 (see p. 245), but most of my visits have been in the pouring rain.

1 9 9 4

The newly created freight companies launched their new liveries during the year; those of Loadhaul and Mainline were particularly striking. Also to make its first appearance was the dramatic lined black livery adopted by Waterman's Railways.

The troubled Class 323 EMUs eventually entered service on 7 February between Lichfield and Redditch, although their problems didn't vanish overnight.

After many years of waiting, diesel enthusiasts were able to celebrate the return to the main line of a preserved diesel, when Class 46 No D172 *Ixion* hauled its first revenue-earning train on 1 October after its expensive overhaul.

The Class 50s finally finished, with No 50033 *Glorious* working the last Class 50-hauled train, from Scarborough to the National Railway Museum on 1 April. Another last was the final Open Day at Old Oak Common on 19 March.

The first of the Class 59/2s, No 59201, later named *Vale of York*, arrived at King George V Dock at Hull. Another locomotive to arrive from abroad was the Brown Boveri gas turbine, which returned to Britain for preservation after over 30 years of exile in Europe.

The Royal inauguration ceremony for the Channel Tunnel took place on 6 May with Eurostar services commencing through the tunnel later in the year. Other positive news was the ordering of the new EMUs for the Heathrow rail link.

In the north, the superb restoration of Hellifield station, after many years of hard work by several interested parties, was celebrated on 18 November.

Crewe electric depot opened its doors to the public on 15 October. The impressive display of motive power included several Class 92s.

The last down service of the day from Leeds to Carlisle on 22 July 1994 heads north between Helwith Bridge and Horton in Ribblesdale on a perfect summer's evening. Sprinter No 156475 is dominated by Pen-y-Ghent in the background.

It is now almost 44 years since there was a regular passenger service over this viaduct, but the line remains open from Buxton to Hindlow for stone traffic. The Branch Line Society organised a special along the branch on 16 April 1994, with two Class 37/4s topping and tailing. Regional Railways-liveried No 37429 Eisteddfod Genedlaethol is at the rear as the train climbs out of Buxton over the viaduct. The line originally went through to Ashbourne and joined the Cromford & High Peak Railway at Parsley Hay.

The 'Worksop Wanderer' on 19 March 1994 was run by the staff at Worksop depot, who, over the years, have organised some excellent events. A Class 58 and a Class 47 brought the train over the East Coast main line before heading cross country to Ayr. The pair was exchanged for two Class 56s, Nos 56124 and 56128 West Burton Power Station, which were working the Ayrshire coalfield at the time, plus Class 37/4s Nos 37408 Loch Rannoch and green-liveried 37403 Ben Cruachan. The train travelled along the old Dalmellington line to Waterside and is pictured on the return journey near Patria.

The Class 50s had a final fling over the West Coast main line and the Settle & Carlisle routes, when Nos D433 and D400 headed the 'Midland Scotsman' special from Birmingham to Glasgow Central on 5 February 1994. Both had been painted into original livery without names, and looked immaculate as they passed Lostock Junction on the outward trip. Unfortunately, the weather was dismal, but a good day out was had by all. No D433 was then repainted back to No 50033 in large logo blue livery with its Glorious nameplates restored. Its final run was on 20 March from York to Scarborough, before being handed over to the National Railway Museum.

During the year, Pete Waterman's collection of locomotives was rapidly increasing. A couple of his Class 20s were painted in this very smart lined black livery and No D8188 (ex-No 20188) visited the East Lancashire Railway for the summer Diesel Gala. The immaculate locomotive is seen passing through Burrs Cutting on a train from Rawtenstall to Bury on 10 June 1994.

The first of the National Power fleet of Class 59/2s, No 59201, arrived at King George V Dock at Hull in February aboard the Haskerland. It was quickly assembled on its bogies and hauled to ABB at York prior to being exhibited at the National Railway Museum, where it was named Vale of York. The date is 18 February 1994.

Class 37/4 No 37407 Loch Long in 'Mainline' livery passes along Colwyn Bay as it approaches Old Colwyn on the 13.30 Holyhead-Manchester service on 27 August 1994. On this glorious afternoon, the Little Orme stands out very clearly at the opposite end of the bay, as does the pier.

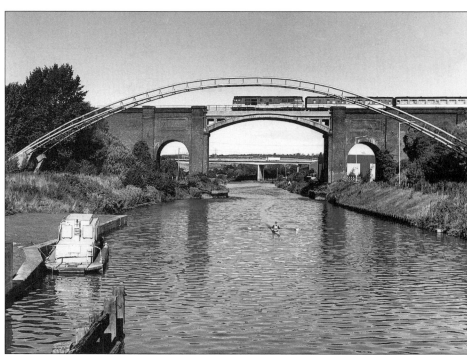

The Saturdays Only 09.19 Liverpool-Bangor service crosses the canalised River Weaver at Frodsham on 17 September 1994 headed by Regional Railways-liveried Class 31/4 No 31421 Wigan Pier as a lone rower heads towards the camera. In the background a lorry can be seen crossing the bridge on the M56 motorway.

After around 26 years in preservation painted in the *LNER* garter blue livery, it was a delight to see Sir Nigel Gresley *appear in the short-lived British Railways lined blue livery of the early 1950s and numbered 60007. Looking magnificent in the evening light of 6 November 1994, the locomotive approaches Woodthorpe Lane, just south of Loughborough on the preserved Great Central Railway.*

Whilst waiting for a Class 507 EMU to turn up at Bank Hall station, Liverpool, on 31 December 1994, I was extremely surprised when this Sandite/de-icing unit No 3 appeared on its way back to the depot.

An excellent open day was held at Crewe electric depot over the weekend of 15/16 October 1994. There was virtually every available class electric locomotive on display together with a few diesels. The opportunity was taken to show the public several of the Class 92s, which were awaiting entry into service; this has proved to be a long wait. This shot was taken on 15 October.

By September 1994, coal was no longer being mined at Kiveton Park Colliery, on the Sheffield-Worksop line, but trains were still running on a regular basis in order to clear the vast dump which had accumulated over the years. Class 58 No 58036, now without coal sector decals, prepares to leave on 29 September 1994 with an MGR train for West Burton Power Station.

The weekly Coalite train was in the hands of Class 58 No 58031 on 23 July 1994. Surrounded by the structures of the plant near Bolsover, the driver carries out a shunting manoeuvre before returning to Worksop.

1 9 9 5

The first Class 92 made it through the Channel Tunnel on 16 February, but many of the class were still doing very little; this allowed No 92009 to be displayed at the National Railway Museum.

An unfortunate accident occurred on the Settle & Carlisle line when a Class 156 unit ran into a landslip and was hit by another unit coming in the opposite direction; this accident resulted in one member of the train crew being killed. Another accident occurred just north of York when Class 47/7 No 47743, at the head of a parcels train, rolled down an embankment and ended up in a field. It landed up in a spot where it was virtually impossible to recover, with the result that it had to be cut up on site.

On the other hand, there were a number of positive events during the year. On 2 June, Class 91 No 91031 achieved the country's speed record of 154mph. More Class 59/2s arrived at King George V Dock in Hull on 4 August and pioneer Class 26, No 26001, was saved by Glasgow scrap merchant Jim McWilliam. The two Royal Class 47s received their special livery during the year. On 1 April, one of the most ambitious railtours for several years

operated when two Class 33 'Cromptons', Nos 33109 and 33116, ran from London Victoria to Inverness and back without any difficulty.

Other events saw the reintroduction of coal trains over the Settle & Carlisle route on 19 August; the train ran for British Fuels from Gascoigne Wood to Mossend for onward movement to Inverness. A superb open weekend was organised at Basford Hall, Crewe, where a large selection of preserved and other locomotives was on display. A total of 11,000 visitors attended the exhibition, paying no less than £25,000 for the privilege.

Freightliner adopted a new livery for its Class 47 locomotives and Direct Rail Services' five Class 20s appeared from the Brush works in their smart new livery. The Aire Valley electrification scheme saw a full service introduced in September, using the refurbished Class 308 units. Finally, in December Wisconsin Central became the new owners of Rail Express Systems.

My own activities were mainly in the northern half of the country, with a disproportionate amount of time spent on the North Wales Coast main line. In addition, I also managed a couple of excellent trips to Canada and the United States.

I had been trying to get this picture for some time; whilst it is not difficult to get a Class 56 on an MGR train leaving Eggborough Power Station passing Whitley Bridge Junction, I had wanted to get No 56094, which is named Eggborough Power Station. *This I achieved on 14 February 1995. I have tried to do the same with No 56123* Drax Power Station, *so far without success.*

Pathfinder Tours ran a special to Immingham Docks and Killingholme on 18 February 1995. Class 56 No 56039 Port of Hull, *which was one of the few painted in 'Loadhaul' livery at the time, headed the train with Class 47/7 No 47739* Resourceful *at the rear. The massive petroleum and chemical complexes in the area show up well on the skyline.*

There were few passengers for the single-car Class 153 unit No 153316 when it called at Betws-y-Coed on the 15.07 Blaenau Ffestiniog-Llandudno service on 9 February 1995. On the right is the model railway which operates during the tourist season, but not on a very wet day in February.

Darlington station, like York and Newcastle, still retains its overall roof. As can be seen, the platforms and the rest of the building are kept extremely clean and tidy. The large clock indicates that the 12.59 service to Bishop Auckland still has four minutes to wait on 10 March 1995. The train is being worked by Class 153 No 153357.

The last nuclear flask to leave Trawsfynydd power station was on 8 August 1995. The train is headed by two Class 31s, Nos 31255 and 31199, and is approaching Blaenau Ffestiniog. As can be seen, a special headboard was carried on the front of the leading locomotive to commemorate the event.

Birkenhead Central and the Merseyrail system seldom seem to feature in the current magazines. I had to visit Birkenhead and so I thought I would see what the station was like, not having been to the town for many years. The three Class 508 units in the picture are consecutively numbered Nos 508126, 508127 and 508128. No 508127 in the station is about to depart for Liverpool, whilst the others are probably awaiting evening rush hour duties. The date is 12 January 1995.

The Special Trains Unit of British Rail ran a final special over the Settle & Carlisle on 31 March 1995. In very dramatic lighting conditions, the train is captured leaving Appleby and crossing the old A66 road. Motive power was Standard Class 4MT No 75014 and Class 7MT No 70000 Britannia. Unfortunately, the '4MT' failed later in the trip and had to be taken off the train. After this picture, I continued my journey north to see the Class 33s on the Highland line the next day.

Ellesmere Port is one of the few stations where trains leave in the opposite direction for the same town or city. The same still applies at Exeter St David's and it used to happen at Chester; no doubt there are others. Pacer unit No 142039 is pictured ready to leave on 25 February 1995 with the 12.22 service to Liverpool Lime Street via Warrington, while the EMU, No 507031, forms the 12.10 service to Liverpool Central via Birkenhead. The Stanlow petroleum complex can be seen in the background.

The five General Motors-built Class 59/2s arrived at Hull King George V Dock from London, Ontario (Canada), in August. The locomotives, still covered, are shown on the quayside. They were attached to their bogies here before being taken to Ferrybridge depot. Some 18 months previously, No 59201 had arrived at the same dock; it can be seen under the crane in the distance on 5 August 1995 waiting to haul the others away. Nos 59203 and 59204 left on the Saturday, and the others on the Sunday. For some reason, 'Loadhaul' sent one of its Class 37/5s, No 37513 to the event, and this piloted the Class 59s to Goole.

Hertfordshire Rail Tours' 'Skirl o' the Bagpipes' 1,153 mile outing from London Victoria to Inverness and back was definitely the most ambitious of the year. Class 33/1s Nos 33116 Hertfordshire Rail Tours in blue livery and 33109 Captain Bill Smith RNR in grey livery were turned out in spotless condition by Stewarts Lane depot. The 10-coach train presented no problems on the climb to Slochd Summit, where the train is passing in dismal weather conditions. The tour, run on 1 April 1995, appeared to operate without a hitch and when I last saw it around Penrith on the return journey, it had never seemed to be more than two minutes adrift of schedule.

National Power Class 59/2 No 59201 Vale of York, with the bell fitted to the cab, heads a rake of new wagons on 21 March 1995 away from Drax power station back to Gasgoine Wood.

One of the new Centro Class 323 EMUs, built at Hunslet in Leeds, enters Birmingham New Street on 27 February 1995 from Redditch en route to Lichfield. The class is used on Manchester and Birmingham local routes, but suffered many problems during tests prior to entering service.

The overhead power was off between Leeds station and Neville Hill sidings on 30 April 1995, so the Class 91s and stock required locomotive haulage into Leeds. One of Pete Waterman's black-liveried Class 47s, No 47703 Lewis Carroll, found itself on these 'drags' and is seen leaving Neville Hill yard and is about to enter Marsh Lane Cutting.

1 9 9 6

The closure of ABB's York Carriage Works was marked by an open day on 27/28 January. Opened in 1844, the works had produced 8,364 vehicles since 1945. Another dramatic change saw Ed Burckhardt's Wisconsin Central Railway become the new owners of BR's freight operations on 24 February; it was subsequently announced that orders for 250 new freight locomotives would be placed with General Motors. Until the new livery of the ex-BR freight operations — known now as English, Welsh & Scottish — was decided, some locomotives re-entered service after overhaul in undercoat and continued in this temporary livery for some time.

The refurbished Class 308s on the electrified Aire Valley services were soon in trouble after an explosion in March, resulting in several sets being temporarily withdrawn. Also in Yorkshire, the first revenue-earning train on the Redmire branch since it was mothballed in January 1993 ran on 10 April, but not without some problems. Freight also returned to the 110-mile long Central Wales line over the 4-6 May Bank Holiday weekend as a result of engineering work on the main line between Swansea and Cardiff.

Other notable events included, on Friday 31 May, the use of Direct Rail Services Class 20s on the Royal Train to Aberystwyth, and, on 3 August, the running of two Class 31s to Fort William. The latter tour was organised by A1A Charters, who have managed to take the type to most parts of England.

There were two unfortunate accidents during the year. One of these was at Rickerscote, near Stafford, when Class 86/2 No 86239 rolled down an embankment, coming to rest inches from a private house, and the second was the much publicised accident at Watford.

Sea Containers, owners of the Great North Eastern Railway franchise, bought the preserved Class 89 electric locomotive in order to reinstate it on services to Leeds and Bradford. GNER also launched its new livery without ceremony on 21 October.

'Deltic' fans got what they had been waiting 15 years for, when No D9000 *Royal Scots Grey* ran a test train on the main line from Glasgow to Tweedmouth. The year also marked the 25th anniversary of the first run of InterCity prototype No 41001; it was these units that were destined to replace the 'Deltics' from the East Coast main line services.

The disastrous Channel Tunnel fire occurred on 18 November, resulting in temporary closure and a major investigation into safety. After a short time services through the undamaged bore were reinstated but full services were not possible until 1997 following both repair to the damaged tunnel and clearance of the freight shuttles.

Finally, new liveries appeared almost every month as Privatisation continued to take effect. This gave plenty of opportunity for photography. For my own part, the USA again produced two good trips, one to the northeastern states and one to California.

Prior to English, Welsh & Scottish deciding on a suitable livery, a few Class 37s, a Class 60 and a Class 56 emerged in undercoat and entered traffic in that condition. The Class 37s were repainted first, but the Class 60 and the Class 56 ran in the livery for at least a year. Class 37/7 No 37717 Stainless Pioneer *passes Scunthorpe on the Lindsey-Leeds (Neville Hill) tanks on 4 April 1996.*

Class 60 No 60022 lost its Ingleborough *nameplates when it emerged in the undercoat livery. It was working the Immingham-Scunthorpe ore trains in April, and is seen passing the now very popular photographic location just to the east of Barnetby with the empty wagons on 3 April 1996.*

Silverwood Colliery had closed some time earlier, but it was decided to collect the large coal dump and use it at Drax and West Burton power stations. Before the trains could be run, a section of track had to be relaid as the locals had removed it for scrap. Trains ran on a daily basis for the first few months of the year and had to be double-headed to the site before being topped and tailed into the old colliery as there were now no run-round facilities. Classes 56 and 58 were the regular motive power. Here coal sector No 56117 Wilton Coalpower *is seen waiting whilst the wagons are loaded on 27 February 1996.*

Class 56 No 56068 became the last locomotive to retain the undercoat livery. It is seen in unfamiliar territory for a member of the class, on engineering duties, on the 1 in 50 gradient between Bowling Tunnel and Bradford Interchange on 28 July 1996. There are no regular locomotive workings on this line, but during July 1996 there were several Sunday engineering possessions, giving the welcome sight of locomotives at Bradford Interchange again.

Mention has already been made on the previous page of the engineering works around Bradford Interchange during July and August. The rare sight of a Class 56 No 56050 in Loadhaul livery leaving Bradford Interchange was captured on 4 August 1996 as it heads back to Healey Mills with the empty ballast wagons.

The AIA Group organised a special named 'Rathan Nan Eilean' on 3 August 1996, which took Class 31/1s Nos 31146 Brush Veteran and 31166 over the West Highland line to Fort William; I believe that this was a first for the class. I decided that it was worth a day trip to get this picture of the pair climbing out of the Horseshoe Bend to the summit at County March on the return journey. The locomotives arrived back at Glasgow Central at about the right time, before heading for fuel for the return journey south.

This was a great day out for Class 59 enthusiasts, as there were four locomotives, from each of the sub-classes, hauling the train during the day. The journey from the Bristol area was handled by Nos 59005 Kenneth J. Painter *and* 59103 Village of Mells. National Power's *Nos 59205 and 59203 also took part. The tour was run to visit the Tinsley depot open day on 27 April 1996. I heard it said by the driver on the return, when told at Sheffield that he had 300 tons plus on the train, that he reckoned he would not require assistance up the bank to Dore. The train is passing Darnall on the outskirts of Sheffield.*

One of the many highlights of the superb summer Diesel Gala on the East Lancashire Railway was the double-heading of the National Railway Museum's 'Deltic', No 55002 King's Own Yorkshire Light Infantry, *with the Deltic Preservation Society's No D9019* Royal Highland Fusilier. *No 55002 had seen very little use since its withdrawal 15 years ago, but No D9019, which is currently based on the ELR, is used as often as possible. The pair produced many dramatic displays during the week, although the pairing was overshadowed by a triple-headed 'Deltic' working at a later event. The date is 4 June 1996.*

After their unexpected Royal Train duties over the Cambrian line a few days earlier, the then complete fleet of Direct Rail Services Class 20/3s returned north from Crewe to their home base at Sellafield heading the Pathfinder tour along the Cumbrian coast on 1 June 1996. The immaculate trio, Nos 20302, 20301 and 20303, head north round the curve at Millom.

The afternoon '1M78' Low Fell-London King's Cross van train was normally hauled by a RES Class 90/0 during this period, although in 1998 it has now become a Class 325 unit diagram. On 15 July 1996 No 90018, looking very smart with its matching red vans, passes Gateforth on the Selby diversion dead on time, as normal, just ahead of a cloud, which was rapidly creeping up the track.

The once superb station buildings at Church Fenton have now been reduced to the terrible bus shelters. West Yorkshire PTE red-liveried unit No 158907 pauses at the station with the 15.13 York-Manchester service (via Bradford and the Calder Valley) on 18 June 1996 whilst three-car set No 158810 rushes by on the nonstop 14.19 Middlesbrough-Manchester Piccadilly service, which will travel via the Standedge route.

1997

If you are into taking colour photography of railways, then 1997 must have been a year to remember. New liveries seemed to be appearing every month and some of them were extremely attractive.

'Deltic' No D9000 *Royal Scots Grey* enjoyed an extremely successful year and exploded the myth that privately preserved diesels break down on every occasion that they venture on to the main line. 'Peak' No D172 *Ixion* only managed a few runs, however, whilst Class 33 No D6593 and Class 50 No 50031 *Hood* joined the list of preserved diesels cleared for main line running. The return of the unique Class 89 from preservation into main line use with Great North Eastern was also a milestone. By the end of the year DRS had purchased no less than 18 Class 20s, and whilst not all will be returning to main line work, it will be interesting to see how they are ultimately utilised.

A very significant, though not very well publicised, event took place on 21 November when Class 92 No 92003 *Beethoven* hauled the last ever British freight before the handover to English, Welsh & Scottish; the service in question was the 23.15 from Dollands Moor to Wembley.

Much to everybody's surprise, the Class 33 'Cromptons' were still at work at the end of the year and there were still some 27 Class 31s operational. Other diesel news saw the Class 59s start work in South Wales and No 59003 was loaned to Germany.

The year will, unfortunately, be remembered for the disastrous accident at Southall, when the 10.32 Swansea-Paddington InterCity 125 service hit an ARC stone train.

The year was one which was full of interest as well as being full of promise for the future from both the train operators and Railtrack. We await future developments with interest.

Pictured not on the duties for which it is specially painted, Class 60 No 60033 Tees Steel Express *approaches Mirfield on the 12.05 Warrington-Lackenby service on 14 September 1997. Two locomotives, No 60033 illustrated here and No 60006* Scunthorpe Ironmaster, *were painted in the light blue British Steel livery and launched at a special ceremony at Scunthorpe on 17 July 1997.*

A couple of Mainline-liveried Class 37s, Nos 37074 and 37371, pass Standish Junction on 15 May 1997 at the head of the Thursdays Only Bridgwater-Sellafield nuclear flask train.

HM the Queen visited Bradford for the distribution of the Royal Maundy Money on 27 March 1997. She arrived at Bradford Forster Square by train from the north and the two Royal Class 47/7s, Nos 47798 Prince William *and* 47799 Prince Henry, *provided the power. Platform space at Forster Square is extremely limited these days, but the operators managed to keep all the local services running without interruption as well as running an empty stock movement with the King's Cross train; as this service was booked to be in the platform at the same time as the Royal Train. The empty stock of the Royal Train is pictured approaching Shipley behind No 47798 and slowing for a signal check to let the Tilcon empties pass with a Class 60 en route for Skipton.*

After test trains, the reopened Redmire branch from Northallerton finally received its first revenue-earning train from the Ministry of Defence on 14 February 1997. The train was top and tailed, with well turned out Class 47/0 No 47033 The Royal Logistics Corps *at the front and No 47213 at the rear. The trains are restricted to 15mph on the branch. Regular trains have run from this date and the line has more recently seen its first railtour since reopening.*

After its unfortunate fire at Berwick on Tweed on its first outing carrying passengers, 'Deltic' No D9000 Royal Scots Grey got the year off to a fine start on 2 January 1997 with a trip from King's Cross to Hull, Leeds and York before returning to London. In seasonal January conditions, the locomotive made a fine sight as it left Selby for Leeds after picking up a pilotman. The locomotive had an extremely successful year and put up some sparkling performances.